I0810555

POSTCARD HISTORY SERIES

Welcome to Omaha

On the Front Cover: Liberty Day. The Buy War Bonds march held on the afternoon of April 6, 1918, marked the one-year anniversary of the United States' entry into World War I and the largest demonstration in Omaha's history. The April 7 *Omaha Sunday Bee* headline proclaimed, "50,000 MARCH LIBERTY DAY." These well-dressed men and women are on Farnam Street's Auto Row. The skeletal structure in the background is the 14-story Nebraska Telephone Building, completed in 1919. The message written on this card—postmarked April 9, 1918, and sent to Chicago—is "Puzzle Picture. Point out the best looking man. One guess only." (Author's collection; photograph by W.W. Scott.)

On the Back Cover: Greetings from Omaha. This early 1950s postcard features Boys Town, Joslyn Art Museum, the South Omaha stockyards, Ak-Sar-Ben, the Mormon Pioneer Bridge (completed in 1952), and Offutt Air Force Base—images symbolizing charity, culture, livestock, national security, sports, automobiles, and faith. Railroads go unmentioned. Howard wrote to Belle in Bowen, Illinois, on this card postmarked from Boys Town on August 21, 1956: "Ate lunch in Memphis Mo. Supper in Council Bluffs Iowa. Staying tonight just outside Omaha Nebr just across from boys Town. Will head up toward the Bad Lands tomorrow. Hope you are o.k - Feel sure you will be." (Gene McConnell.)

POSTCARD HISTORY SERIES

Welcome to Omaha

Oliver B. Pollak

ARCADIA
PUBLISHING

Copyright © 2018 by Oliver B. Pollak
ISBN 978-1-4671-2865-0

Published by Arcadia Publishing
Charleston, South Carolina

Printed in the United States of America

Library of Congress Control Number: 2017956536

For all general information contact Arcadia Publishing at:
Telephone 843-853-2070
Fax 843-853-0044
E-mail sales@arcadiapublishing.com
For customer service and orders:
Toll-Free 1-888-313-2665

Visit us on the Internet at www.arcadiapublishing.com

To Omaha,
tangible, real, and human,
our home for 42 years,
atmospheric extremes,
cold, stormy, hot, humid,
delicious spring and fall, prune and rake leaves
undaunted, though perhaps bent by tornadoes and snow,
a place to learn, play, and grow.

Contents

Acknowledgments

Thank you to Doyia Carpenter; Phyllis Chester; Kay Calamé Dalstrom; Harl Dalstrom; Dave and Helen Edwards; John Farr; Michelle Gullett, librarian with the *Omaha World-Herald*; David and Chris Hicks; Beryl Weiner and Joyce Craig; Bruce Garver; the late Hilda Graham; Pat Kelleher; Bill Lo; Jim McKee, indefatigable writer for the *Lincoln Journal Star*; postcard artist Gene McConnell; George Piness; Steve and Margo Riekes; Marty Shukert; Les Valentine and Bob Nash, the University of Nebraska at Omaha Library Archives; Martha Grenzeback and Amy Capes, Omaha Public Library; Kathy Aultz and Ana Somers, Douglas County Historical Society; Bill Gonzales, Durham Museum photograph curator; Patricia LaBounty, Union Pacific Museum; registrar Sarah E. Haines, Joslyn Art Museum; Mary-Jo Miller, Nebraska State Historical Society; the Nebraska Library Commission; John Powell, The Newberry Library; Karen S. Shafts, Boston Public Library; the New York Public Library; Thomas Lynch and Benjamin L. Clark at Boys Town Hall of History; the Omaha Chamber of Commerce; Internet postcard sellers; and prior Arcadia Publishing authors. Jeff Ruetsche and Liz Gurley, with Arcadia Publishing, were very accommodating from inception through editing. Karen, my wife and editor for over half a century, patiently encouraged me and made this work better than what I handed to her. Of course, all mistakes, omissions, and errors are my own.

Unless otherwise noted, all images are from the author's collection.

Introduction

My introduction to and first impression of Omaha occurred in May 1974 at a job interview. The airport was smallish but growing. The humidity could make a fish blush, similar to Mozambique. Lunch in a caboose recycled as a dining car evoked nostalgia. Light traffic at rush hour, an introduction to the 20-minute city. Broad swaths of green belts. A place to settle down, isolated but in the middle of things. Fast forward 42 years, we moved to California.

Where is Omaha? In the Midwest, on the Middle Border, in the atlas gutter, Edge of the Great Plains, the Heartland, one of many inland empires, the great American desert, lost, flyover country, a location in progress, best kept secret, road to somewhere, an old frontier, Where the West Begins, where the East peters out, the Heart of America, BerkStock Nation.

Location location location—a sense of place, rootedness, reminiscence, and nostalgia. Postcards, photographs, stereopticons, lantern slides, panoramas, and engravings were designed to leave an impression of Omaha's proudest icons. The 1993 book *Reading National Geographic*, by Catherine Lutz, details the complex negotiations involved in choosing which images to print in that magazine. Postcards may introduce clouds, flags waving in a breeze, cars, people, and imaginative styling.

This collection of postcards presents primary sources for self-projected images. They are advertising, aiming to place Omaha in the best light. The existence of a hotel postcard after 1905 meant that the hotel sought patrons. This book features four postcard genres: conventional single view, multiview, large letter postcards, and souvenir foldouts.

City directories, telephone books, newspapers, magazines, billboards, and painted signs reveal further information beyond the scope of these pages. Obituaries of hotel owners, managers, night clerks, and elevator operators color hospitality history.

Postcards were enormously popular after 1905, almost like Twitter today. Postcard advertising reminded patrons to pass the word along to potential customers. Business cards, calendars, and pens were also used toward this aim.

The messages on postcards sent between friends, children, parents, and grandparents are vignettes of everyday life. The precious messages sent through the postal system provide insights into private and public life, the mundane, the quotidian, and the worldly. Communications between collectors—known as deltiologists—were frequent as they exchanged cards, asked for what they wanted, and returned thank-you postcards.

Postcards reveal changes of streetscapes and cityscapes in the urban scene. Commerce, urban planners, and suburban developers took advantage of the opportunities of population growth within the context of profit margins.

This book is based on what visitors saw in the past, but no longer exists. Gertrude Stein's statement about Oakland, "there is no there there," acknowledged that the home of her youth had been demolished. This book is a record of transport, urban life, demolition and redevelopment, fires, and tornadoes. In the words of George Hacker, a past president of Landmark Inc., "taking stock of Omaha's architectural retention is a bleak endeavor." The redevelopment of the urban core, tax incentives, and blighted districts resulted in the loss of Jobbers Canyon. Businesses, industries, and hotels come and go. Some have survived to be listed in the Historic Register.

Hotels touted their amenities, refinements, and constant improvement. Amenities expanded to include indoor plumbing, individual baths and showers, elevators, dining areas, bars, display rooms, fans, air conditioning, coin-operated (and then free) radio and television, Wi-Fi, iPhone docking stations, indoor and outdoor swimming pools, parking decks, exercise rooms, porters, bellhops, valets, writing areas, concierge service, laundry, barbershops, billiards, shoe shines, event planners, room service, maids, hot tubs, Turkish baths, saunas, coffee bars, exercise areas, minibars, luxury bathroom items, boutiques, cookies, free newspapers, pet-friendly areas, bicycles, and art. Suffice it to say, the transition from stables to garages, feed to filling stations, and outhouse to bidet reflected rising expectations.

Merchandising the business and the city involved postcards, letterhead stationery, envelopes, telegraph blanks, laundry lists and bags, blotters, notepads, luggage tags, sewing kits (needles, threads, and buttons), shoehorns, cocktail napkins, and the unsanctioned mementos—desk sets, hangers, laundry bags, bottle openers, ashtrays, teaspoons, pens, even bottles of ink (ballpoint pens arrived in the late 1940s), towels, "Do Not Disturb" signs, and key fobs, which—despite free return postage—guests kept. In the hotel trade, they were "souvenir hunting," which owners consider a cost of doing business. The Hotel Paxton gift shop sold souvenir five-inch-long golf clubs. Matchbooks cross-advertise hotels and restaurants as well as familiarizing guests with hotel chains and affiliated hotels, social commentary, and special qualities in an attempt to distinguish them from the rest of the industry.

Innovations like steam heat became expected and ceased to be mentioned as a special hotel feature, just like the in-room telephone. Merchandizing demanded being alert to the new and trendy. Non-smoking rooms, floors, and entire hotels were still well in the future.

Whether architecture is music frozen in time or music is liquid architecture (thoughts attributed to Goethe), it sets lofty rhythms. Brick and stone striations on the buildings are sheet music. Buildings can attract and repel just like music. People can get used to what they once rejected.

The first hotels, wooden frame structures or "settlement hotels," indicated arrival but not necessarily being here to stay. Brick and stone indicated permanency. Hoteliers underbuilt and then expanded as occupancy demand increased, resulting in the building of more stories or the annexing of adjacent properties, even digging tunnels between the properties. Architects with authority and grace gave the impression of stability, safety, and longevity.

Many postcards are staged, retouched, and manipulated to reflect the ambiance, style, fashion, comfort, and familiarity the hostelry industry desired. Hotel exteriors, lobbies, and guest rooms set them apart from the competition. Fancy, sleek, European-style cars on Omaha streets were unlikely. There are postcards of restaurants, but not the kitchens. Sketches, photographs, newspaper illustrations, postcards, hotel promotional literature, advertising envelope covers, and matchbooks may conflict with reality. Towering signs loomed large over the streets below.

A.K. Sandoval-Strausz characterizes hotels as luxury, commercial, middle-class, marginal, resort, railroad, and settlement. The hierarchy of comforts between settlement hotels and first class is vast and ranges between a myriad of functional, albeit less distinguished lodging, the boardinghouse, lodgings, rooming houses, sleeping rooms, workingmen's hotels, rooms, and short-term apartments or flats.

The worker's voice is sometimes heard. Chas wrote to Ethel in Detroit, Kansas, in November 1909: "This is a picture of the house where I stay. My room is the second window above the bicycle." Julia wrote to Eva in Villisca, Iowa, in green ink on a Douglas Street Bridge streetcar card around 1910: "I am rooming nearer to my work now."

Visitors to towns need accommodations. The Chamber of Commerce and visitor guides provided occupancy suggestions for traveling salesmen and tourists. "Vacancy" and "No Vacancy" signs appear on placards and in neon. Tenants, transients, and those attending weddings and funerals need lodging. The homeless—buffeted by seasons with the frostbite of cold and dehydration of heat—resort to flophouses, missions, dormitories, the Salvation Army, abandoned buildings, cabins, campgrounds, trailers, campers, mobile homes, or relocating to more accommodating climes.

The duration of the appellation "New" is problematic, as a structure may hang on for many years and get remodeled as the "New Arcade Hotel." Few buildings are prefixed with "old." "Old" is used if it adds panache, as in Omaha's Old Market and Bellevue's Olde Town.

Hotel names have suggestive texture and connectivity to the glamor of exalted metropolises and Western world dominance. Grand, Grand Central, Ritz, Carlton, New, Plaza, Commodore, Empire, Colonial, Wellington, Windsor (Omaha and Lincoln), Victoria, and Castle suggest royalty, aristocracy, authority, heroes, railroad executives, and pretensions. Eppley, Barker, Mercer, Iler, Millard, Rome, Loyal, Harley, Conant, Hill, Paxton, Redick, Henshaw, and Hilton reflect the owner or proprietor's self-praising first or family name. Grand, the most popular hotel prefix, was followed closely by St. (Saint). The term Hotel had replaced House by the 1880s.

Hotel reputations rely on word of mouth, recommendations, advertisements, travel agents, and print endorsements from publications such as Crofutts, Baedeker, Frommer's, Fodor's, Michelin, Rick Steves, Lonely Planet, Rough Guides, and AAA Tour Books. Yelp and TripAdvisor dominate social media today. Maintaining a reputation was and still is vital to survival. The fraternity of traveling salesmen, not unlike Professor Harold Hill in Meredith Wilson's *The Music Man*, picked up information about towns along the rail line.

The Thursday, May 19, 1887, edition of the *Omaha Daily Bee* printed four columns about hundreds of Presbyterian ministers and elders attending the General Assembly of the United States in the city. They came from over 20 states as well as the Dakotas and Washington (which did not become states until 1889) and Indian Territory. They stayed at the Millard, Arcade, Paxton, Cozzens, Metropolitan, Canfield, Planters, Barker, and Windsor hotels. Most were put up in private homes.

In 1856, the Hamilton House, a brick building at Douglas Street between Fourteenth and Fifteenth Streets, employed "half a dozen colored people" from St. Louis as servants. African Americans served diners at the Merchants Restaurant and many other establishments but were not welcome as paying guests.

Thousands of visitors flock to Omaha each May and June. Ak-Sar-Ben racing season, the Berkshire Hathaway annual stockholders meeting, and the College World Series fill hotels, bed and breakfasts, and the homes of friends. Lodgings in Omaha, Council Bluffs, and the general area are often booked months in advance.

It takes many hands, often hidden, to run the hospitality industry. Flurries of newspaper advertisements—often with gender and race restrictions—for positions such as desk clerks, night clerks, porters, bellhops, elevator operators, bookkeepers, cooks, dishwashers, maids, managers, restaurant servers, food purveyors, coffee boys, parking lot attendants, building maintenance, charwomen, housekeepers, repairmen, and waiters indicated new hotel and restaurant openings. Many job interviews and sales pitches occurred in hotels.

Hotel construction, a speculative enterprise, followed economic cycles. Boom and bust, slump, downturns, recessions, panics, depressions, and recoveries almost defied planning and exposed hotels to disruptions that could leave construction sites abandoned and foreclosed. Some hotels had good fortune and high occupancy rates. Some were victims of optimistic overbuilding followed by a downward business cycle, bad management, sunken reputations, or failure to update amidst changing neighborhoods, clientele, and standards. Catastrophic building fires, especially on winter's coldest days, were horrifying. Some hotels acquired unsavory reputations as newspapers reported people arrested, injured, or killed on their property.

Hotels and the hospitality industry are masters of hype, overstatement, superlatives, and hyperbole. Reporters were induced to give good reviews. New, renovated, refurbished, and fireproof were all part of the parlance of the trade. Newspapers published "Personals and Arrivals," "In the Hotel Corridor, " "Nebraska Guests at Leading Hotels," and other chatty accounts about newly registered guests, the rich and famous, and many more less-renowned characters.

Financial viability meant responding to local and cyclical challenges. Financial stability and continuity of management cannot be assured. Miscalculations occurred. Overheads, loan payments, maintenance, occupancy, and competition were constant concerns, several of which ended in lawsuits and bankruptcy. Guests skipping out without paying the bill were sued. The Saratoga in Florence, in 1856, was a case of build it and they did not come; finances delayed the opening of the Grand Central Hotel for three years. The McTauge of 1895 became the Henshaw in 1896 and the Dillon Diplomat in 1962; it closed in 1974. The upscale Madison boardinghouse opened broke on arrival in 1898. The much lauded Fontenelle opened in 1915 and closed in 1971, shortly after the Hilton opened; it was demolished in 1983.

Hoteliers and investors built, bought, leased, traded, and sold hotels and partnered to increase income. Before World War II, downtown hotels and family-owned roadside "motels" referred guests to one another. Cooperative merchandizing and word of mouth was for a slower age. The American Automobile Association (AAA), founded in 1902, facilitated trip planning.

Hotels and office buildings vacillate, change their character. They were modified to house long-term residents and transient guests or to serve as apartments, seminaries, or warehouses. Finance, opportunity, and the market dictate business models. For instance, the Schlitz offices became a hotel, the Mercer a jobbing house, Dellone became Omaha General Hospital, Herndon became Union Pacific headquarters, Cozzens a medical institute, and Paxton government-funded programs for women and elderly housing.

Alcohol, bars and lounges, restaurants, and main floor retail bays—all hotel profit centers—supplemented the small profit margin earned by renting rooms. Liquor law enforcement plagued hotels.

Building a hotel involved real estate brokers, financing, syndicates, banks, architects, builders, raw materials, brickyards, lumber, hardware, construction crews, bricklayers, stonemasons, carpenters, plumbers, electricians, owners, lessors, managers, syndicates, and consortiums. The time between announcement, ground-breaking ceremony, building, and opening can be years. Some hoteliers had interests in several hotels in Omaha and elsewhere.

Untold numbers of people have taken trains, cars, buses, and airplanes and crossed bridges, then lain their heads down to sleep in hotels that were simultaneously unfamiliar and familiar. They were travelers, tourists, people on the go. Their expectations of safety and security were sometimes disappointed. Poor sanitation, theft, break-ins, physical violence, police raids for disorderly offenses, alcohol, drugs, and the occasional death disrupted their stays. Fire was the worst—a nightmare and graveyard for guests, staff, volunteer and professional firefighters, and insurance companies. Wooden buildings can fall to matches, candles, gas lights, kitchen equipment, and spontaneous combustion. Declaring something "fireproof," an insurance term, does not make it so, even with sprinkler systems, smoke detectors, fire alarms, fire escapes, aerial ladders, fire codes, and no-smoking ordinances. Omaha hotels had several serious fires and numerous smaller conflagrations.

The *Omaha World-Herald* and the *Omaha Daily Bee* typically announced hotel openings in the Sunday business, building, and real estate sections. A combination of chest beating, news, promotion, advertising, and public service announcements listed the vendors and furnishers for wiring, lighting fixtures, safe and iron works, plumbing, lathing, plasterers, brick makers, masonry, concrete, roofing, mosaic flooring, wallpaper, architects, bedding and linens from Brandeis, mattresses, furnishings, financers, Nebraska Telephone company, fireproofing, restaurant, cutlery, laundry, barbershop, facilities, and retail tenants on the main floor. Management took special pride in furnishings from Chicago. Irvin A. Medlar Co. was the leading hotel stationery printer in Omaha.

Although some characterize Omaha at its worst as dirty, wicked, racist, and corrupt, with a selfish elite, the city is also home to generosity, philanthropy, community, and concern for the greater good and generations to follow. Postcards show a veneer of Omaha's better side. Matchbooks and menus reveal information the institutions wanted to share with customers.

Omaha business leaders printed the motto "The Convention City of the West" on many postcards. Not all hotels had postcards. Perhaps regulars, word of mouth, and newspaper advertisements sustained occupancy. The Hotel Boquet, located at Fifteenth and Howard Streets, advertised in 1914 in the *Alliance Herald*: "Headquarters for Stockmen. European Plan."

Hotel postcards were free advertising. In 1910, they cost about 1¢ each, or 30 for 25¢, plus 1¢ postage. In 2017, a typical price is eight cards for $9.99, and postage is 34¢. Postcard publishers addressed purchasers, and purchasers addressed family and friends. They wrote in ink, it ran light, and they dipped the pen in the bottle.

One

Pioneers, Salesmen, and Tourists

Getting to and leaving Omaha has been accomplished throughout the years via walking, horseback riding, riverboats, stagecoaches, animal-drawn wagons, railroads, automobiles, buses, trucks, and airplanes. At the beginning of its story, Omaha, located on the frontier, was a "Gateway to the West." By the end of the 19th century, Omaha promoted itself "The Convention City of the West."

The biggest impediments to travelers were distance and the Missouri River. The transcontinental railway conquered distance. Rowboats and ferries crossed the river. During the winter, ice supported intrepid travelers. Wooden bridges were replaced by metal bridges that could support railroads, streetcars, automobiles, and trucks.

Pioneer travel was rough and uncomfortable. Wood frame settlement hotels sufficed at the beginning. Brick and stone structures indicated confidence in permanency. Runners and touts met passengers getting off the train, extolling the value of their establishment. Standard time zones, introduced in 1884, facilitated railway scheduling and safety.

The telegraph and transcontinental railroad created an increasingly diverse and sophisticated infrastructure. Financiers in New York; legislators in Washington, DC, and Lincoln, Nebraska; and entrepreneurs relished opportunities for personal gain. The railway epitomized robber baron capitalism.

Several postcards reveal trolley, tram, and streetcar tracks. These disappeared in the 1950s as the automobile and oil industry exercised supremacy. Some bemoaned rising exhaust emissions, gridlock, parking squeeze, poor public transportation, and hope for economic and environmental light rail and bike paths.

One can still take the train to the West Coast. The "California Zephyr" departs from the Omaha Amtrak station at 1003 South Ninth Street. One day and 17 hours later, passengers arrive in Emeryville across the bay from San Francisco.

This chapter covers pioneer settlement, the 1898 Trans-Mississippi Exposition, the 1913 tornado, the Great Depression, World War I, and World War II, and technology that evolved from horse and wagon to train, automobile, and airplane—events and transformations that engaged Omaha citizenry and visitors.

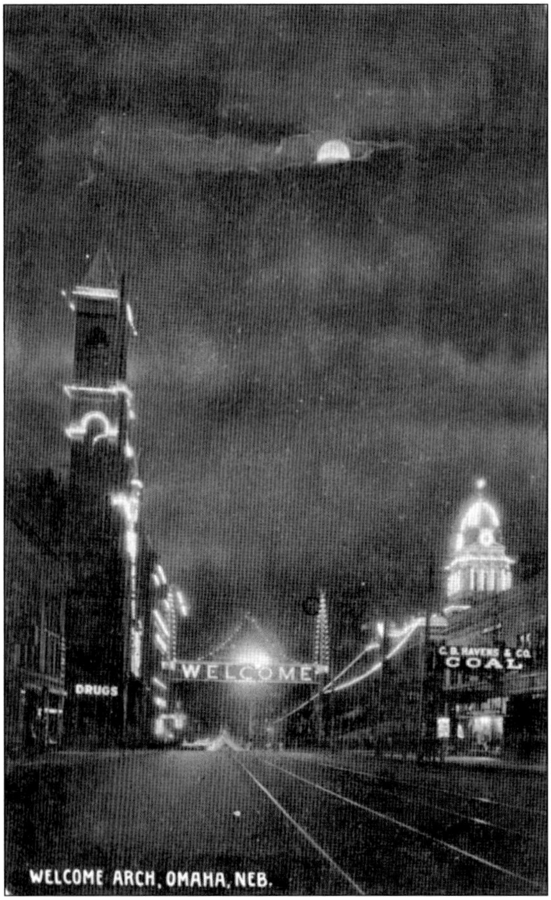

WELCOME ARCH LIT AT NIGHT. This "Welcome" to Omaha wrapped the altruism of Midwestern friendliness in economic self-interest. Columbus, North Platte, and Denver had similar structures. Visitors brought money to Omaha, stayed in hotels, ate, shopped, and sought nighttime entertainment, all fueling the local economy. Commerce thrived amidst American mobility. This sign between the five-story City Hall and Douglas County Courthouse dates from 1908. C.B. Havers & Co. Coal is visible on the right. This sign was not really an arch.

WELCOME AT THE CIVIC CENTER. This view is from the same angle, but much has changed—not just that it is daytime. On the right (the south side) is the new Douglas County Courthouse designed by John Latenser and built between 1909 and 1912; this replaced the old courthouse that dated from 1882 and was razed in 1913. On the left, the City Hall tower looms, flags fly, and seven horse-drawn carriages line the curb.

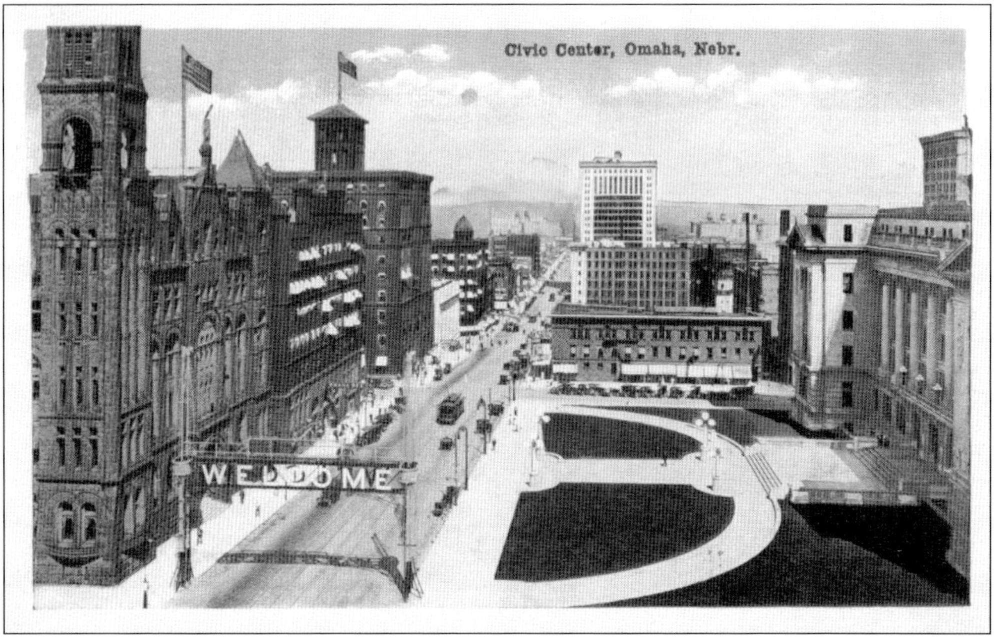

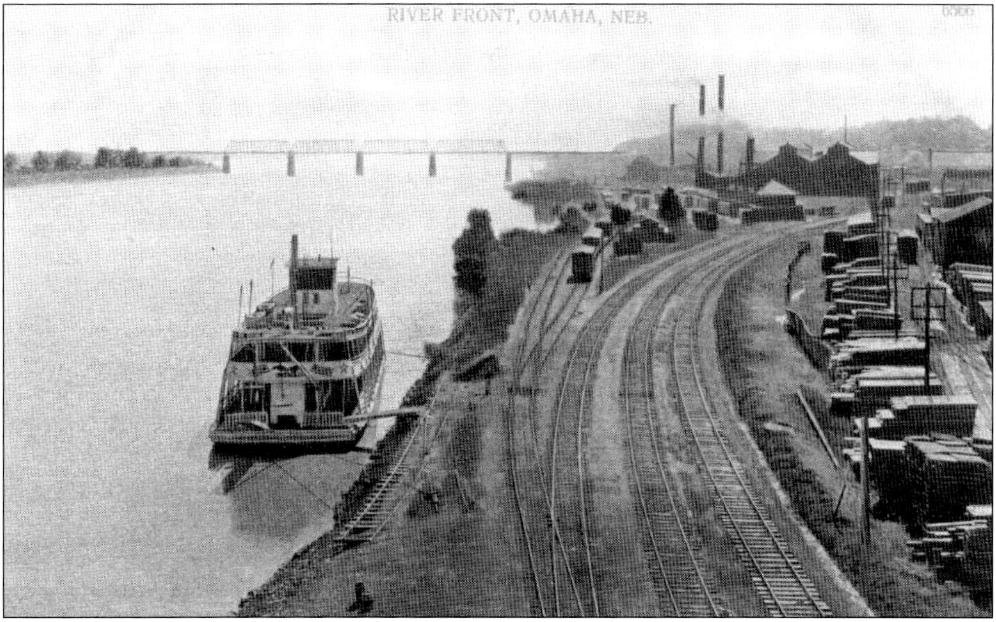

RIVERFRONT AND STEAMER AT OMAHA. The Ohio, Missouri, and Mississippi Rivers comprised a riverine transportation network. The Missouri River connected Omaha to Kansas City, St. Louis, New Orleans, and Sioux City. Omaha surpassed Bellevue, Florence, and Nebraska City as freighting and shipping centers. The flexibility of the railway improved upon these "natural highways." This riverboat faces the Union Pacific Bridge and smelters.

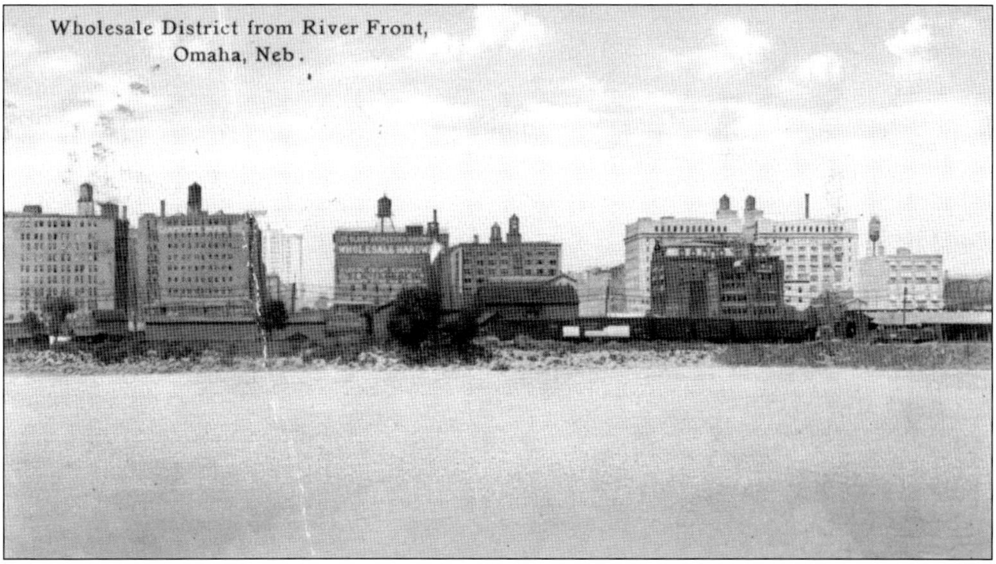

WHOLESALE DISTRICT FROM RIVER FRONT—JOBBERS CANYON. Commerce combined with culture. Baedeker, a German publisher, began printing travel books in 1827. In the 1893 first American edition, James F. Muirhead recommended Omaha's Millard, Murray, and Dellone hotels and Council Bluffs' Grand, Danforth, and Pacific Hotels. In 1909, Baedeker recommended the Paxton, Rome, Henshaw, Millard, Murray, and Merchants hotels. This card sent from Denver to Pennsylvania reported, "When we got to Lincoln we had 7 cars on the train, but 5 now, as we divided into sections on account of hills."

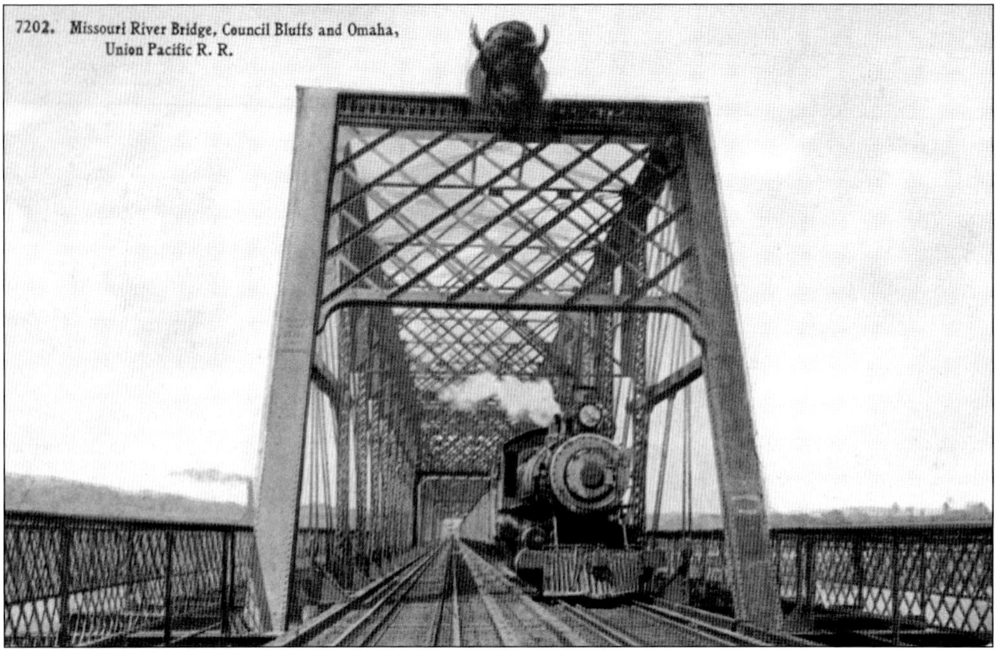

MISSOURI RIVER BRIDGE. Railroad bridges are vital arteries. Ferrying trains and crossing on ice in the winter was a stopgap. Baedeker described this 1886 railway bridge as a "fine iron Bridge, more than ½ M. long, erected at a cost of $1,000,000." A bison crowns it in this view.

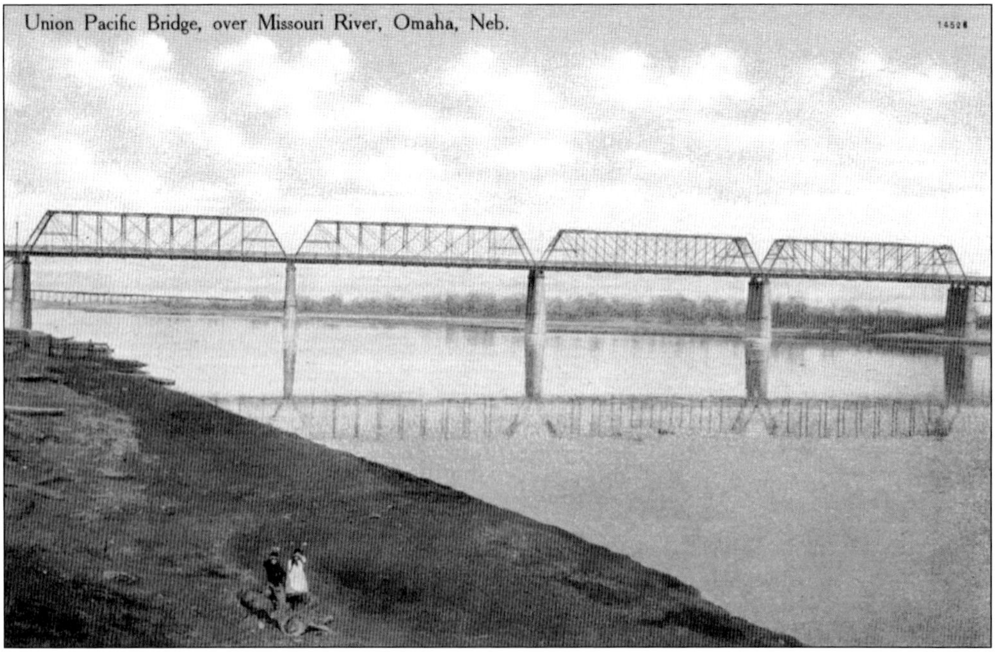

UNION PACIFIC BRIDGE OVER MISSOURI RIVER. This view of the 1886 bridge is presented in a playful painterly and picturesque fashion. The trusses are reflected in the water. A man and a woman amble on the sandy shore with driftwood at their feet. The river is low, evoking a serene and bucolic vision reminiscent of the work of European impressionists.

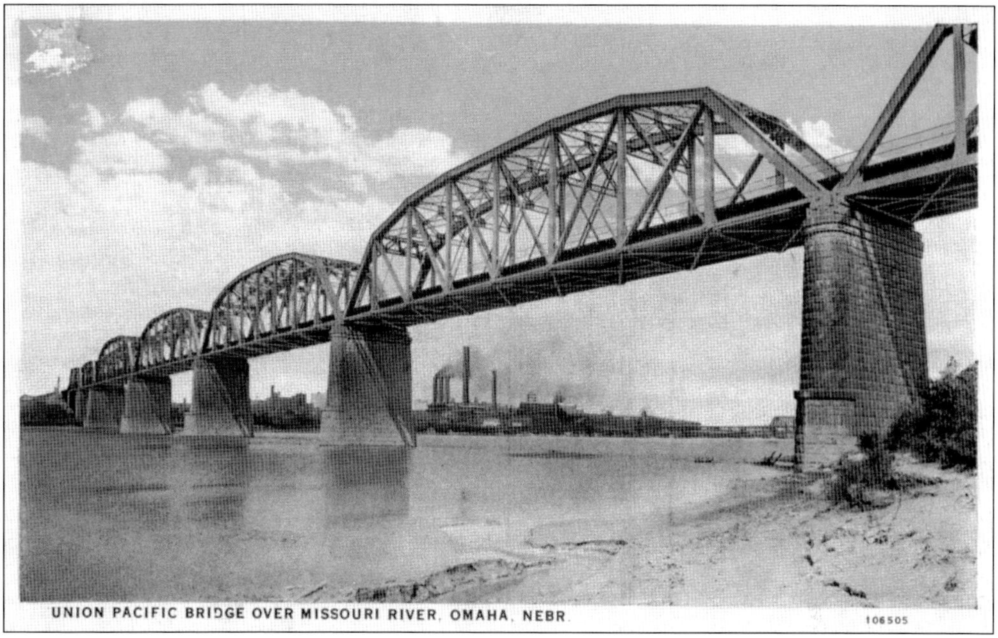

Union Pacific Bridge and ASARCO. In the background of this postcard featuring the 1916 bridge, the American Smelting and Refining Company (ASARCO) is smelting lead. The plant closed in 1997, and the riverfront has since undergone environmental cleanup and redevelopment including Gallup University, public art installations, and the 3,000-foot 2008 Bob Kerrey Pedestrian Bridge.

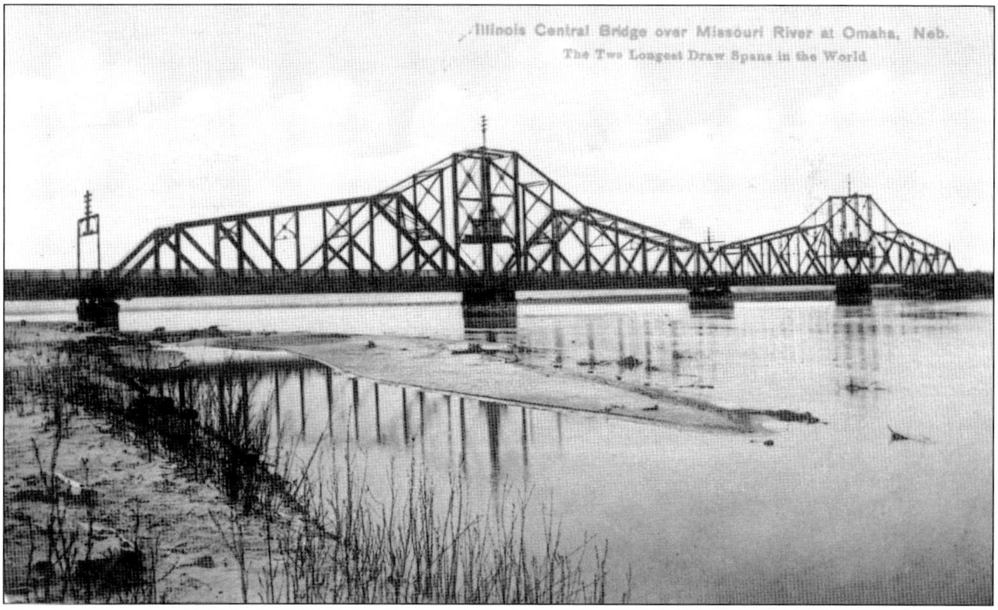

Illinois Central Bridge over Missouri River. Built at Twenty-Eighth Street and Woodland Avenue east of Abbott Drive, this bridge has changed ownership and is not currently in operation. Airplane passengers can see it when taking off and landing at Eppley Airfield. The card's sender, "F.O.S.," wrote on July 30, 1911, to Miss Lucile in San Francisco: "Turned me down again didn't you. I had to come alone after all."

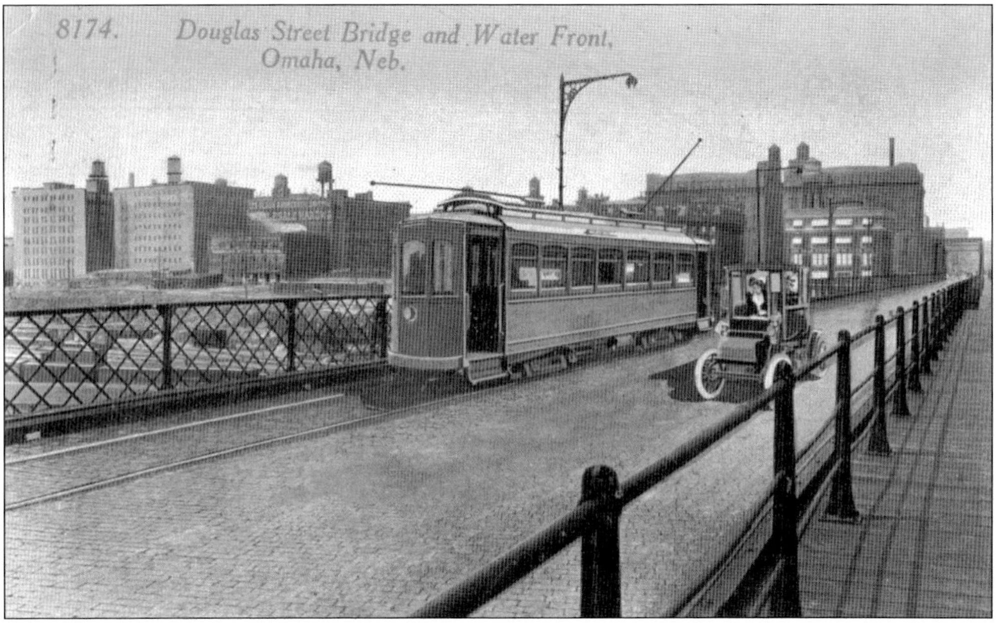

DOUGLAS STREET BRIDGE. The Omaha and Council Bluffs Street Railway Company built the first road bridge (which later became part of the Lincoln Highway) across the Missouri River between Council Bluffs, Iowa, and Omaha in 1888. The streetcar connected the two cities. Streetcars, horses, and wagon traffic have been replaced by automobiles, trucks, and buses. In the early 20th century, a large "Welcome to Omaha" sign hung from the trusses.

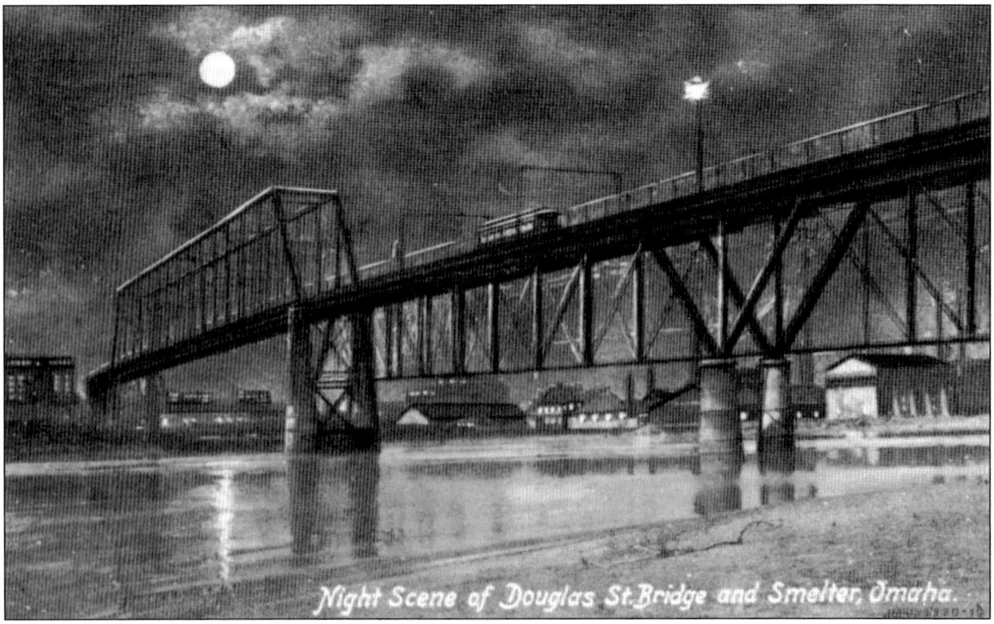

NIGHT SCENE OF DOUGLAS STREET BRIDGE AND SMELTER. Night scenes were a popular postcard genre. Walter in Omaha wrote to Chadron in August 1909, revealing human foibles: "Received your card some time ago and wrote an ans. But forgot to mail the card. Carried it around in my pocket so long that I spoilt it." Interstate 480 took the place of the Douglas Street Bridge in 1966.

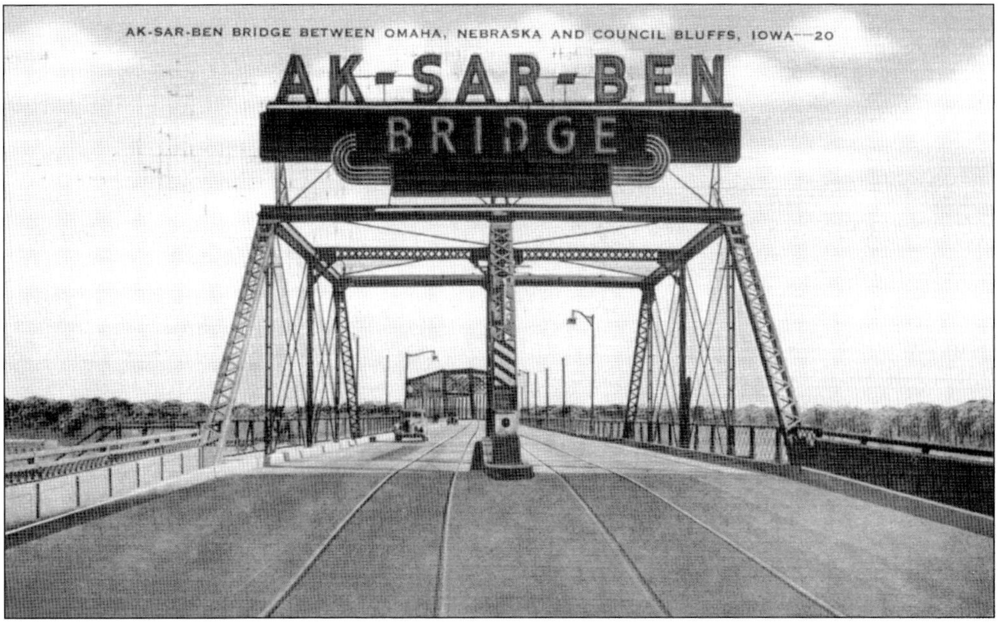

AK-SAR-BEN BRIDGE. The Douglas Street Bridge became the toll-charging Ak-Sar-Ben Bridge in 1938. In 1939, toll totals averaged $1,117 per day. In September 1947, tolls ended, saving drivers 15¢. Politicians met at the Fontenelle before going to the bridge in 12 Army cars. On this card, Dora wrote to Betty in Elkhart, Indiana: "This is now a free bridge since last Thursday, still haven't taken advantage but will shortly. They celebrated with fireworks & parades."

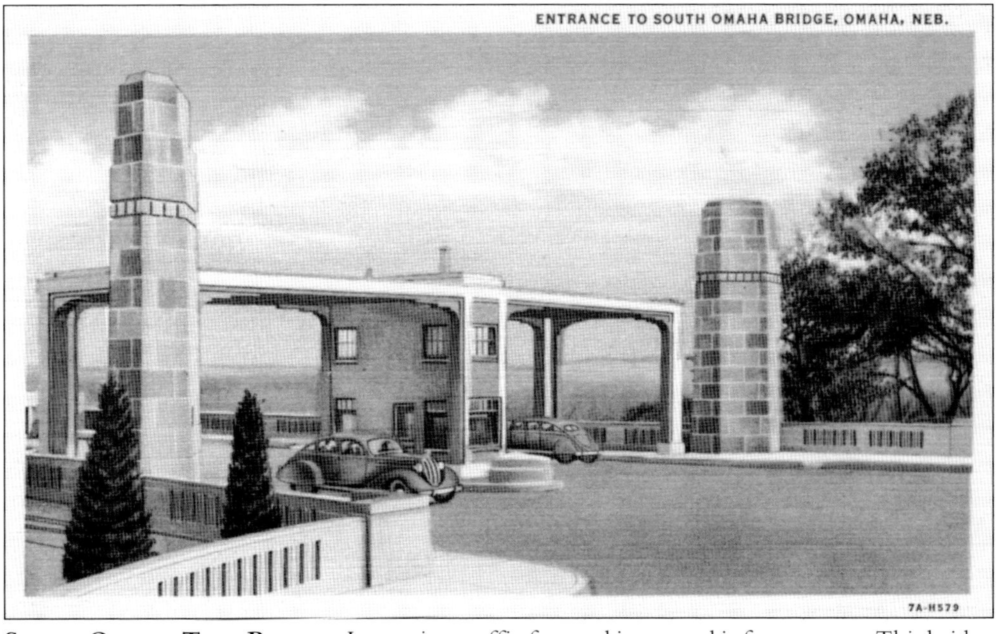

SOUTH OMAHA TOLL BRIDGE. Increasing traffic fostered improved infrastructure. This bridge opened in 1933, and tolls ended in 1947. It was renamed the South Omaha Veterans Memorial Bridge in 1995 and demolished in 2010. The Mormon Pioneer Memorial Bridge (pictured on the back cover), located on Omaha's northern edge (where Mormons crossed the Missouri in 1846), opened in 1952. Tolls were eliminated in 1979.

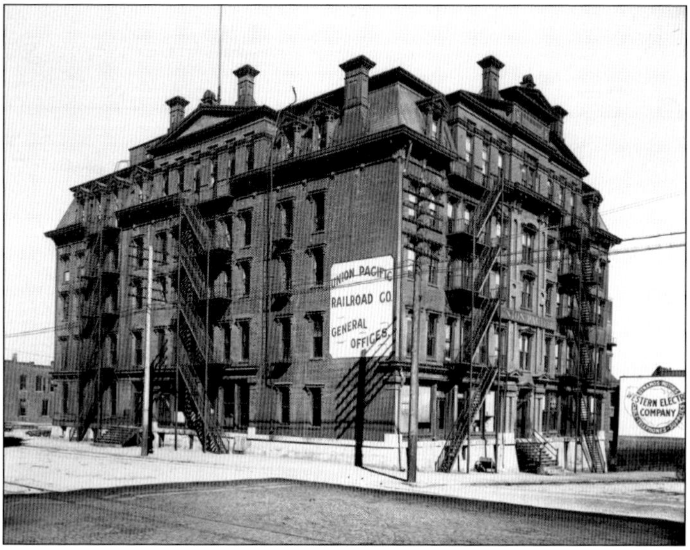

HERNDON HOUSE—UNION PACIFIC HEADQUARTERS. Union Pacific (UP) acquired the Herndon House, located at Ninth and Farnam Streets (and discussed in chapter two), as its headquarters in 1870. UP added a fifth story with a mansard roof. The fire escapes date from around 1910. UP moved to a new building at Fifteenth and Dodge Streets in 1911. (Durham Museum, Bostwick-Frohardt Collection.)

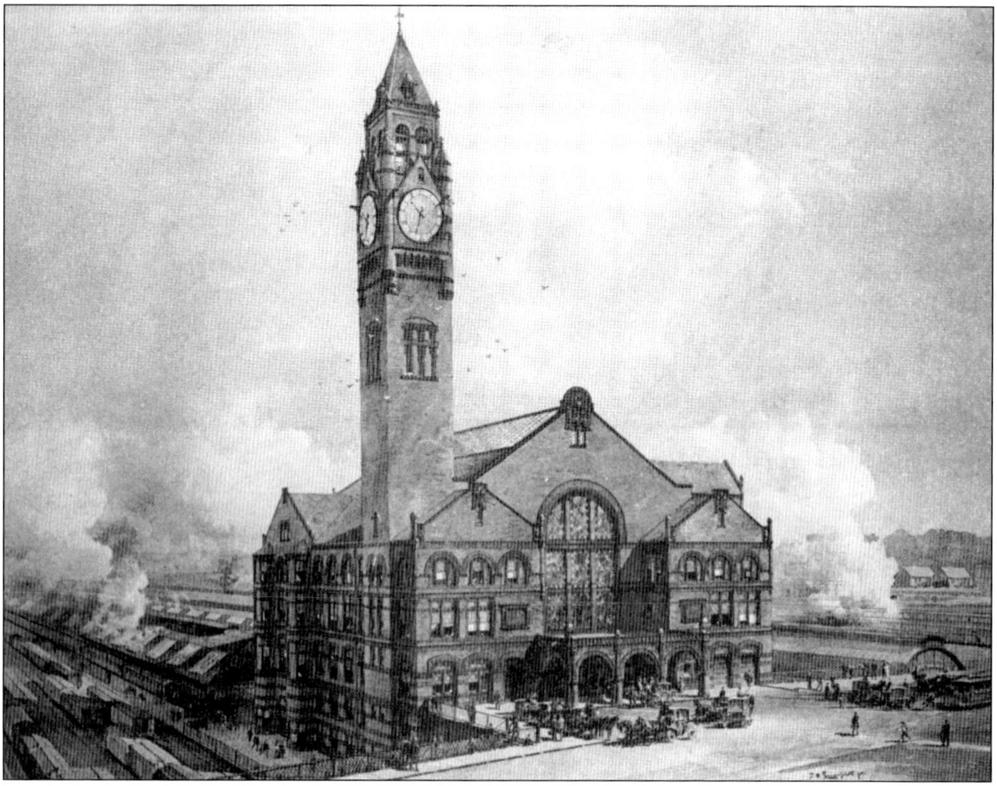

SKETCH OF THE UNION PACIFIC STATION. Architects produced at least two depot sketches between 1872 and the 1880s. In this one, there are several horse-drawn carriages waiting for passengers on Tenth Street. The 1874 *Croffut's Trans-Continental Tourist's Guide* reported that omnibuses took passengers to hotels for 50¢. Streetcars cost 5¢ and left the station every five minutes, passing the principal hotels. This sketch (with a tower) evokes grandiosity akin to that of the 1880 Omaha City Hall and 1898 post office, both of which were demolished in 1966. (Omaha Public Library.)

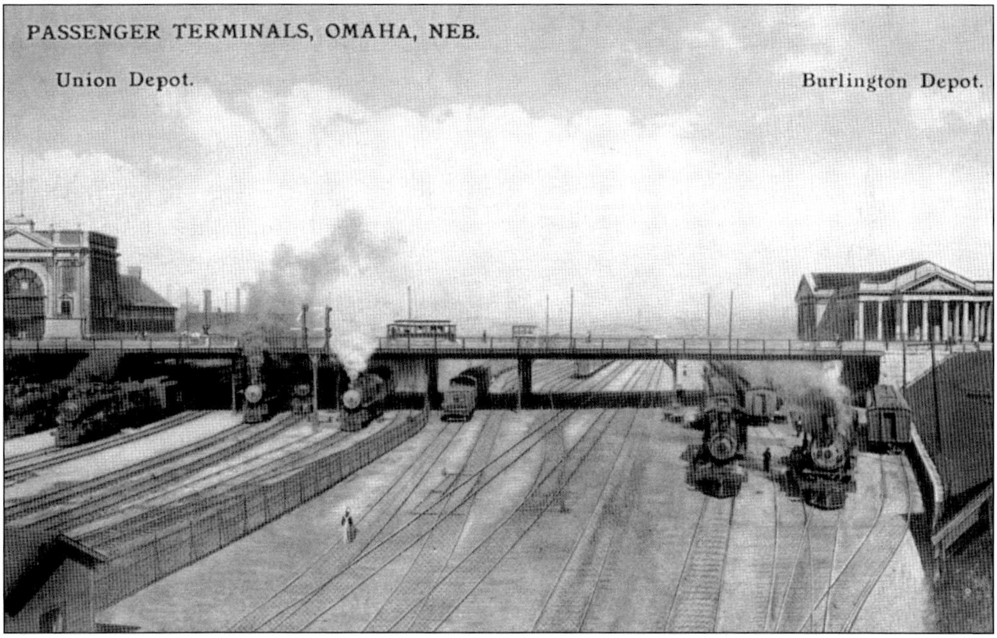

PASSENGER TERMINALS. The Union Pacific and Burlington stations have at least 12 tracks between them, and almost all contain locomotives or rolling stock. The differences in late 19th-century financial conditions between the Union Pacific and the Burlington meant they could not cooperate to build one station. The bridge, the Tenth Street viaduct, has a streetcar on it. A passenger wrote in 1913 to a relative in Los Angeles: "Dear Mama. Left Omaha last eve. Crossed Missouri River into Iowa. Crossed Mississippi River into Illinois this AM. Soon be in Chicago. Love to all."

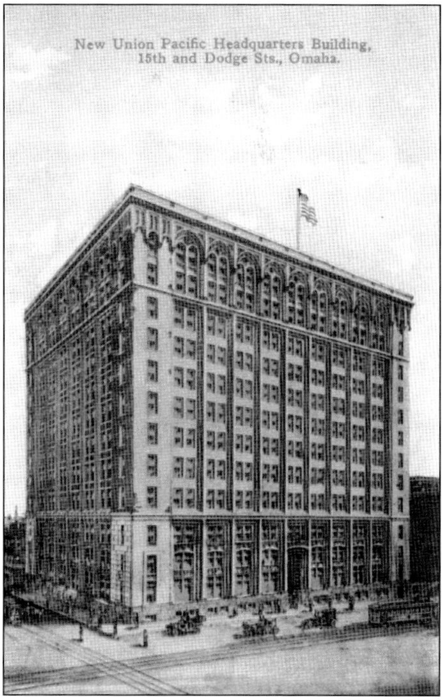

NEW UNION PACIFIC HEADQUARTERS BUILDING. This 1911 view depicts streetcar tracks, a trolley, pedestrians, a horse carriage, an automobile, and a moderate breeze at Fifteenth and Dodge Streets. A more flamboyant Union Pacific headquarters card states, "This handsome and massive structure houses the general offices of the Union Pacific Railroad. The neon-lighted sign on the roof is more than forty feet high." This building was demolished in 2008 after UP moved across the street in 2004 to its current headquarters at 1400 Douglas Street.

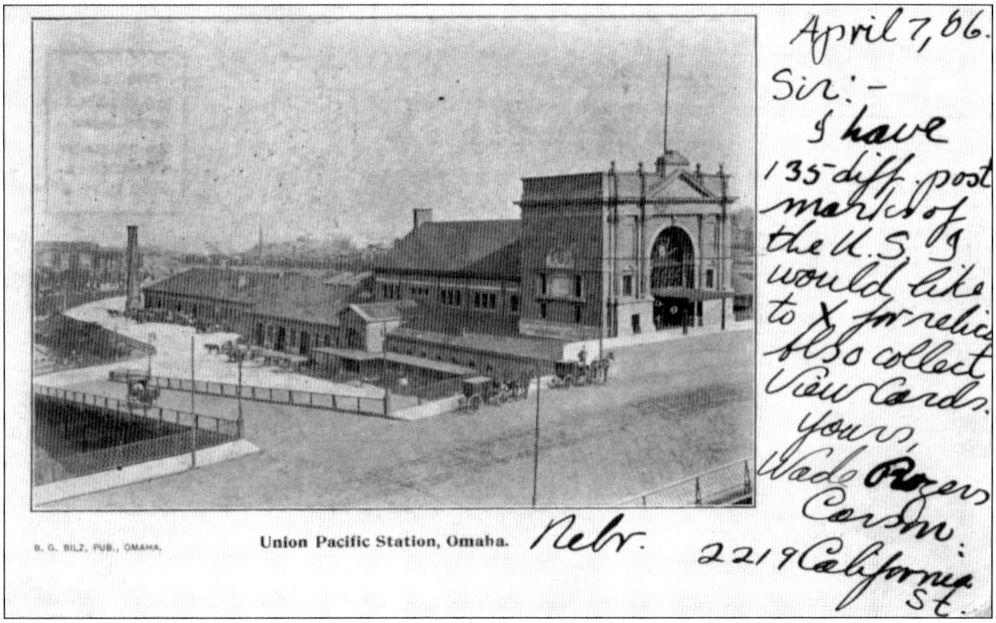

UNION PACIFIC STATION "COWSHED." This station, designed by Chicago architect Charles Frost and completed in 1899, replaced the "cowshed" dismantled in 1890. This view from Tenth Street shows three horse-drawn vehicles. Wade, an Omaha postcard collector, wrote to Walter in North Carolina on April 7, 1906: "Sir: I have 135 diff postmarks of the U.S. I would like to X for relics also collect view cards. Yours, Wade."

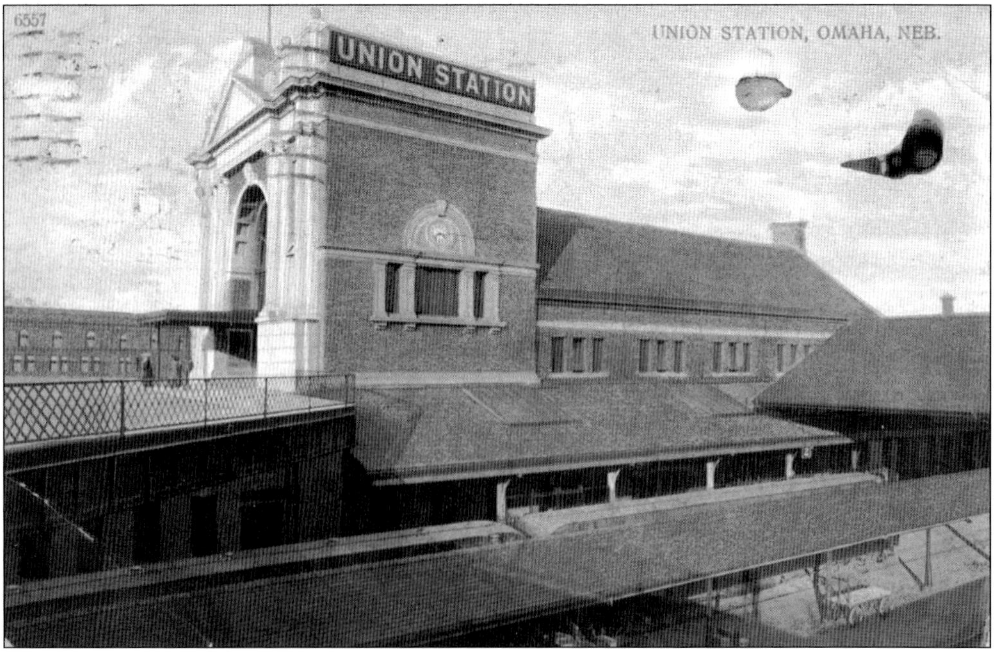

UNION STATION IN FEBRUARY. Mary wrote in February 1908 to Miss Edna in Chicago: "This is where I came into Omaha. It is a good looking place on the outside at least." Perhaps February weather was being kind. Another wrote more critically: "This picture is a joke, it is all mud around the depot."

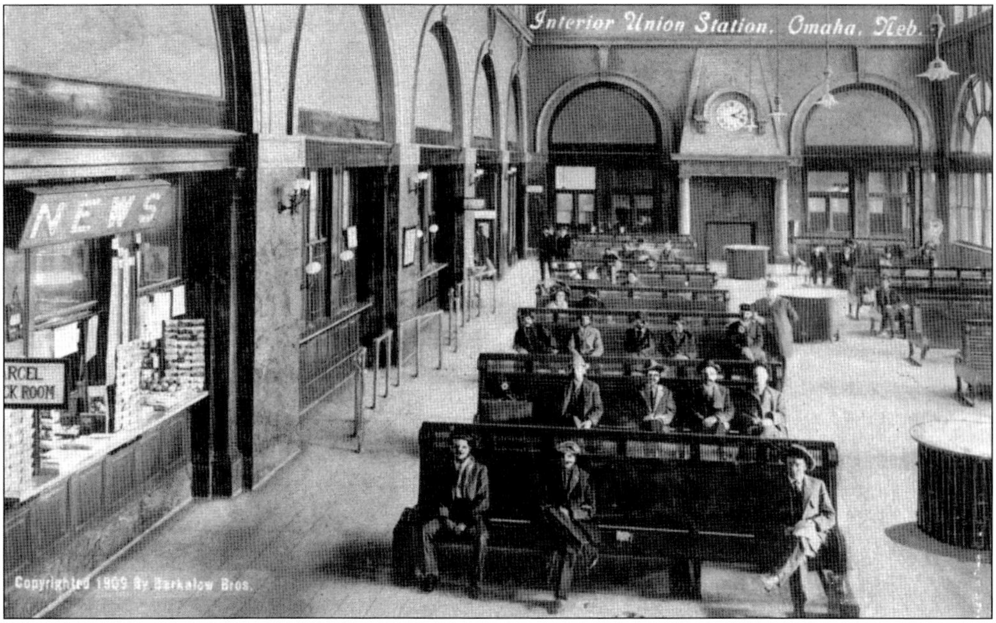

Interior of Union Station. A lot of traveling time is spent in waiting rooms. On the left is a parcel check room and newsstand. Twenty-nine people sit on benches—about three are women. In the 1870s, the station had an "emigrant house" for passengers who paid 25¢ for a plain meal and good lodging.

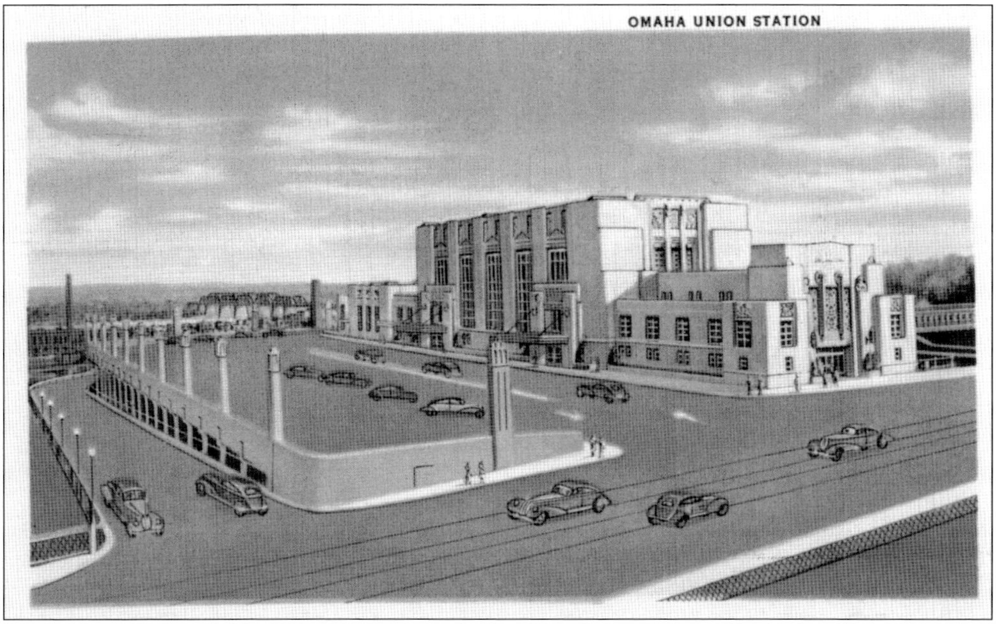

New Union Station. This Art Deco station was designed by Gilbert Stanley Underwood and opened in 1931. Above the entrance are the words "Dedicated by the railroads of Omaha to the service, comfort and convenience of the people." Amtrak opened in 1971. The station became the Western Heritage Museum in 1975 and the Durham Museum in 1996 (to honor donors Marge and Richard Durham). At the museum, children play on engines, carriages, and cabooses; seniors reminisce; and soda jerks run the fountain.

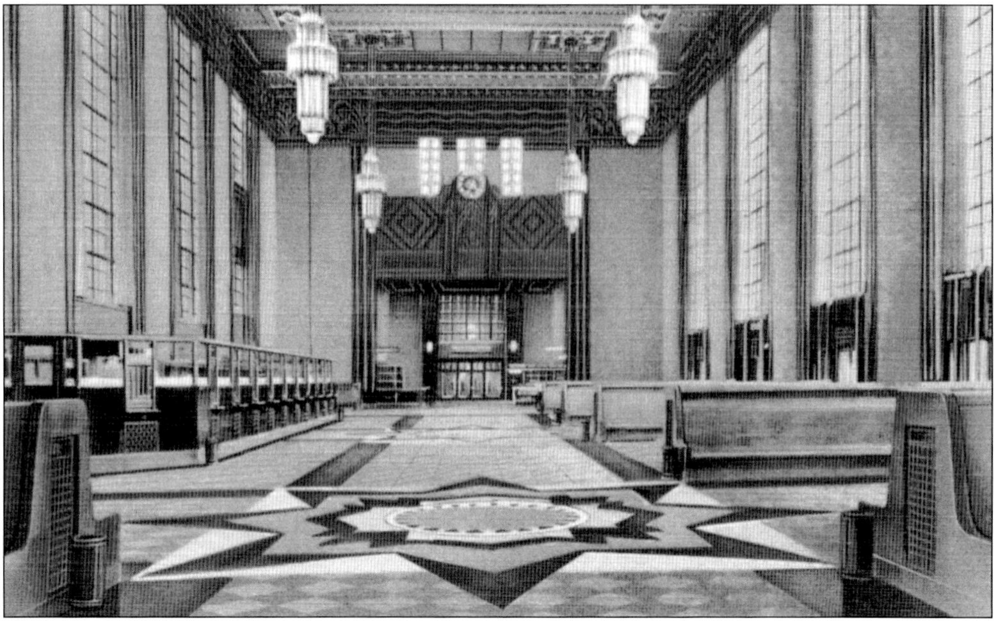

MAIN WAITING ROOM, UNION STATION. Large rooms demonstrate architectural skills and awe passengers. In May 1944, Lydia wrote to Gervais in Oregon: "Hello Darling—X marks the spot where mother & I are sitting now. There are lots of people in here too. We get the train for Falls City 8:10 in the morning. We both had a good supper here. The dining room is straight ahead. We are both well and not a bit tired. Take good care of yourself dearest. Lots of Love."

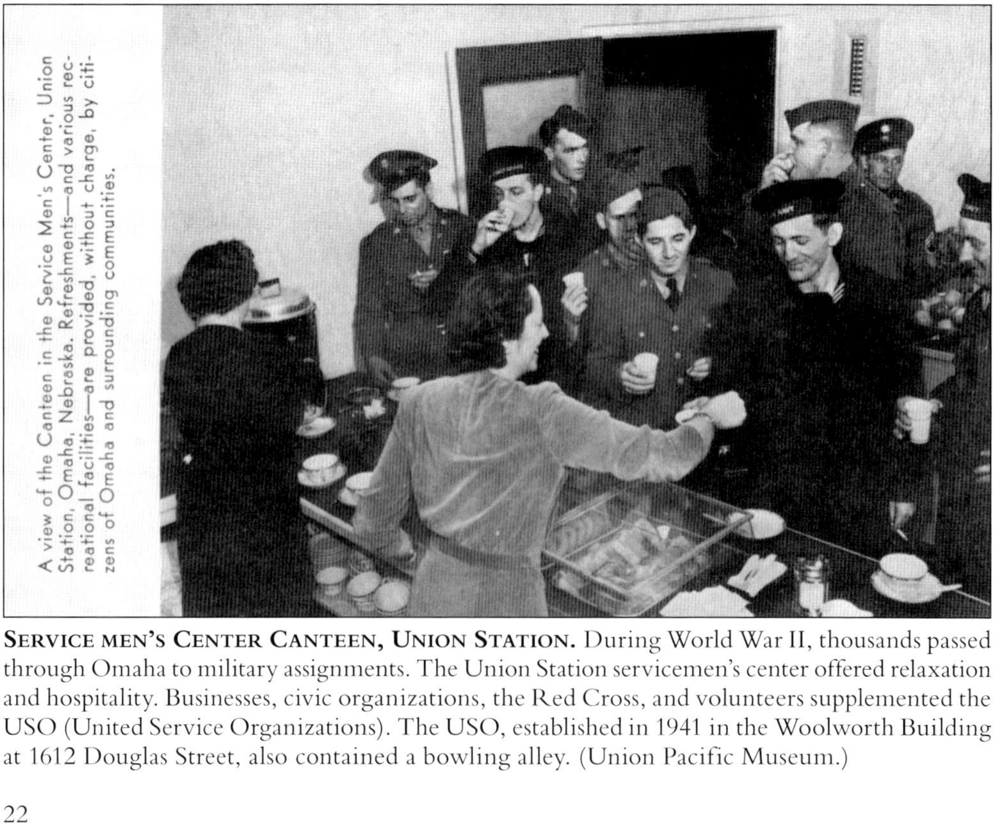

SERVICE MEN'S CENTER CANTEEN, UNION STATION. During World War II, thousands passed through Omaha to military assignments. The Union Station servicemen's center offered relaxation and hospitality. Businesses, civic organizations, the Red Cross, and volunteers supplemented the USO (United Service Organizations). The USO, established in 1941 in the Woolworth Building at 1612 Douglas Street, also contained a bowling alley. (Union Pacific Museum.)

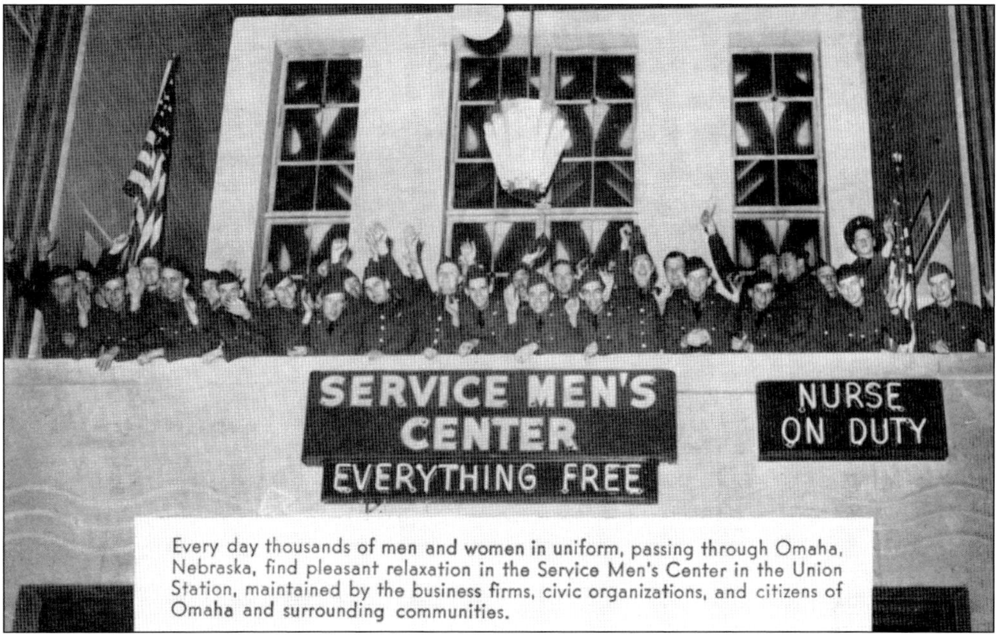

SERVICE MEN'S CENTER, STATION MEZZANINE. Union Pacific prepared this card. The *Omaha World-Herald* reported in January 1945 that hospital trains rated the highest hospitality. Resourceful women provided bowls of ice cream. Next to food and postcards, stationery and magazines made the biggest hit on hospital trains. Ak-Sar-Ben provided 20,000 postcards of the coliseum. Giving troops postcards began during World War I. (Union Pacific Museum.)

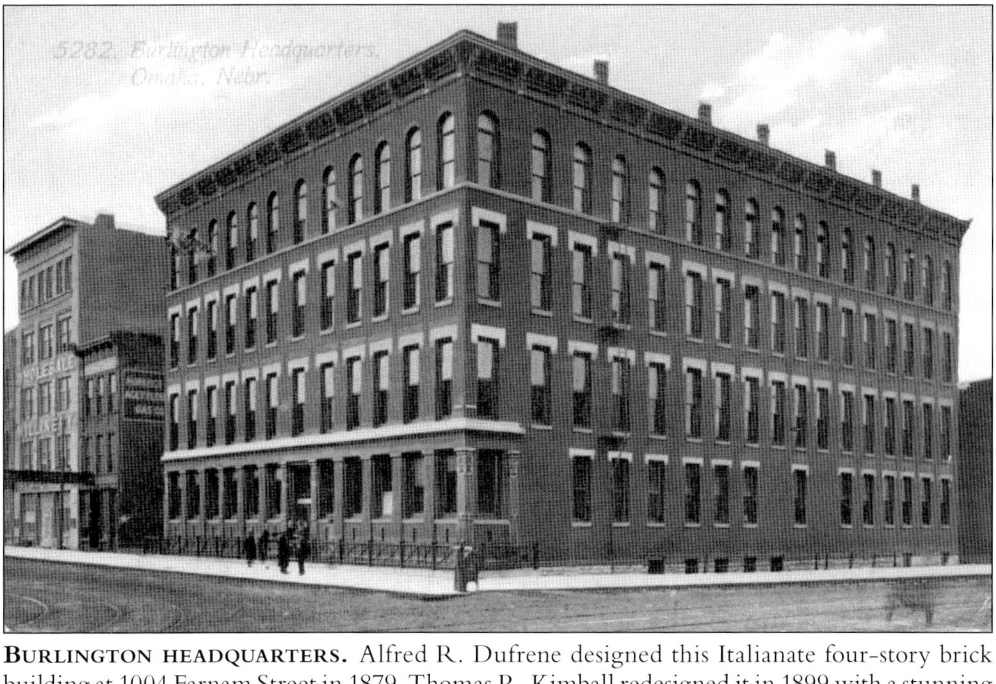

BURLINGTON HEADQUARTERS. Alfred R. Dufrene designed this Italianate four-story brick building at 1004 Farnam Street in 1879. Thomas R. Kimball redesigned it in 1899 with a stunning central atrium. The railroad vacated the premises in 1966. It sat empty for several years and was rehabilitated in 1983. Burlington Place is now an office building on the Gene Leahy Mall.

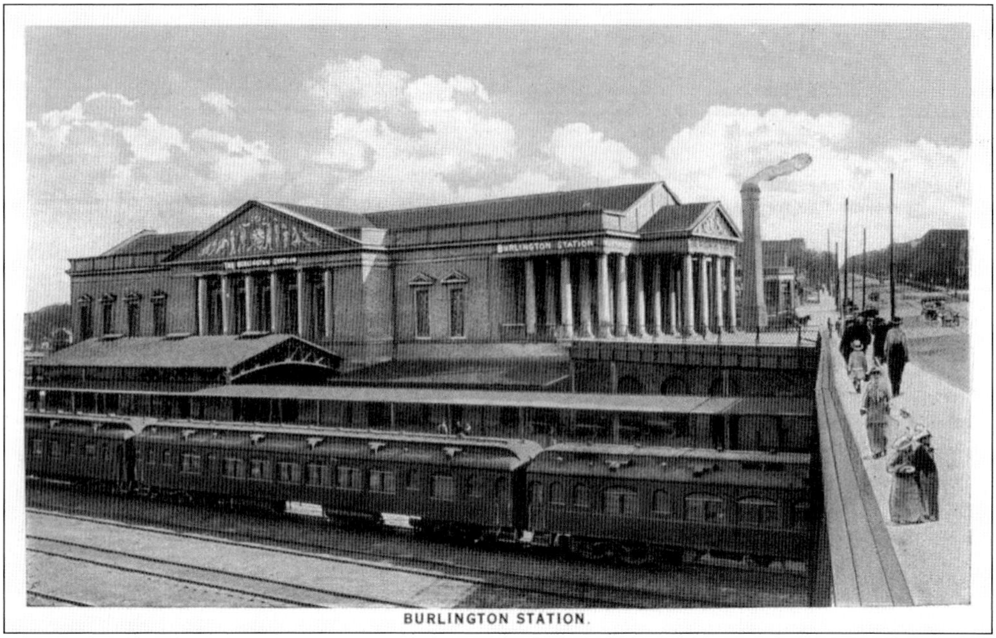

BURLINGTON STATION, 1920. Thomas Rogers Kimball designed this Italianate Indiana limestone station that opened in 1898—just in time for the Trans-Mississippi Exposition. The exterior columns at the Tenth Street entrance were made of Colorado granite, while the interior columns were Sienna marble. George wrote in July 1910 to Carol in Dixon, Illinois: "This is the Depot that I got off at when I came from Kansas City. It is a nice one. Everything is lovely in Nebraska."

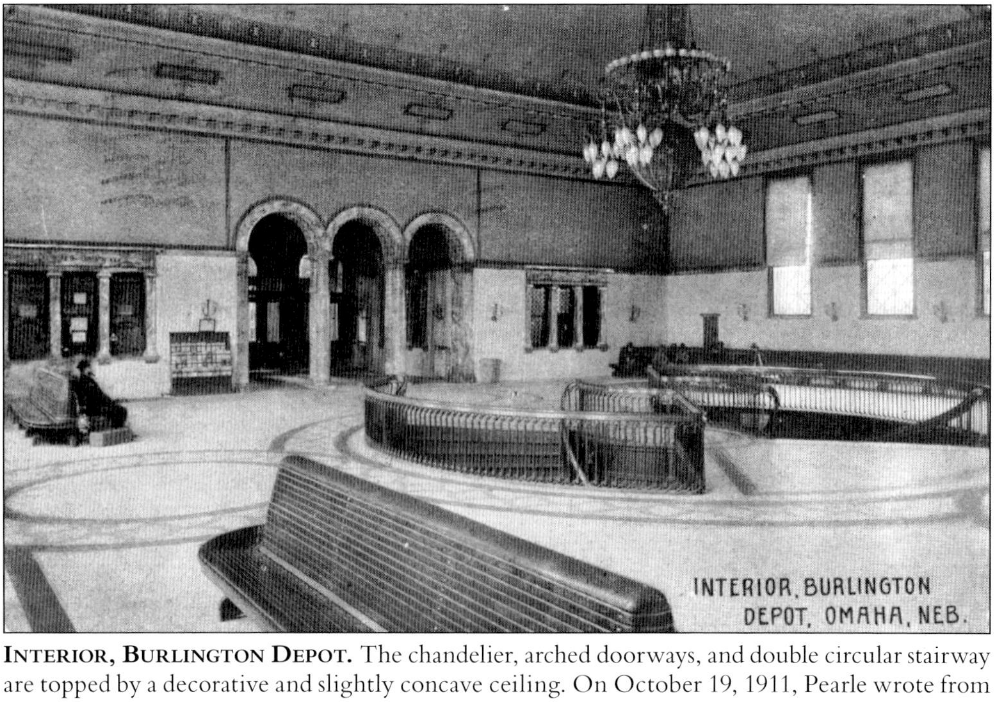

INTERIOR, BURLINGTON DEPOT. The chandelier, arched doorways, and double circular stairway are topped by a decorative and slightly concave ceiling. On October 19, 1911, Pearle wrote from Fresno to Carrie in Milledgeville, Illinois: "Omaha was a lovely place . . . Wish you were here eating English walnuts, pink white apples, figs and watermelon."

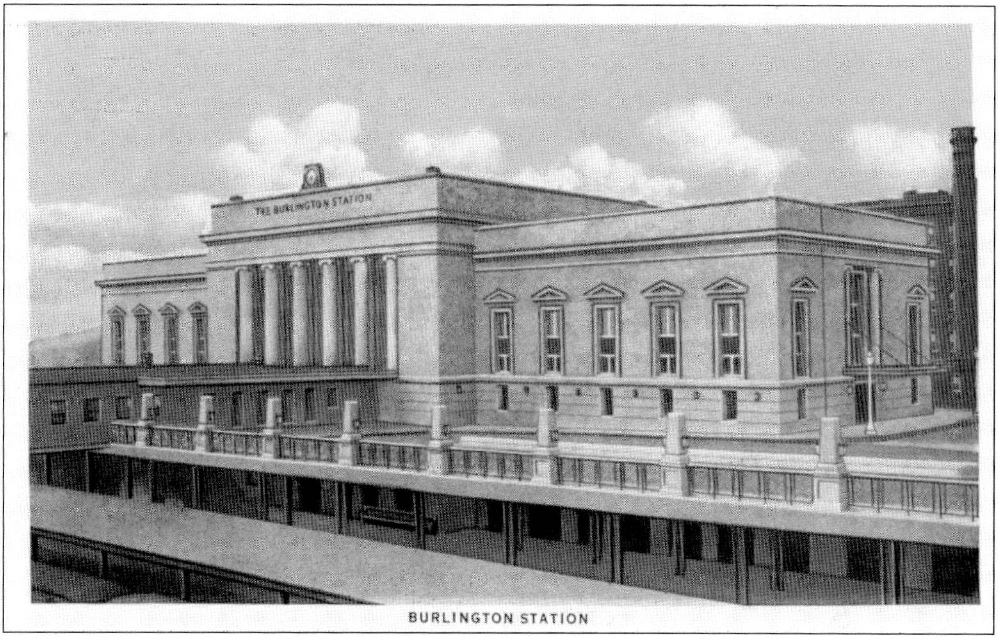

Renovating Burlington Station. The Burlington station was remodeled in 1929–1930 with a cleaner neoclassical revival motif to be competitive with Union Pacific's prospective grand edifice. The old exterior columns went to Memorial Stadium in Lincoln. The roofline was raised over the main waiting room. The station closed in 1971 and stood vacant until 2015, when it became the home of television station KETV.

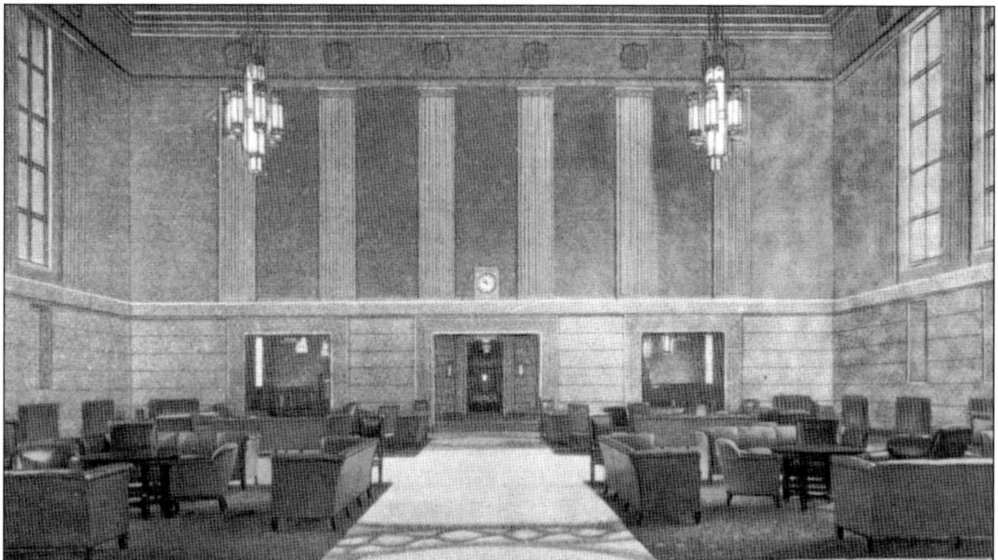

Main Lobby, New Burlington Station. Union Station employed Southwestern colors and right-angled decoration. Burlington employed circular motifs. Michael wrote to Sheila at Saint Catherine's Hospital in Omaha on September 6, 1944: "Eating dinner. Having a wonderful time. Wish you were hear [*sic*]." The circular motifs of the arches, floor, stairway, and chandeliers were preserved by the architects who renovated the building for KETV in the 2010s.

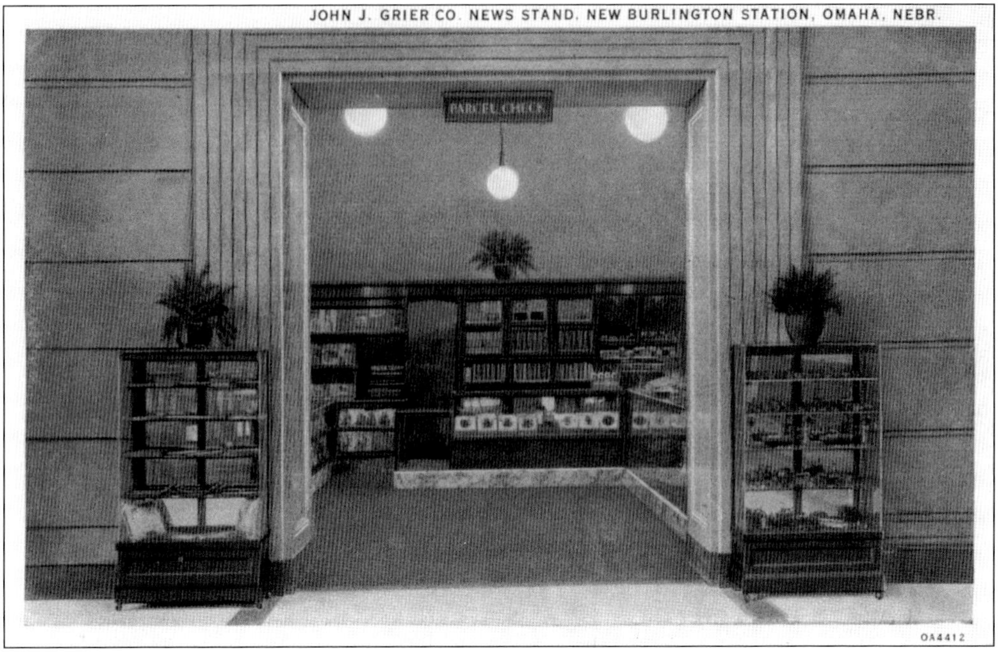

John J. Grier Co. Newsstand, New Burlington Station. Newsstands and bookstores are common in railway stations and airports. Travelers pass time by reading or snoozing. First-class passengers received complimentary newspapers and magazines. This finely-appointed room with wood and glass cases has a "parcel check" sign over the door. The entrance cases flanking the door are on wheels; the right one contains model toy boats and tractors for adults to purchase for children who will ask, "Daddy, what did you bring me?"

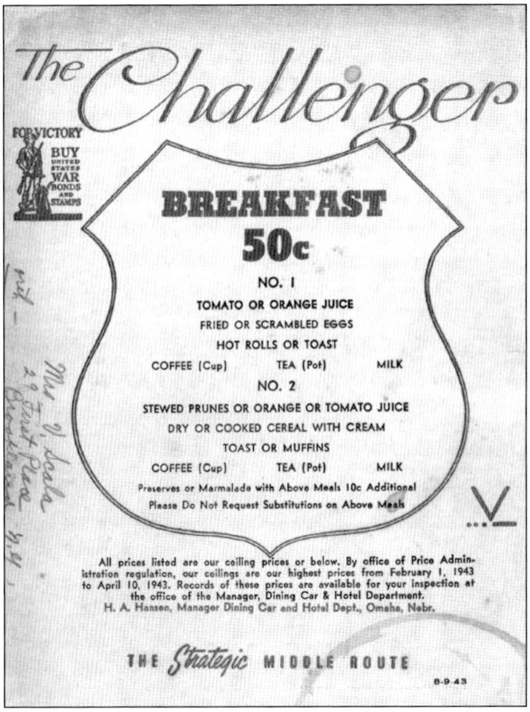

The Challenger Breakfast Menu. The Union Pacific's *Challenger* steam locomotives were built between 1936 and 1944. The *Challenger* route used diesel engines with Domeliners in the 1950s and 1960s. This menu is from the earlier era. Chalkboards and printed menus illustrate meal choices and prices. Dining cars opened early and closed late. This wartime menu complies with Office of Price Administration regulations and promotes war bonds. On the "Strategic Middle Route," 50¢ bought a middle-of-the-road menu of eggs, toast, prunes and coffee. An attractive children's menu catered to youngsters. (Union Pacific Museum.)

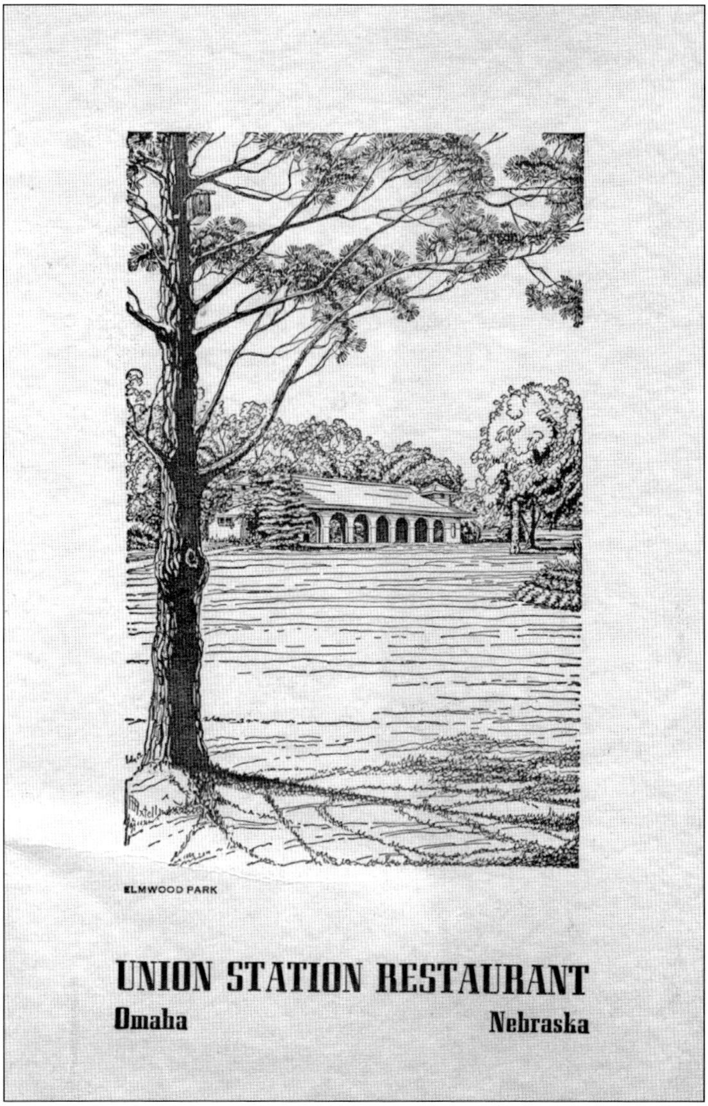

UNION STATION, 1947 MENU. Railways served food in stations, at stops along the line, and on the train (including lunchboxes). Passengers used the restaurant while waiting for trains. A sign in the Omaha Depot in 1877 read: "LUNCH BASKETS FILLED FOR 23 CENTS. TAKE NOTICE BLACK HILLERS." The Black Hills gold rush occurred in 1877. The front of this 1947 menu maintains a motif of technology and the natural world. The illustration follows a European tradition of using pastoral and architectural art on menu covers—in this case, the pavilion at Elmwood Park (see page 122). The impressive 1947 menu featured appetizers of Spiced Salmon en Wine, Crab or Shrimp Cocktail, or Cornucopia of Smoked Tongue, while $1.75 would buy Calf's Liver Saute with Rasher Bacon or Fricassee of Young Chicken, Parsley Dumplings. For $2, one could have French Fried Gulf Shrimps, Caper Mayonnaise or Pan Fried Soft Shell Crabs, Columbia Butter, and US Choice club Sirloin cost $2.25. All meals came with salad, potatoes, vegetable, dessert, and coffee (or tea or milk). The specials were One-Half Cold Fresh Cracked Crab or Fresh Columbia River Salmon Steak for $1.50. Parents could share their portion with children "without extra cost or half portions served at two-thirds price to children under twelve years of age." (Union Pacific Museum.)

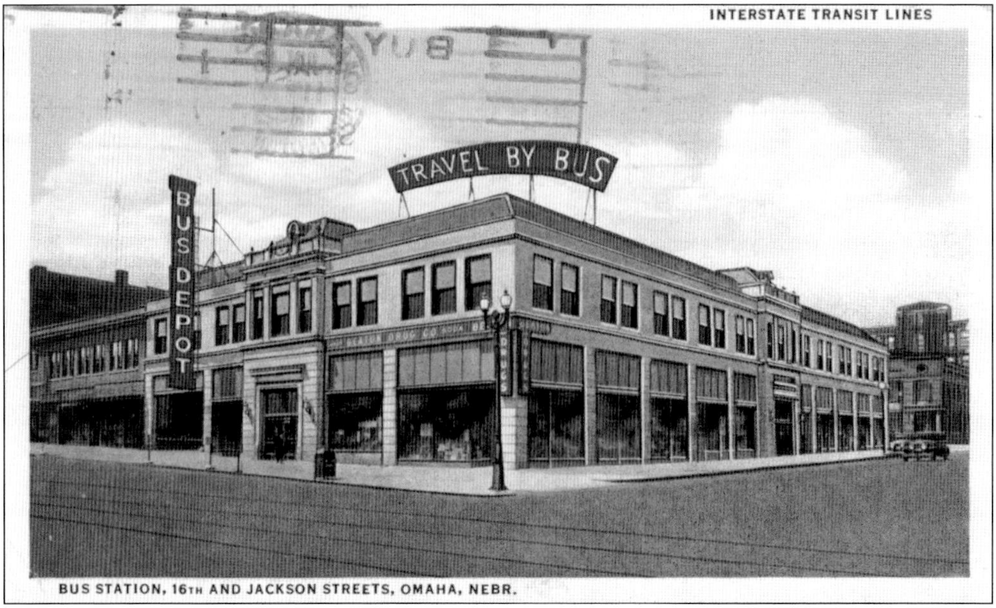

BUS STATION, SIXTEENTH AND JACKSON STREETS. Busses reached remote locations. Recall Cary Grant in *North by Northwest* being dropped off at an isolated location. Architect George L. Fisher's design complements the Aquila Court. They expected passenger traffic to rise from 43,000 to 100,000 per month. This card states, "Among Omaha's fine new buildings is a union bus depot for the rapid and efficient handling of this class of travel." Beaton Drug Co. is on the corner. During the Great Depression, bus companies lowered fares to attract passengers. (Omaha Public Library.)

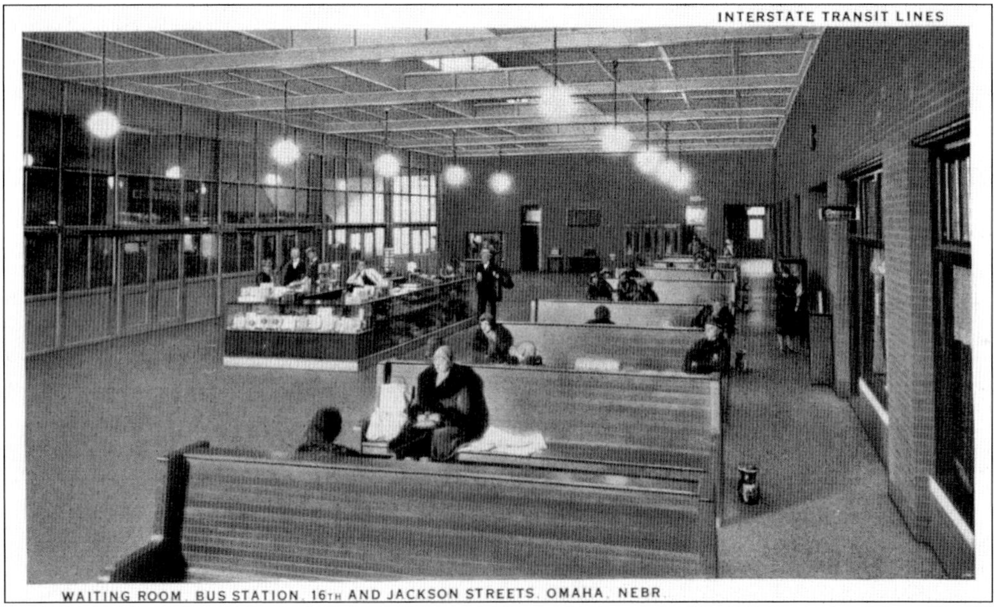

WAITING ROOM, SIXTEENTH AND JACKSON STREETS BUS STATION. Bus schedules, departures, and arrivals were printed and mounted on the wall. In 1936, the *Omaha World-Herald* reported that Omaha's three bus terminals handled more than 100 buses per day: "The uncomfortable hard-riding busses of the early 1920s were a far cry from the luxurious, modern streamlined busses of today, with their elevated seats."

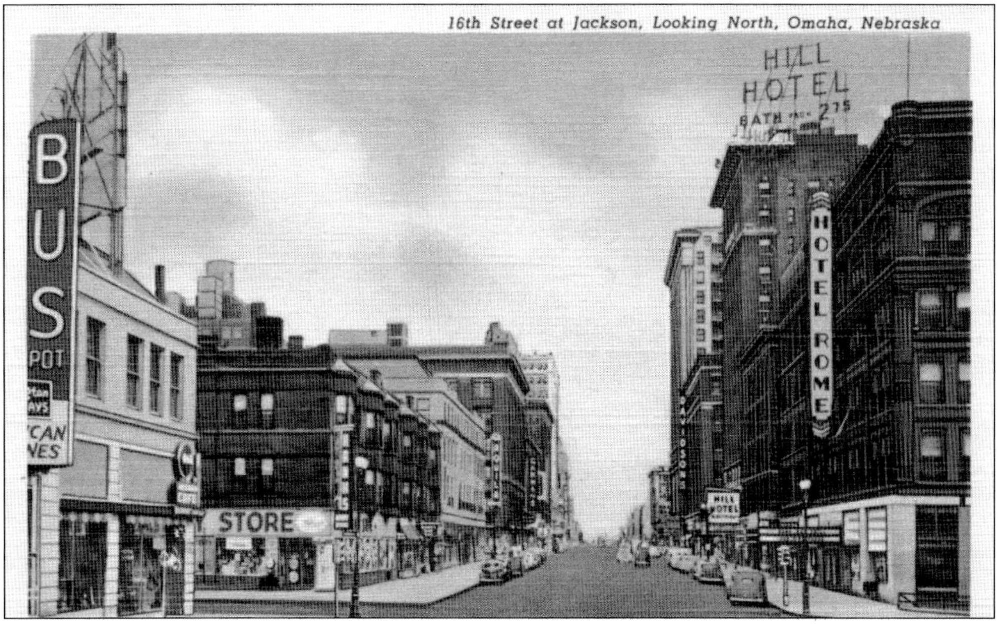

SIXTEENTH STREET AT JACKSON STREET, LOOKING NORTH. The Burlington Trailways Bus Depot is on the left. Like Union Pacific, the Burlington had bus interests. Trailways and the blue Megabus continue to connect Omaha to Des Moines and Chicago. The signage shown here includes Hotel Rome and Hill Hotel, Davidson's furniture, Aquila women's clothing, Carman's, and a café. This 1940s street scene shows lampposts, traffic lights, and free parking.

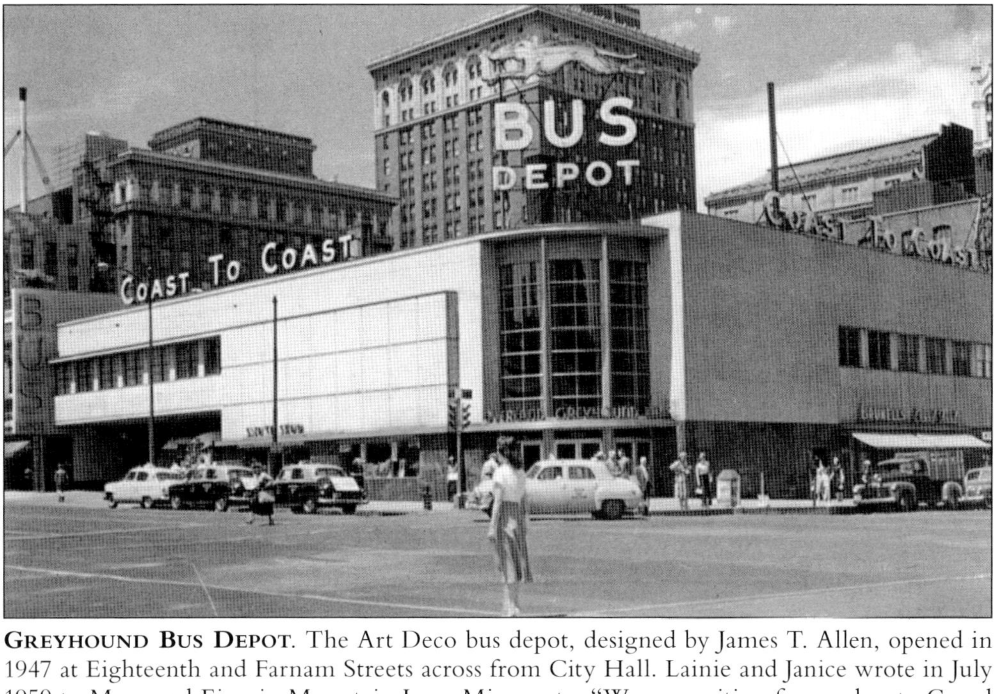

GREYHOUND BUS DEPOT. The Art Deco bus depot, designed by James T. Allen, opened in 1947 at Eighteenth and Farnam Streets across from City Hall. Lainie and Janice wrote in July 1959 to Mary and Eino in Mountain Iron, Minnesota: "We are waiting for our bus to Grand Island. We have had air-conditioned Scenic Cruisers all the way so far. Most of the passengers are going to California and Denver. The buses are filled."

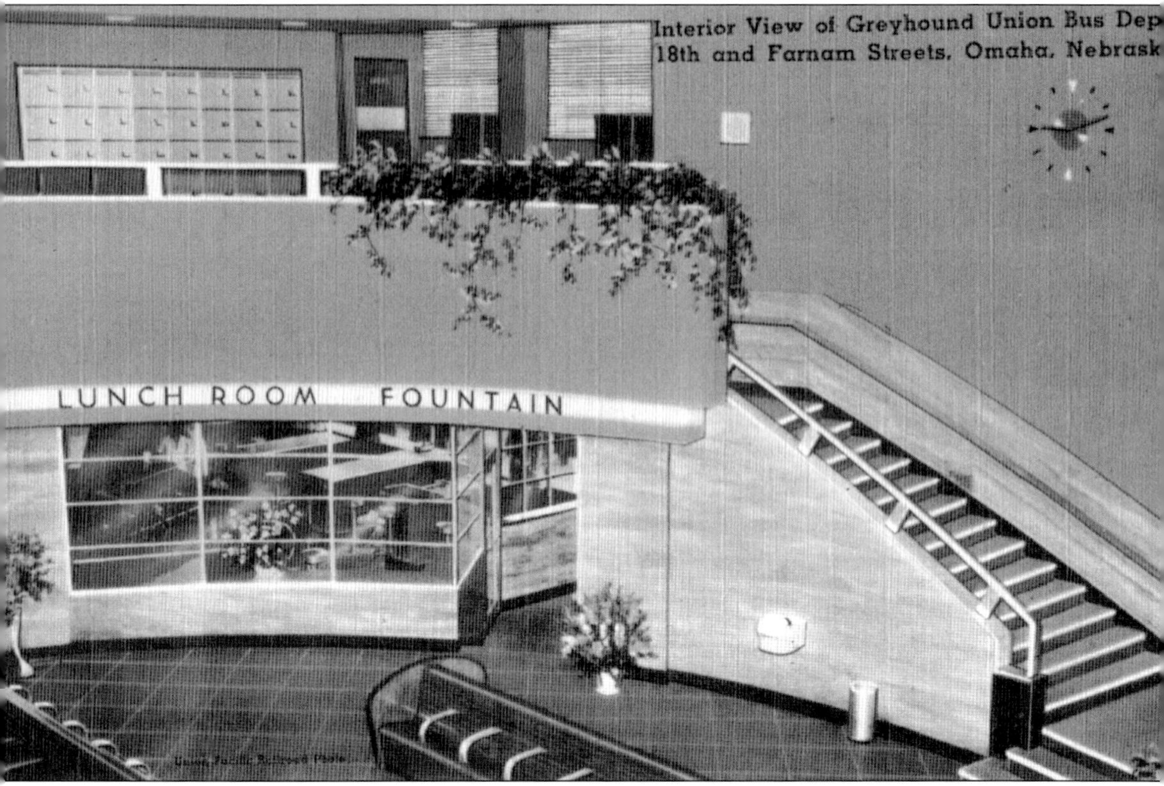

INTERIOR, LUNCH ROOM AND FOUNTAIN, GREYHOUND UNION BUS DEPOT. This postcard proclaims, "This ultra-modern terminal is one of the country's finest. Even the phone booth was air-conditioned." In 1952, Brunells' Good Food had the food franchise in the depot and advertised for "men who want permanent employment. Experience not necessary." Minimum wage was 75¢ per hour. In 1978, Burger King got the bus terminal franchise. Today, vending machines or food trucks serve these needs. The current bus station is at 1601 Jackson Street.

Two

Frontier Village to Regional Metropolis

Between 1854 and 1900, Omaha progressed from being a frontier village to a regional metropolis. Omaha's population grew from 1,861 people in 1860 to 140,452 in 1890. The 1890s depression caused a decline to 102,555 in 1900. It rebounded in 1910 to 124,096, and to 191,601 in 1920.

Omaha's first hotel—the St. Nicholas (or the Claim House), a log cabin built by the Council Bluffs and Nebraska Ferry Company in 1854—was at Twelfth and Jackson Streets and was probably named after New York's five-story, 500-room St. Nicholas Hotel, the first to cost more than $1 million, which opened in 1853. Accommodations at the Hamilton Hotel were described as follows: "The upper part of the house was one large bedroom, filled with bedsteads ranged against the walls, and about once a week this room was cleaned out for ball-room purposes." Omaha pioneers Byron Reed and Aaron Cahn performed music.

The 1866 City Directory listed 10 lodgings. In 1870, there were 8 hotels and 36 houses. "Houses" became "hotels." Names like Cedar Rapids, Chicago, Colorado, Elkhorn Valley, Pennsylvania, Wyoming, Germania, and Scandinavian guided travelers to regional and language familiars. The Schlitz, Karbach, Western, Vienna, and Drexel had German-speaking management. In March 1898, the *Omaha World-Herald*, anticipating the Trans-Mississippi Exposition, identified 34 hotels with 2,530 rooms and capacity for about 6,300 guests. The *Official Guide Book to Omaha, Trans-Mississippi and International Exposition* listed 42 hotels, boardinghouses, addresses, and prices and endorsed the Millard, Dellone, and New Mercer. Promoters reported Omaha, Council Bluffs, and South Omaha lodgings were sufficient to care for about 50,000 guests. With boardinghouses and private rooms, "at least 100,000 visitors can be easily and comfortably cared for at one time." Prices ranged from 25¢ to $5 per day. American plans served breakfast, lunch, and dinner, while European plans included only breakfast.

Omaha portrayed itself as "The Convention City of the West." Hosting fairs, exhibitions, and expositions made Omaha a destination and encouraged business and construction. Omahans visited the Chicago World's Fair in 1893. The Olympics were revived in 1896. Fairs were in the air. Omaha's greatest enterprise, the 1898 Trans-Mississippi Exposition, enticed throngs of visitors. The official guide listed 57 organizations holding annual conventions in Omaha, including cricket, dentists, florists, poultry, beekeepers, "Old-Time Telegraphers," homeopathy, Knights Templar, undertakers, funeral directors, the National Convocation of Women's Clubs, and the National Council of Women. In 2020, Omaha will host the American Bus Association with roughly 3,500 participants.

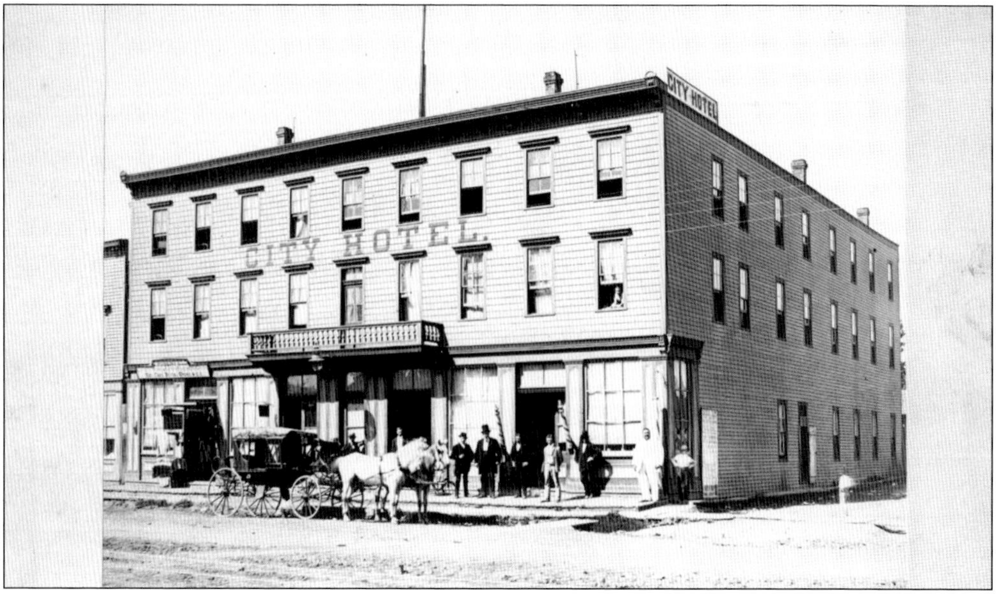

CITY HOTEL. This wood-frame three-story settlement hotel on Tenth Street between Farnam and Harney Streets probably opened in 1854. Rosenfeld Clothing occupied the main floor. In 1874, the *Omaha Daily Bee* announced, "This house, lease and furniture, for sale!" Housing a growing population fueled entrepreneurs' imaginations for stopgap measures. In 1857, twelve men purchased the sidewheel steamer *Washington City* for $15,000; it could house 250 while moored. (Omaha Public Library.)

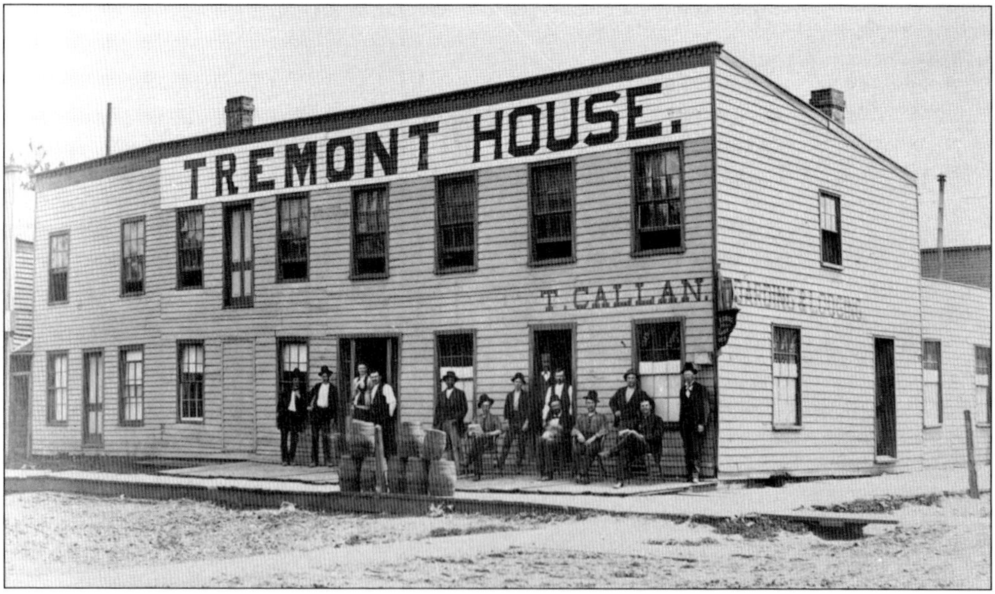

TREMONT HOUSE. This photograph of the two-story hotel at Sixteenth and Capital Streets dates from about 1860. In 1873, day board cost $1 per week with "good livery stable convenient." Tremont is a familiar hotel name. Boston's Tremont, built in 1829, has been called the "truly grand hotel." According to John Jakle, it had 173 guest rooms and occupied an entire city block. The dining room seated 200. Davy Crockett and Charles Dickens stayed there. Lincoln, Nebraska, also had a Tremont. (Durham Museum, Bostwick-Frohardt Collection.)

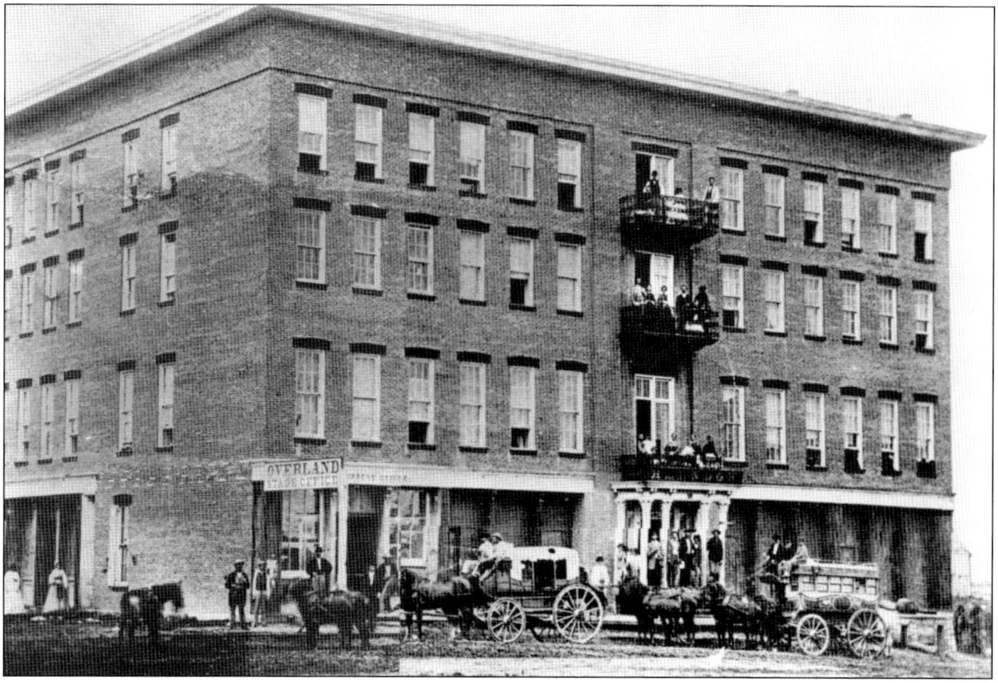

HERNDON HOUSE. The Omaha City Council, wanting a substantial hotel, donated land to the lowest-bidding hotel builder. Public land grants induced private enterprise to invest, similar to tax credit stimuli. Free land went to churches and parks to encourage morality. The four-story, $75,000 brick hotel at Ninth and Farnam Streets was finished in 1858 and was "the first of any size in Omaha." The Overland Stage and Express had offices in the Herndon. Herndon became the International Hotel in 1868 and Union Pacific Headquarters in 1870. (Durham Museum, Bostwick-Frohardt Collection.)

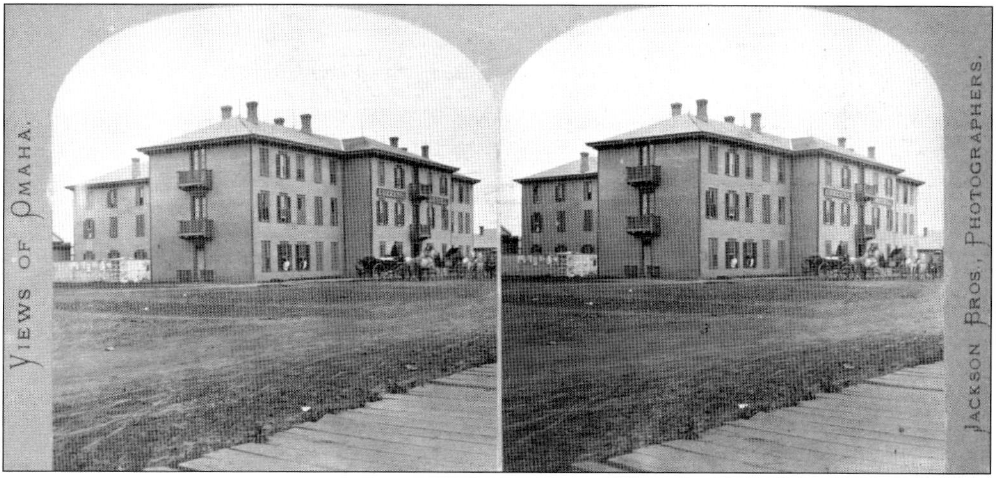

COZZENS HOUSE HOTEL. Stereoscopic views date from the 1830s. The irascible railroad tycoon George Francis Train built this hotel at Ninth and Harney Streets in 60 days in 1867 at a cost of $60,000. It had 120 rooms. It sat empty during the 1870s. J.D. Iler purchased it in 1881, and George Canfield renamed it Canfield House and ran it until the mid-1890s. It was renamed Jenning House and became the Omaha Medical Institute and then the Presbyterian Seminary. It was demolished in 1902. (New York Public Library Digital Collection.)

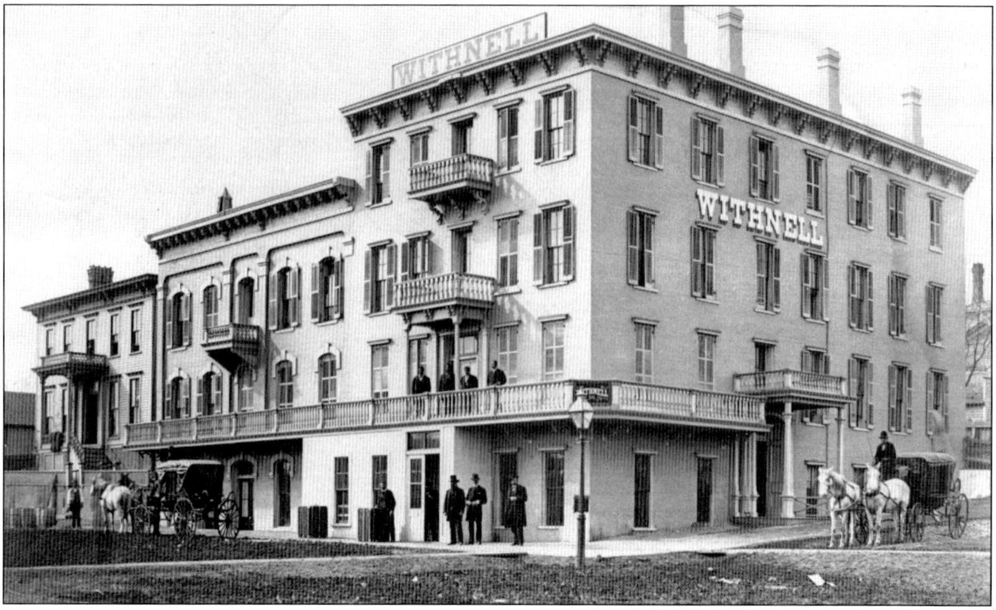

WITHNELL HOUSE. Built in 1868, this served as a hotel from 1878 to 1882 to meet demands after the Grand Central burned. Oscar Wilde stayed here on his American lecture circuit. He came to Omaha via Sioux City. The Social Art Club sponsored his Omaha lecture at the Boyd Theater on March 21, 1882. The Withnell went through three building stages. (Durham Museum, Bostwick-Frohardt Collection.)

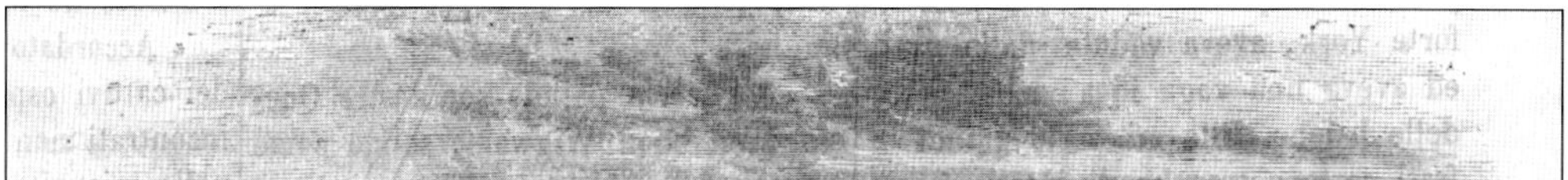

FARNAM STREET FROM SIXTEENTH STREET EAST. This image, a leaf from an Italian magazine, dates from about 1868. There are wooden sidewalks, frame and brick buildings as high as four stories, and two churches. Horse-drawn wagons and pedestrians ply the well-kept street running east to the Missouri River. There are no bridges, street poles, or streetcar tracks. An 1866 view has fewer buildings and a rough street. An 1889 view has streetcar tracks.

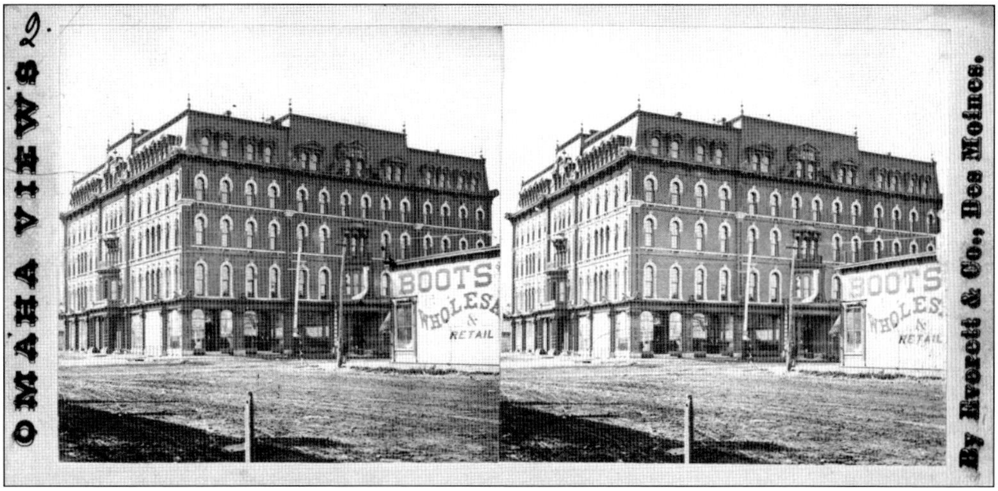

GRAND CENTRAL HOTEL EXTERIOR. This ill-fated five-story brick hotel, started in 1870 at Fourteenth and Farnam Streets, had financial problems that delayed its opening until 1873. The "largest hotel between Chicago and San Francisco" may have had the muddiest streets. It had an elevator. It burned down, killing five firemen, on September 4, 1878. Grand Central was a popular name, attested to by Grand Central Station in New York City, which opened in 1871. Nebraska City's Shoff House became Grand Central Hotel in the 1870s. (Omaha Public Library.)

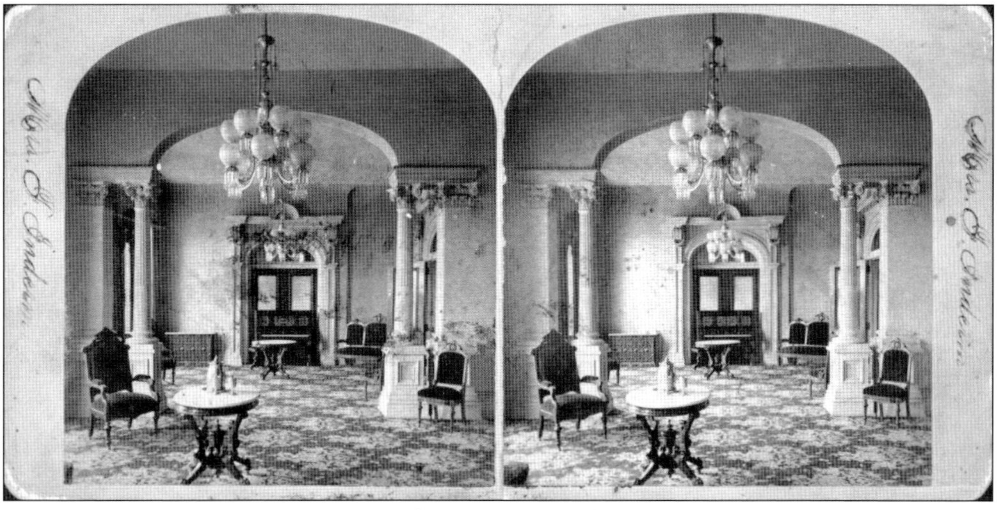

GRAND CENTRAL HOTEL PARLOR. The Grand Central was truly grand and palatial. Lighting, columns, and concave arches divided the room and enclosed the double-hung door with glass windows. Floor treatments and furniture suggested classic elegance. (New York Public Library Digital Collection.)

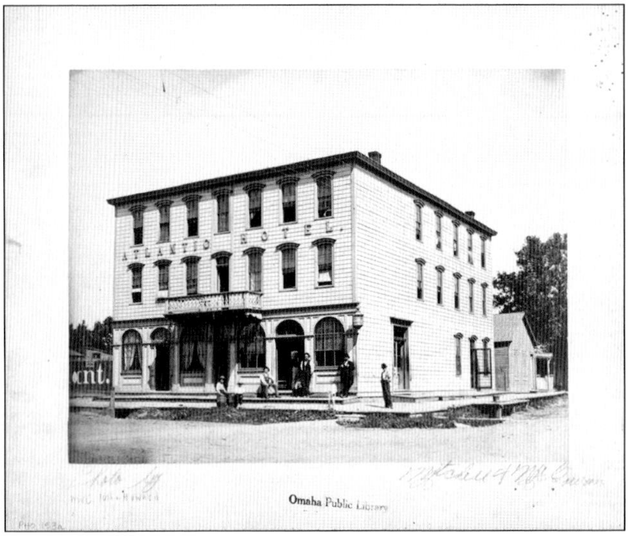

ATLANTIC HOTEL. This three-story hotel with wood siding at the corner of Tenth and Howard Streets advertised in the *Omaha Daily Bee* in March 1878: "Rooms all refitted and newly furnished," a claim often repeated by hoteliers. The sample room provided space for wholesale and retail salesmen to display their wares: farming and household labor-saving equipment, clothing, and sundries. If the hotel filled all its rooms, the sample room housed overflow guests. Larger hotels had as many as 10 sample rooms. (Omaha Public Library.)

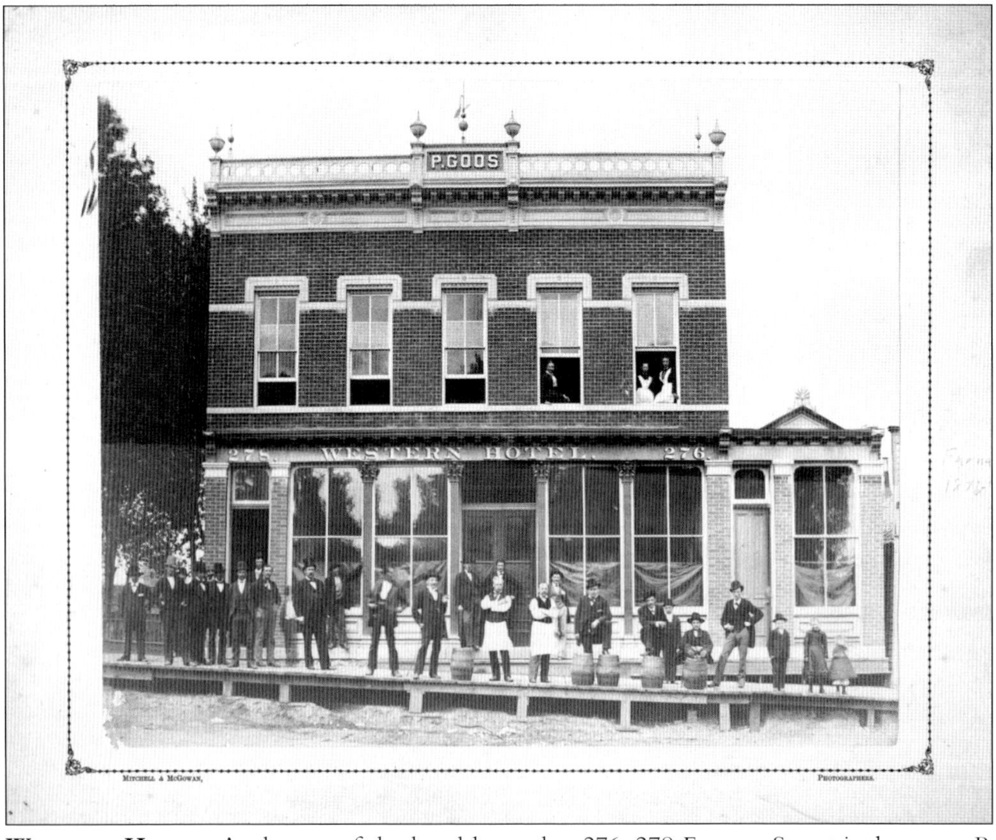

WESTERN HOTEL. At the top of the hotel located at 276–278 Farnam Street is the name P. Goos. Peter Goos, born in Holstein, Germany, in 1838, came to the United States, settled in Plattsmouth, and moved to Omaha in 1865. He opened a saloon, billiard hall, and boardinghouse at Fifteenth and Farnam Streets, where the Merchants Hotel was later located. He built the Goos Hotel at Fifteenth and Jackson Streets, and it later became the Savoy Hotel. Goos died in 1916, and his funeral services were held in German. (Omaha Public Library.)

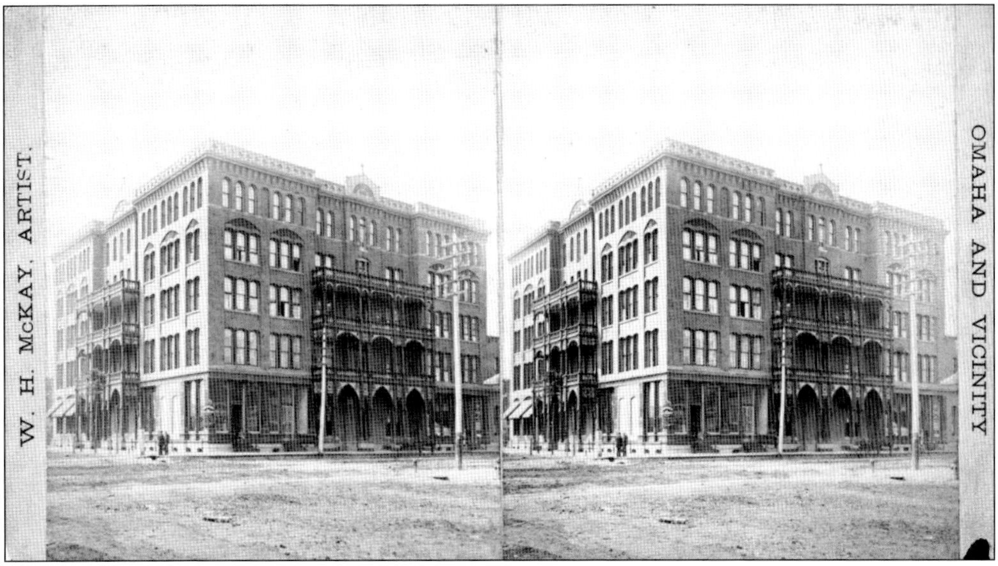

PAXTON HOTEL. One benefit of the stereoscopic view is that it records things pretty much as they are and eliminates, for the most part, artistic retouching. The Paxton, Henshaw, and Loyal hotels produced promotional cards. People enjoyed viewing and sharing mass-produced stereo views in their parlors. (Omaha Public Library.)

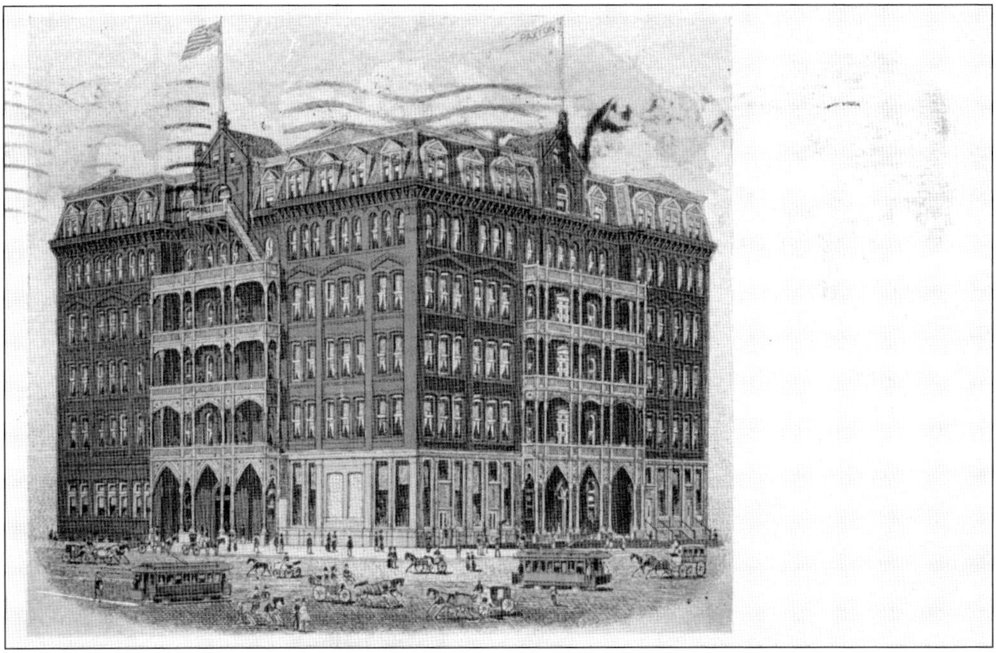

THE IMAGINARY PAXTON HOTEL. The Paxton, named for prominent businessman William A. Paxton, has been at the southwest corner of Fourteenth and Farnam Streets since 1882. The original Paxton is on land formerly occupied by the Grand Central Hotel. This card (postmarked 1909), shows six stories with a mansard roof, balustrades to four floors, sidewalks and streets busy with pedestrians, electric streetcars, and no less than eight horse-drawn wagons. The Paxton did not have a sixth-floor mansard roof.

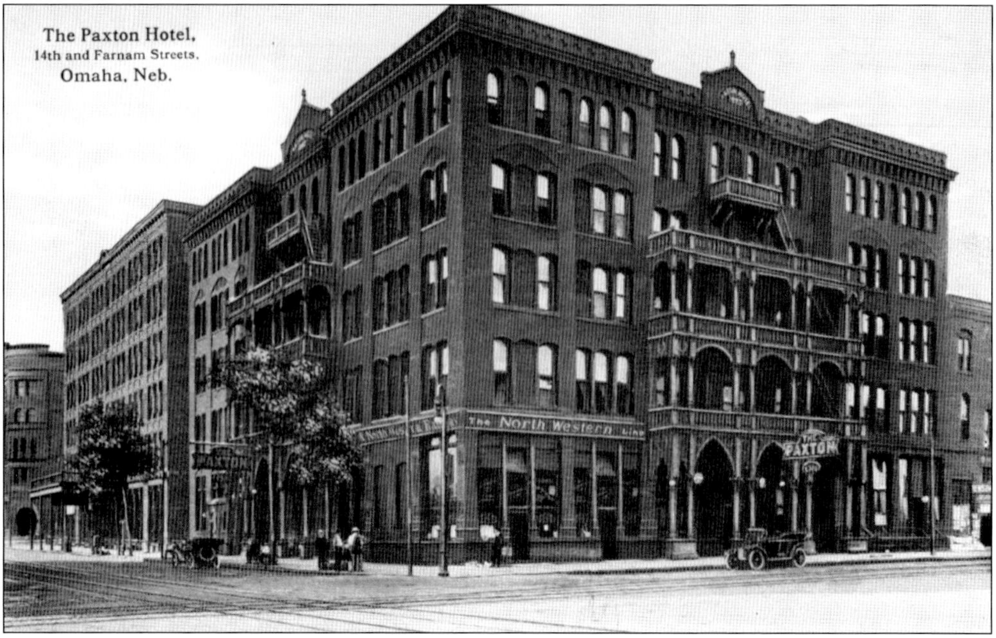

THE REAL PAXTON HOTEL (ABOVE) AND THE MURRAY HOTEL (BELOW). The above postcard—and all other Paxton postcards and stereographs—depict a five-story building with porches on three floors. The elaborate imaginary card has trolleys and horse-drawn carriages. This more accurate card has automobiles and two trees lining the street. The Murray Hotel is on the left. Jessie wrote to Rev. R. Harlow in Muncie, Indiana, in June 1912: "We arrived here all ok. Sat. night we had a misunderstanding at St. Louis and staid [*sic*] there all night. We all felt pretty tired." The eccentric Tom Murray built the six-story Murray Hotel in 1888 at Fourteenth and Harney Streets. After 1889, the Paxton Hotel was sometimes called the Paxton-Murray Hotels. Though they were separated by a 20-foot alley, they frequently appeared on the same postcard. In 1912, the Kitchen Brothers, Richard and Ralph, then owners of the Paxton, purchased the Murray Hotel and connected the buildings. Realtors declared it an "ideal location for a million-dollar hotel." The time was not ripe for such a venture (although The Fontenelle achieved that distinction in 1915). The Murray was demolished in 1935.

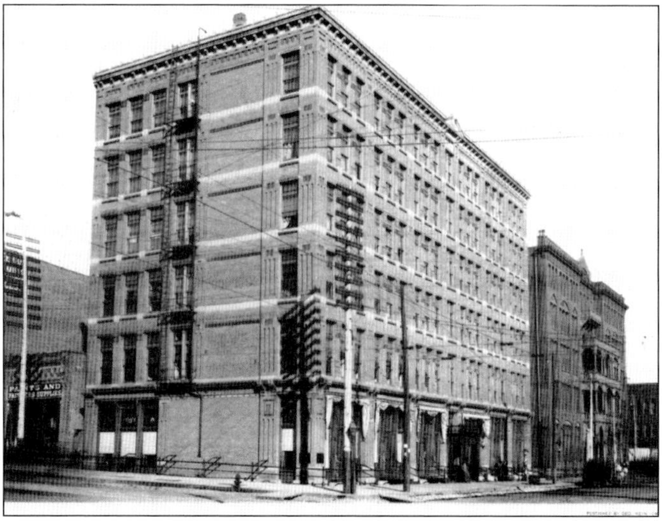

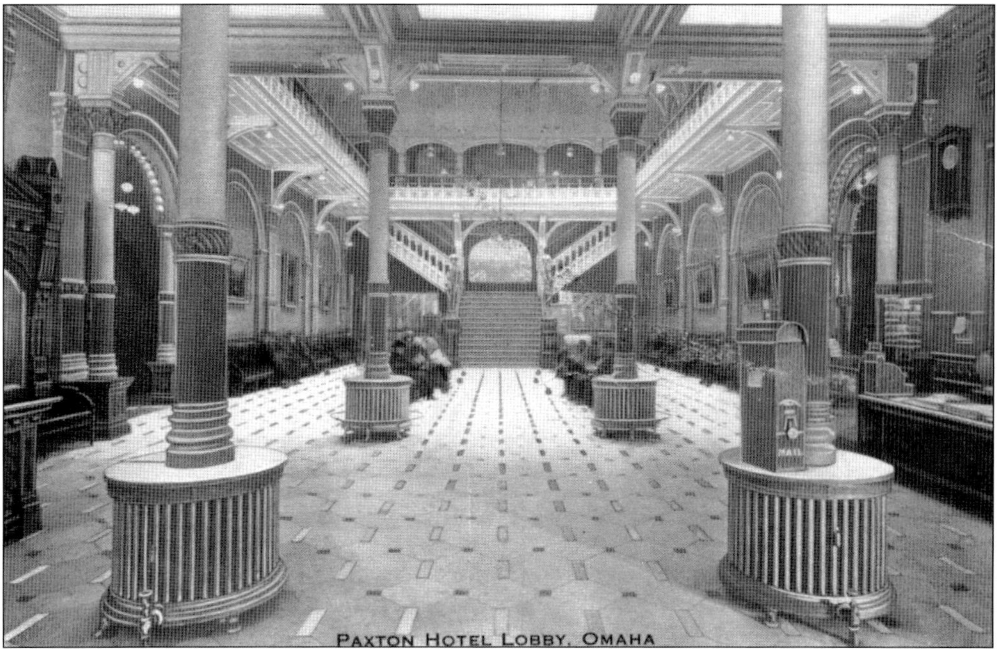

PAXTON HOTEL LOBBY. Lobbies set the tone for the hotel experience. They can be welcoming, stuffy, pretentious, or forbidding. This vision presents a high-ceilinged room with a reception desk, seating area for 30, five brass spittoons, art on the walls, columns with radiator heating units at the bases, a green mailbox, a regulator clock, a newspaper rack, a cash register, a gallery or mezzanine, and a tiled floor with imaginative (perhaps retouched) colors. The seated people appear to be reading. Spittoons gave way to ashtrays.

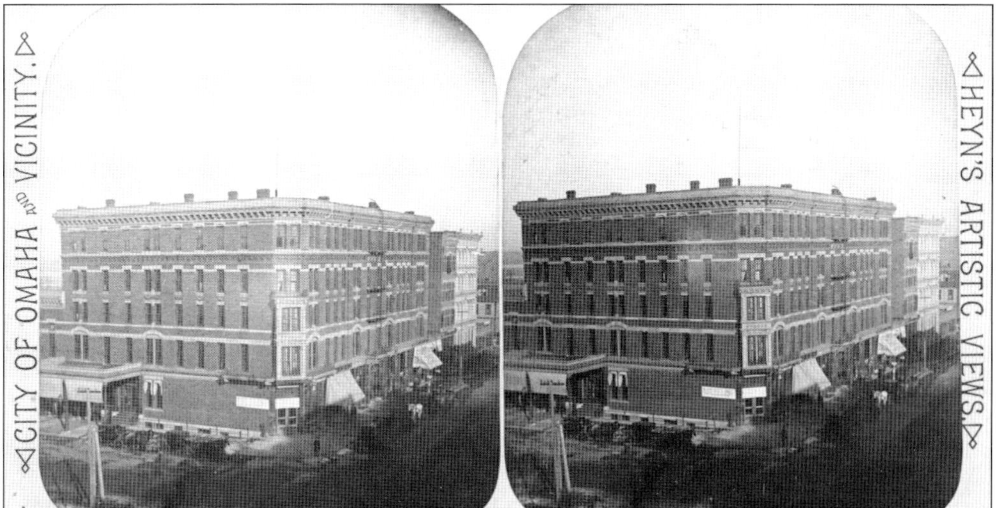

MILLARD HOTEL STEREOGRAPH. This hotel opened in 1882 at Thirteenth and Douglas Streets. Ezra Millard had real estate, banking, and Union Pacific interests. The $150,000 cost included "fire proof" construction and safety measures to prohibit the "communication" of fire. The furniture came from Chicago. It had a bar, billiard room, barbershop, six handsome stores, and a private entrance for women. A fourth story added a year later increased the number of rooms to 170. (Omaha Public Library.)

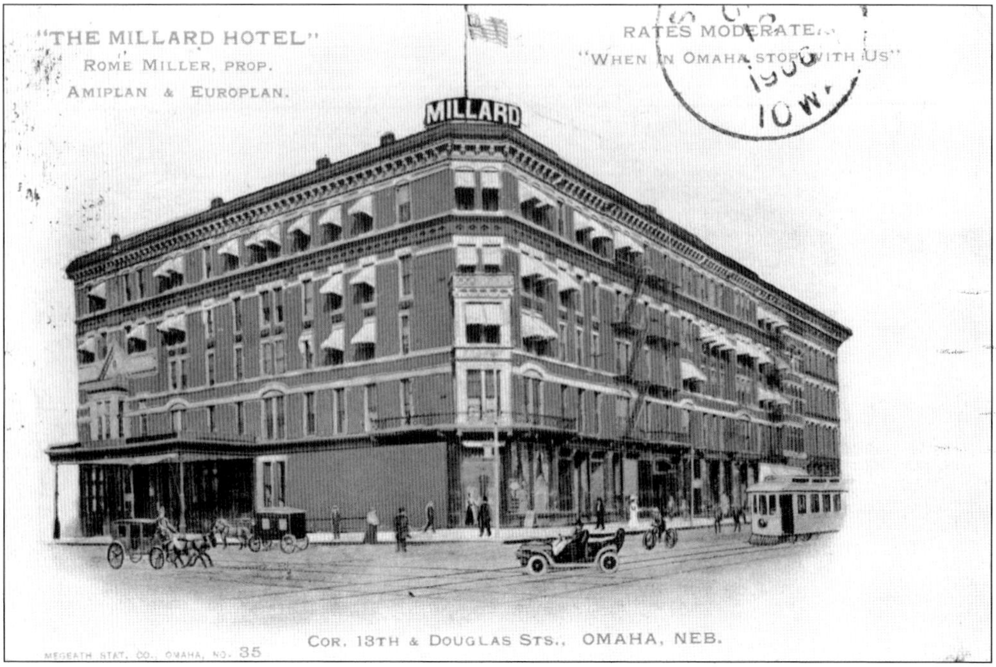

MILLARD HOTEL. Rome Miller managed the Millard Hotel, which offered American and European plans. On October 14, 1911, a guest wrote to Verona, Pennsylvania: "Dear Mae & Dorothy; I arrived here safely at 10-30 tonight. Am stopping at Hotel Rome. Am well, yours." That's right; this Millard card was mailed from the Rome. Despite "fire-proof construction," the hotel burned down in February 1933 in subzero weather. (Omaha Public Library.)

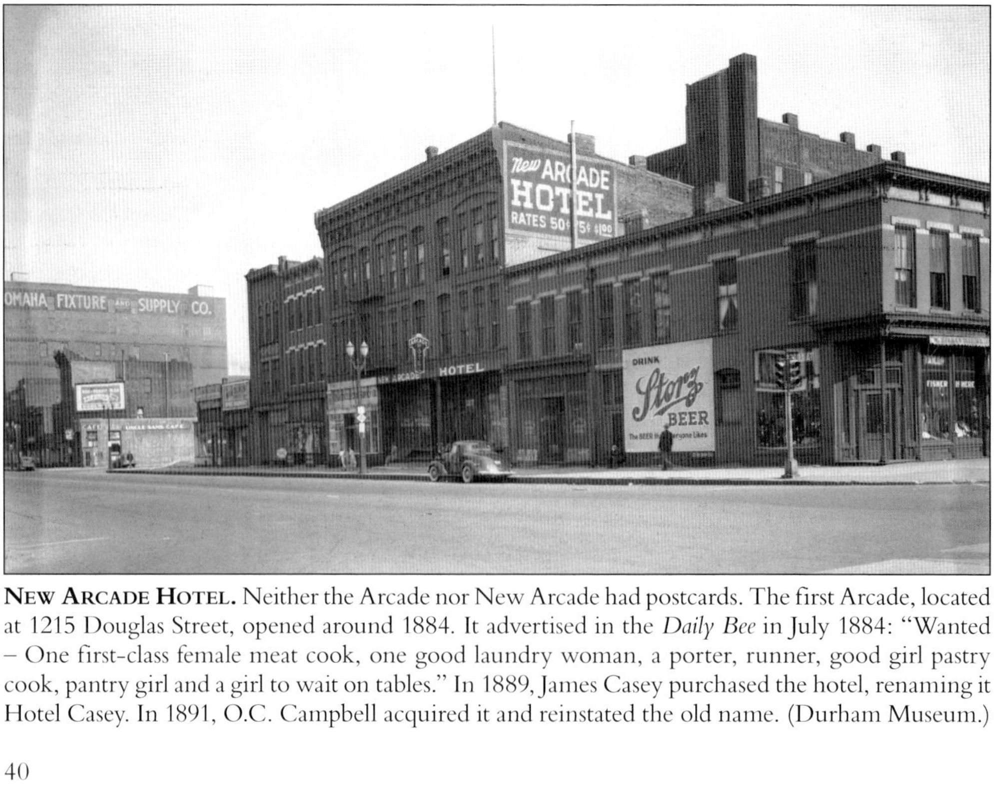

NEW ARCADE HOTEL. Neither the Arcade nor New Arcade had postcards. The first Arcade, located at 1215 Douglas Street, opened around 1884. It advertised in the *Daily Bee* in July 1884: "Wanted – One first-class female meat cook, one good laundry woman, a porter, runner, good girl pastry cook, pantry girl and a girl to wait on tables." In 1889, James Casey purchased the hotel, renaming it Hotel Casey. In 1891, O.C. Campbell acquired it and reinstated the old name. (Durham Museum.)

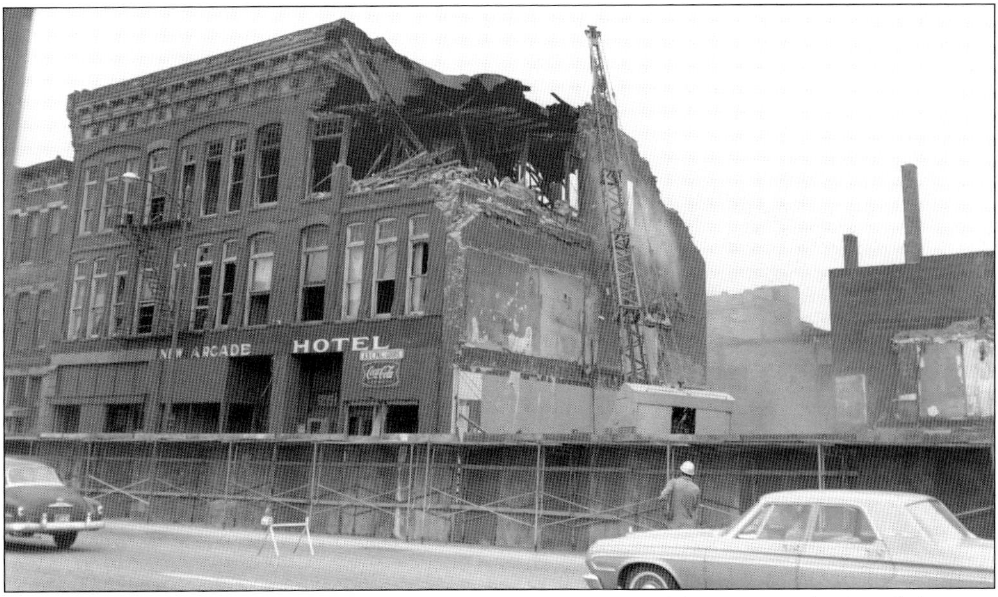

Demolition of the New Arcade Hotel. After it was remodeled in 1945, the Arcade became the New Arcade. "Old men of the pensioner class sit about the lobby. One said he had lived there 40 years." In 1948, the hotel advertised "working men's rooms." A fire in 1964 weakened the structure, and demolition ended its life, an act that would occur repeatedly as downtown buildings aged. John Savage took this photograph. (Durham Museum.)

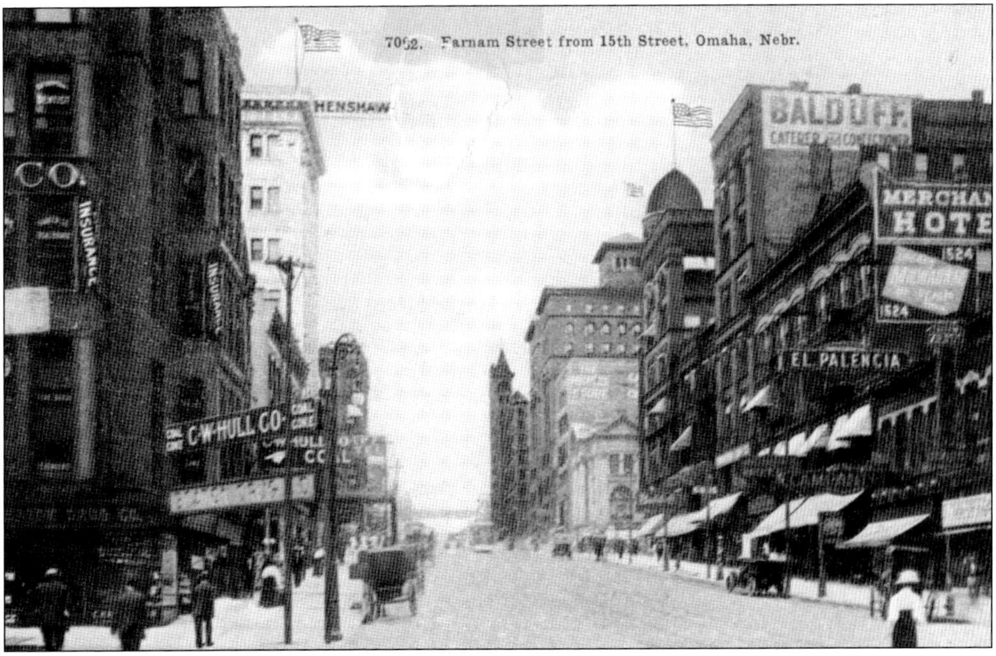

Merchants Hotel. Merchants Hotel was built around 1887 on Farnam Street between Fifteenth and Sixteenth Streets. This 1920 card shows Merchants Hotel on the right and Henshaw on the left (with an overhanging sign). Three flags, probably added to the image, blow in the wind. Both cars and horse-drawn carriages are on the street. Retail signage includes El Palencia, a Cuban cigar brand; C.W. Hull, coal and coke; and Balduff Caterer and Confectioner.

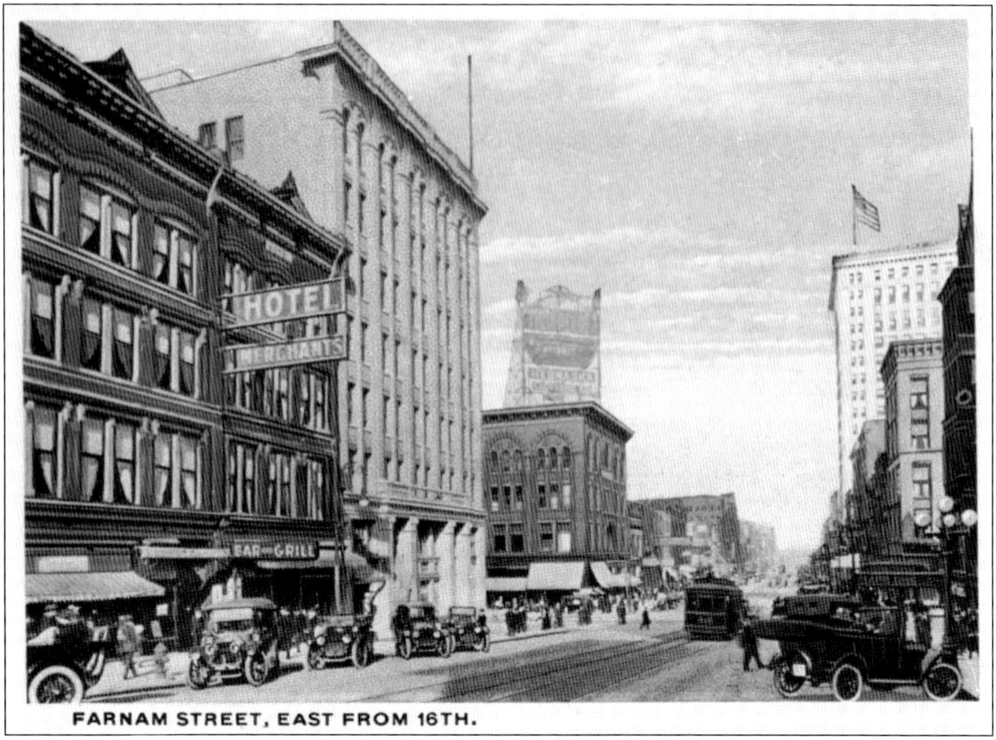

Farnam Street Looking East from Sixteenth Street (above) and Merchants Hotel Restaurant (below). The above view of Merchants Hotel comes from a miniature souvenir foldout containing 16 three-by-four-inch views. The bar and grill signage is clearly visible, there are many pedestrians, at least eight cars on the street, a streetcar, and no horse-drawn carriages. The black-and-white postcard below shows the dining room and predominantly black serving staff at Merchants Hotel. Postcards and newspapers offer insight into race and labor relations. Most photographs featured an all-white kitchen staff. In 1902, four white hotel workers' unions went on strike at the Henshaw Hotel over "colored" labor; African Americans, who were not members of the unions, were fired. In the latter half of the 20th century and beyond, food preparation—from farm to kitchen to table—has relied heavily on immigrant labor.

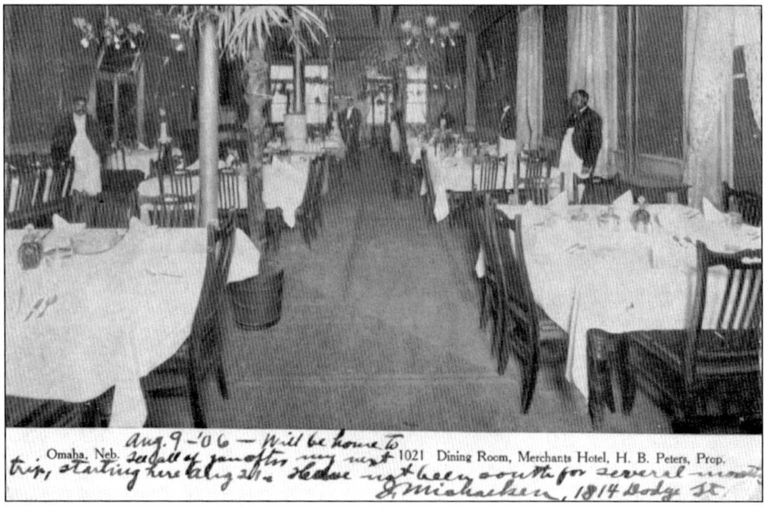

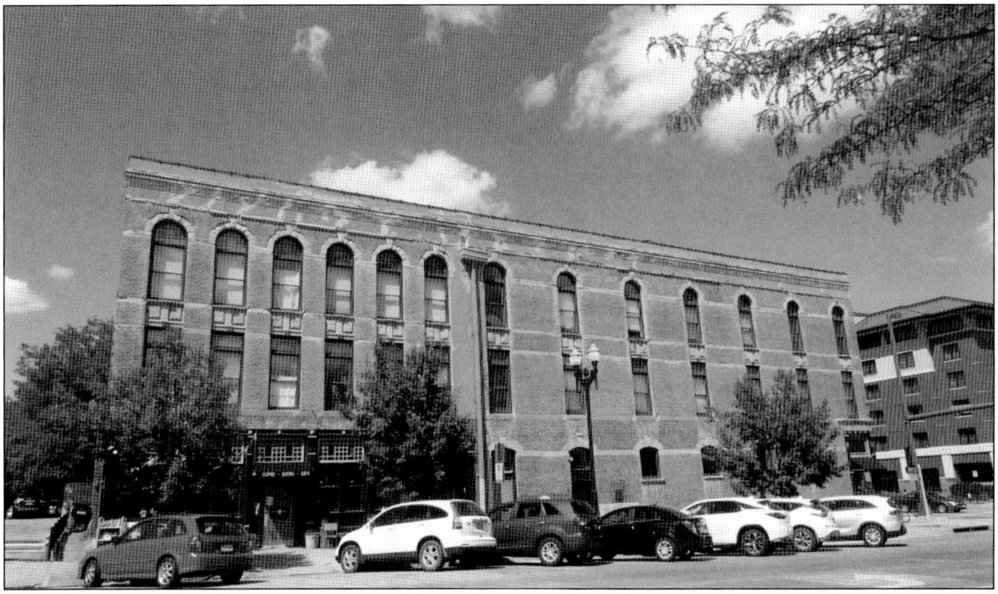

WINDSOR HOTEL. A bronze historical plaque on the building at Tenth and Jackson Streets indicates the hotel's construction in two phases during 1885 and 1887. With its location near the Union Pacific and Burlington stations, the restaurant and bar attracted passengers enduring layovers. This was designed to be a workingman's and railroader's hotel. It later became the Windsor Inn, then closed in 1979. It is now Windsor Square. An open-air market flourished behind the hotel until 1964. In 1994, the Saturday open-air market reopened. Embassy Suites is located across Tenth Street.

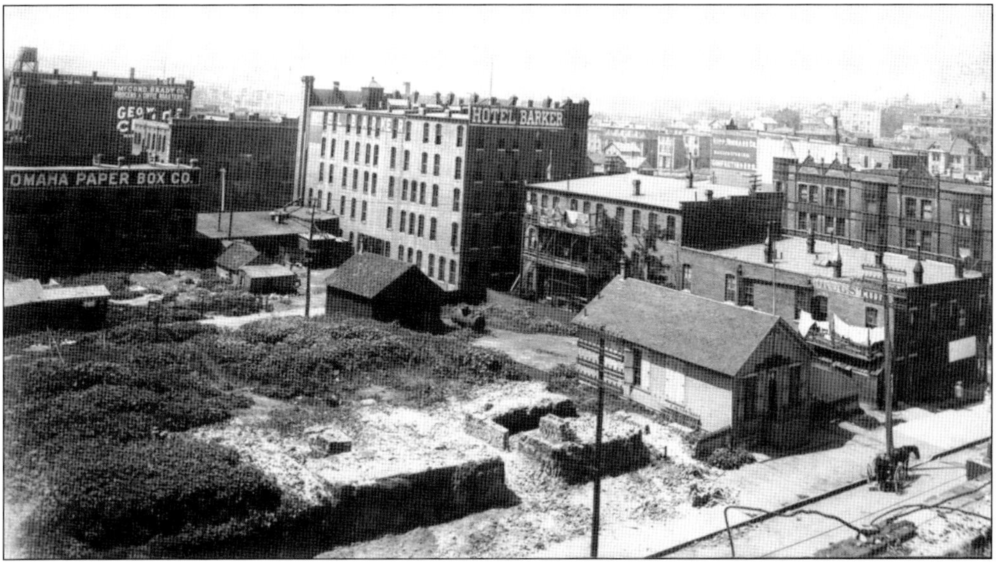

BARKER HOTEL. This five-story brick building on the northeast corner of Thirteenth and Jones Streets was owned by the Barker brothers and leased to F.A. Balch; it opened in March 1887. It had a passenger elevator, 103 sleeping apartments, and electric annunciators. It advertised as a first-class hotel: "There is no extra charge for steam heat and the rooms are always warm." Rates were $1 per day and up. A billiard room and barbershop were in the basement. (Durham Museum, Bostwick-Frohardt Collection.)

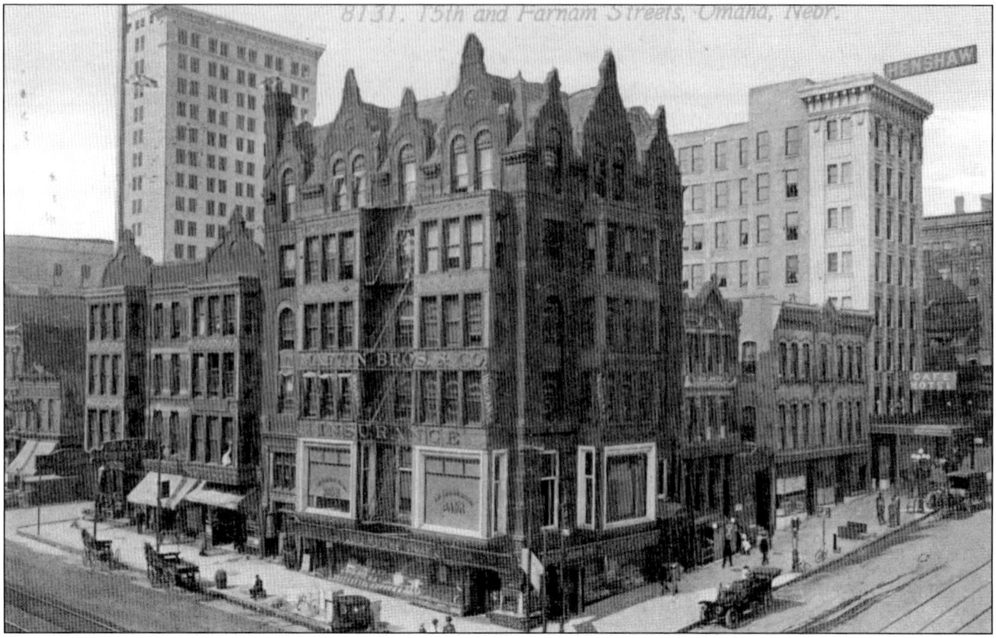

FIFTEENTH AND FARNAM STREETS. This 1912 view of downtown Omaha shows a shoe store, the 16-story City National Bank (built in 1910; now contains 132 apartments), Robertson Café, a man washing a second-floor window, and the six-story Martin Bros. & Co. Insurance building with a bank and cigar store. Around the corner are an open iron cellar delivery grate and the eight-story Henshaw Hotel and Café. Also visible are many signs, two streetcar tracks, flat and peaked roofs, men and women wearing hats, three horse-drawn wagons, two horseless carriages, and two bicycles.

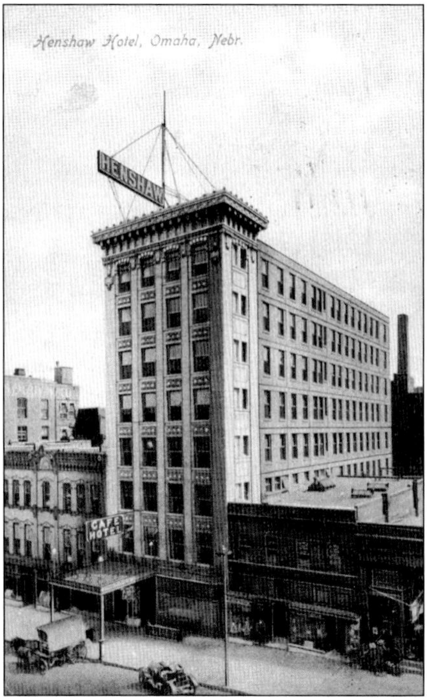

HENSHAW HOTEL. James McTague opened the McTague European Hotel in the converted Redick Block at 1509–1511 Farnam Street in May 1895. He advertised in North Platte, Red Cloud, and Iowa newspapers. The hotel's Oyster and Grill Rooms and Ladies' Restaurant were renowned. McTague fell behind in payments, was sued, and closed the hotel. C.W. Reed, former owner of the Dellone, purchased the hotel and renamed it Reed's European Hotel. Joseph Henshaw took over in October 1896, renaming it Henshaw Hotel. McTague's finances recovered in St. Louis; his 1926 obituary stated, "Coffee Made Him Rich."

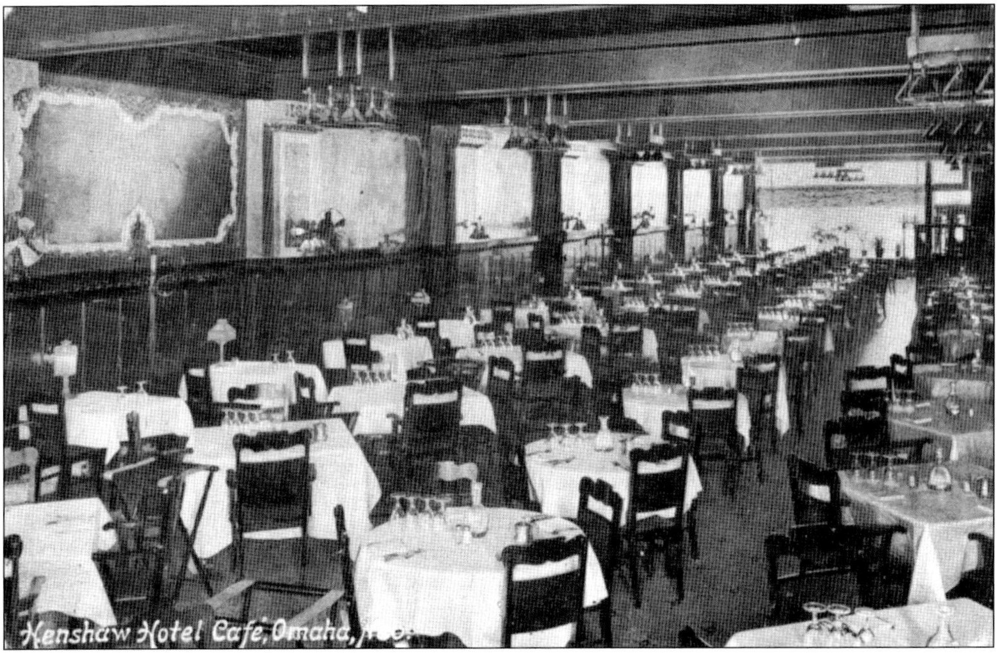

HENSHAW HOTEL CAFÉ. The Henshaw Hotel Café became a cafeteria in 1921, claiming to be "the finest west of the Mississippi River." The Rotary Club, formed in 1916, met in the Rathskeller. Chas wrote Art in 1909 about Henshaw's Lounge bar, "I'll tell you this some place to eat. Look at all those glasses going to waste. How are you?" On another card, Mrs. Gage wrote Mary in Michigan in 1909: "Dear friend. Arrived safely, am certainly seeing Omaha. It's a pretty place. Am having a good time. Laura has company from N.D. and they keep me on the go all the time."

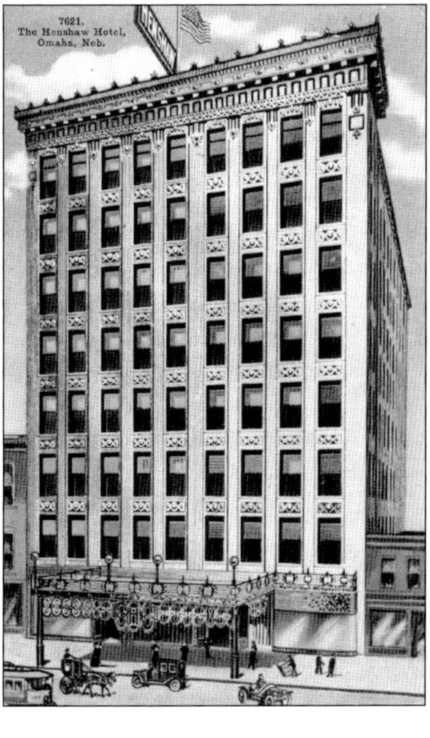

THE HENSHAW HOTEL WITH NINE WINDOW ROWS. As early as 1908, the Henshaw Hotel owners planned to complete a "duplicate" or "twin" of the hotel. In 1911, the Redick brothers, owners of the Henshaw, discussed doubling its size. They advertised in 1912: "Capacity Tripled next year." This card, postmarked "1915 RPO San Francisco, San Jose, Los Angeles," simply states, "Love from Grace" and is addressed to Florence in Detroit. A 1916 *Omaha World-Herald* promotional sketch depicts the Henshaw's expansion to nine window rows.

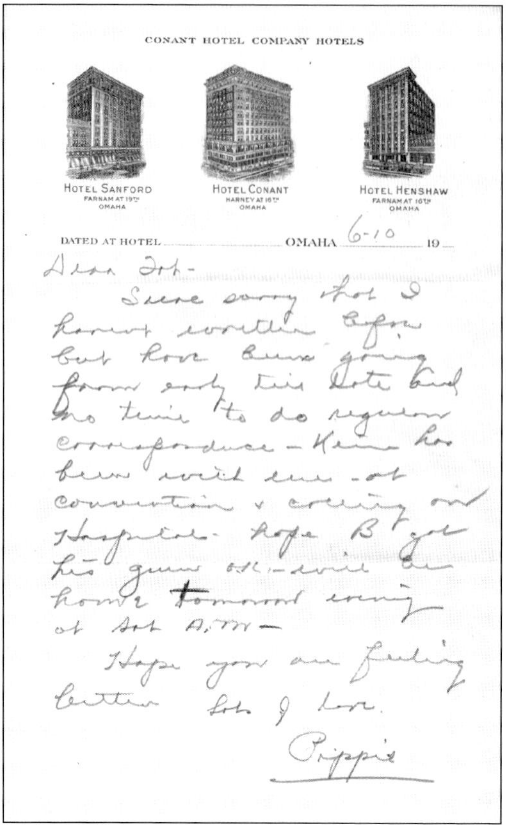

CONANT HOTEL COMPANY HOTELS

HOTEL SANFORD
FARNAM AT 19TH
OMAHA

HOTEL CONANT
HARNEY AT 16TH
OMAHA

HOTEL HENSHAW
FARNAM AT 16TH
OMAHA

DATED AT HOTEL .... OMAHA 6-10 19..

Dear Dot-
Sure sorry that I haven't written before but have been going from early till late and no time to do regular correspondence - Karl has been with me - at convention & calling on Hospitals - hope B't got his gun ok - will be home ~~tomorrow~~ evening at 8:00 A.M. -
Hope you are feeling better. Lots of love.
Pippie

1926 CONANT HOTEL COMPANY LETTERHEAD. Conant Hotel Company acquired Henshaw Hotel in 1921 from George Petros. A 1921 *Omaha World-Herald* photograph of the building being scrubbed clean of urban grime shows four window columns. Conant Hotel stationery in 1926 depicted the building with six window columns. Faced with at least three different depictions, Winston Churchill might have called this a riddle wrapped in a mystery inside an enigma, or some such. The decline of traveling salesmen during the Depression almost led to the closing of the Henshaw in 1933.

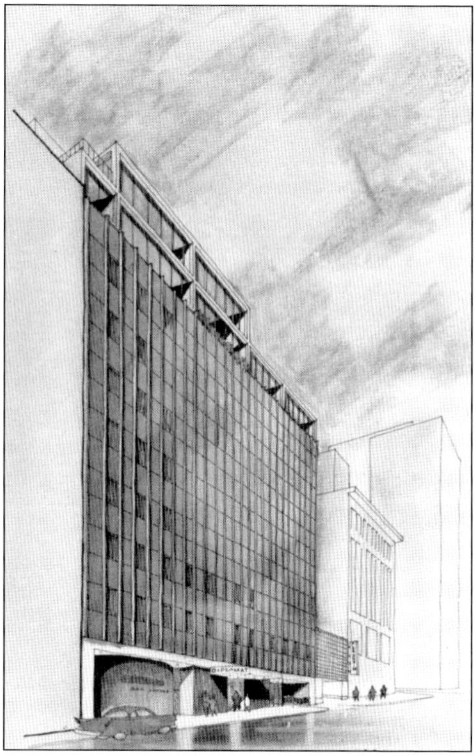

DILLON'S DIPLOMAT. Robert W. Dillon leased the Henshaw Hotel in 1962. He deferred expansion until demand rose, which it did not. In April 1974, the 137-room Diplomat Motor Inn, lounge, and restaurant closed. "Business hasn't been good downtown," Dillon said. "I was losing more keeping it open than it will cost me to pay the rent and take my medicine." The lease expired in 1975. Dillon owned the Aquarius Lounge at Seventy-second and Pacific Streets and Holiday Inns in Minnesota and Iowa. In 1977, the four-column Diplomat became Central Park Tower, which had housing for the elderly and disabled.

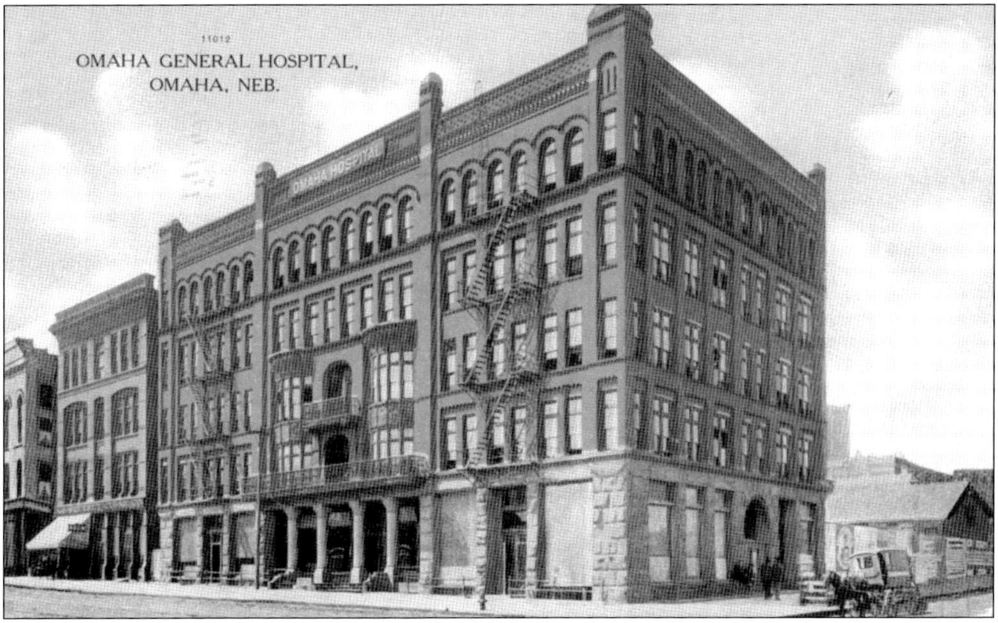

DELLONE HOTEL/OMAHA GENERAL HOSPITAL. This stone-and-brick hotel opened at Fourteenth and Capitol Streets in 1891. It claimed to be the state's only fireproof hotel, and with the new annex, also the largest. The mid-1890s depression led to foreclosure in 1896. In 1905, the International Christian Institute turned it into a nonsectarian general and maternity hospital. (Omaha Public Library.)

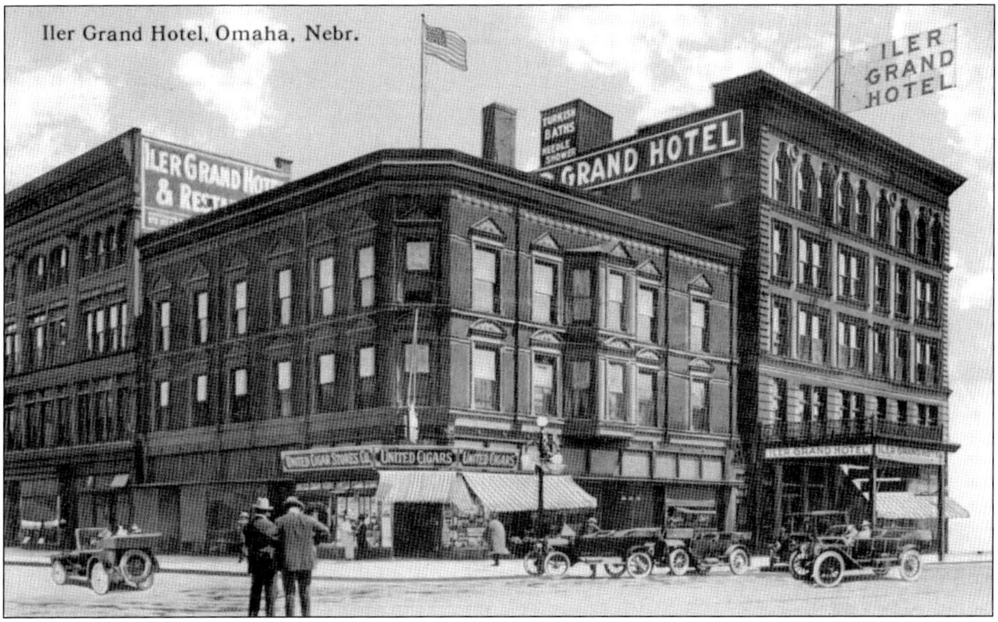

ILER GRAND HOTEL. This hotel opened in 1898 at Sixteenth and Howard Streets. Five signs identified it. Owner Peter Iler, a distiller, promoted the hotel's waters—"Electro Therapeutic, Turko-Russian, Roman, Plunge, Needle and Shower, Plain Baths, Sea Salt, Bidet and Turkish Baths"—open all night. Ladies had access on Tuesday and Friday from 10:00 to 5:00. United Cigar Stores occupied the corner.

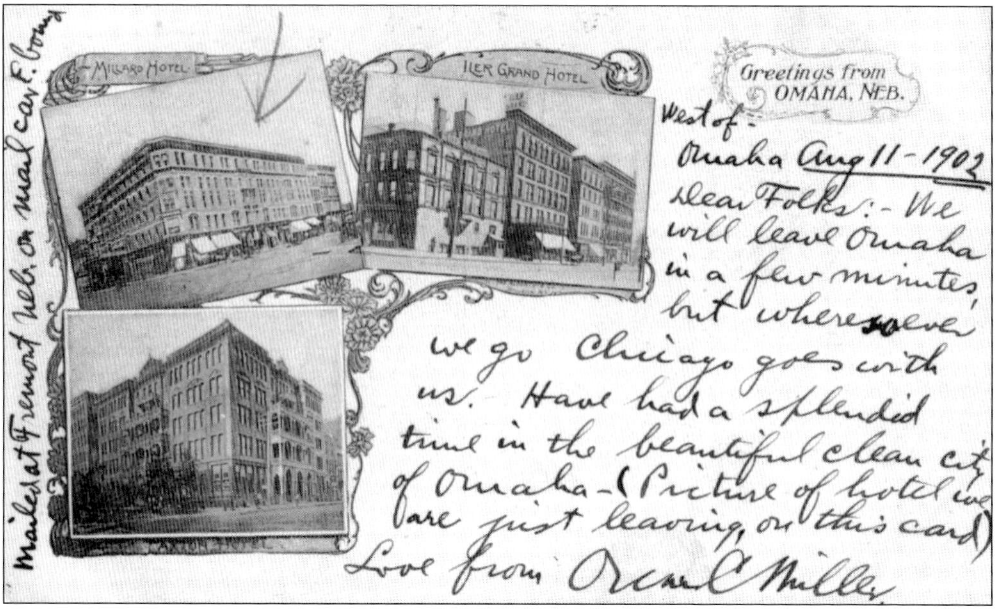

Greetings from Omaha. This triple-view card, a marvel of cooperative advertising, includes the Millard, Iler Grand, and Paxton Hotels—all built between 1882 and 1899 and named after prominent Omaha businessmen. The sender mailed the postcard from Fremont, 33 miles from Omaha; perhaps his travels left a trail of cards. All of these structures were gone by 1934.

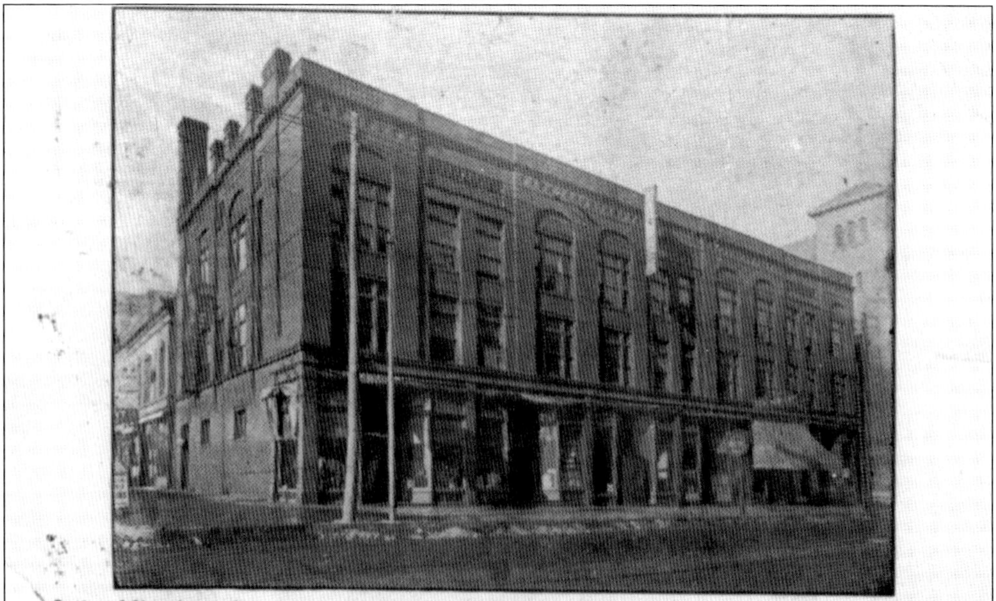

Karbach Hotel. This three-story brick building at Fifteenth and Howard Streets dates from around 1890. Born in Germany in 1839, Peter J. Karbach came to Omaha in 1859 and went into business with his brother Charles J. Karbach. They had a wagon and blacksmith shop. They claimed the hotel was at the "Center of Shopping and Theater Districts." Peter Karbach's 1898 obituary described him as unostentatious and unpretentious.

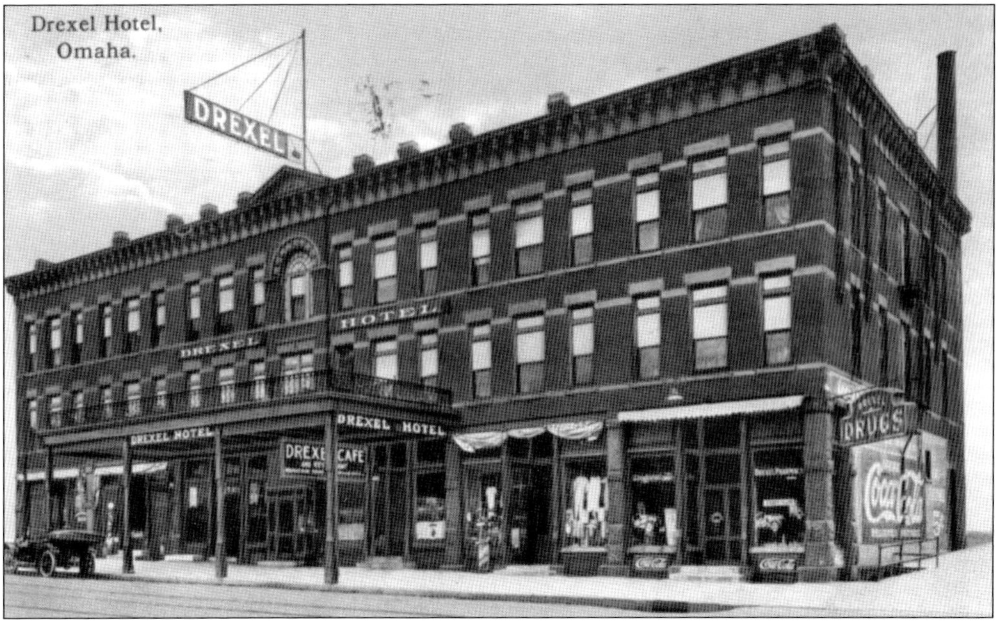

DREXEL HOTEL. This hotel was built in the early 1890s at Sixteenth and Webster Streets by German stonecutter Frederick Drexel, who came to Omaha in 1856. He had interests in undertaking and died in 1894. An advertisement in the *Omaha World-Herald* on July 10, 1915, read, "Wanted—A wide-awake agent to place a perfect steering device used on Ford cars. Call J.S. Williamson, Drexel Hotel after 9 am Saturday." This card, sent to Atlantic City in July 1916, contains a plaintive message: "got the blues so cant write much this time . . . I am awful lonesome may go home next week." (Douglas County Historical Society.)

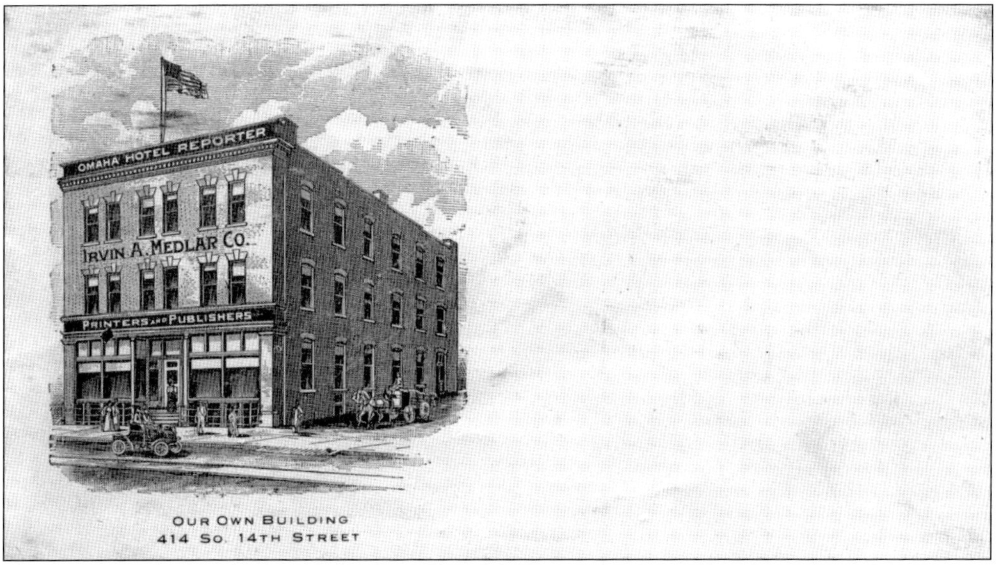

IRVIN A. MEDLAR COMPANY. Irvin A. Medlar, a Union veteran, arrived in Omaha in 1891. He worked at Omaha Printing Company until fire destroyed it. He opened his own shop in 1892 and moved to 414 S. Fourteenth Street in 1905. He published the *Omaha Daily Hotel Reporter* (printed for the hotel trade), served in the Nebraska legislature, and rose to office in regional hotel associations. Medlar died at age 68 in 1938.

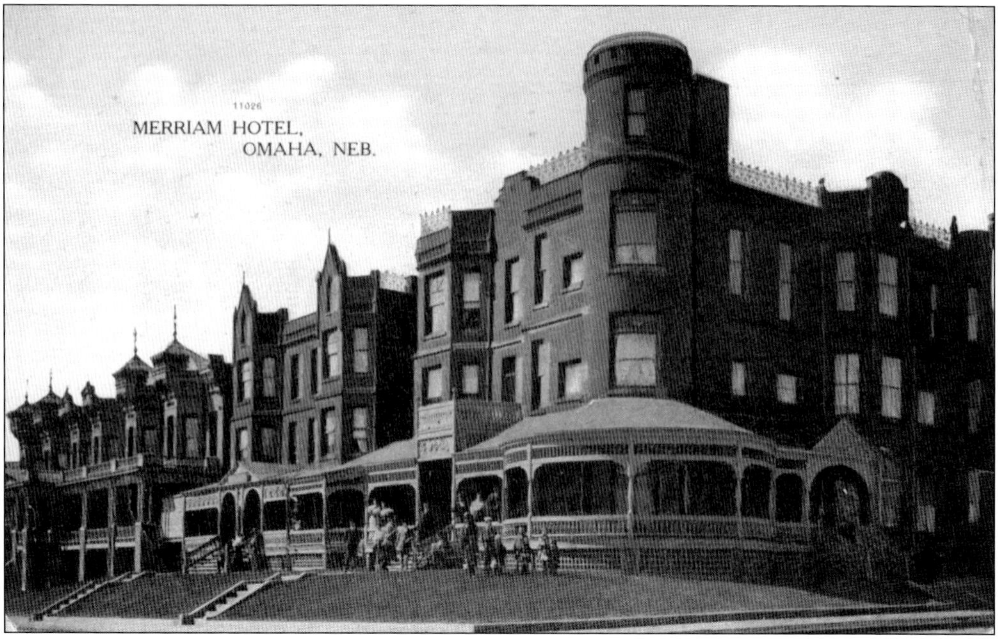

MERRIAM HOTEL. This hotel, located at Twenty-fifth and Dodge Streets, appeared in the *Omaha World-Herald* "In Society" column of December 11, 1897, which reported a whist party with over 100 women in attendance hosted by Mrs. Benjamin F. Crummer, mother of physician and medical history book collector Le Roy Crummer. In 1899, the hotel advertised, "The Merriam—First Class Family Hotel," and in November 1931, "Live comfortably and economically in clean bright rooms and apartments." The message on this card (sent to Bridgeport, Connecticut) reads, "You see I have not forgotten you, Elliott."

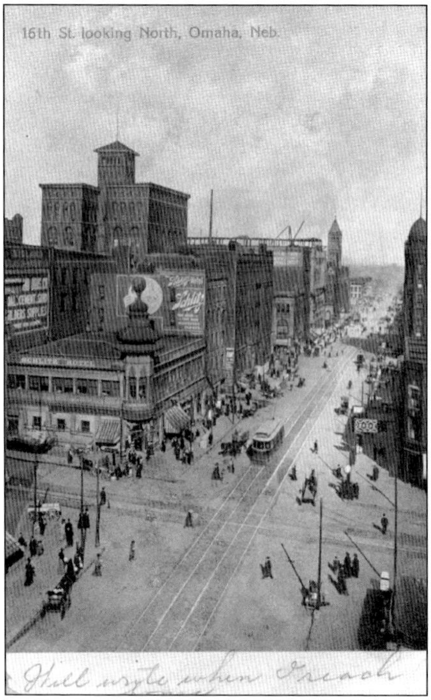

SCHLITZ HOTEL. The two-story Schlitz building at Sixteenth and Harney Streets was converted into a hotel in 1896. Milwaukee's Schlitz brewery dates from 1849, and its four-story Schlitz Hotel from 1890. Around this time, Germans were Omaha's largest immigrant group. This view includes streetcars, trolley tracks, pedestrians, horse carts, telephone poles, and wall signs. The message on the card, addressed to Cumberland, Tennessee, and postmarked October 1907, states, "Am here this week taking in sights. Big parade last evening. Will write when I reach home." The Schlitz Hotel was later torn down for the larger Conant Hotel.

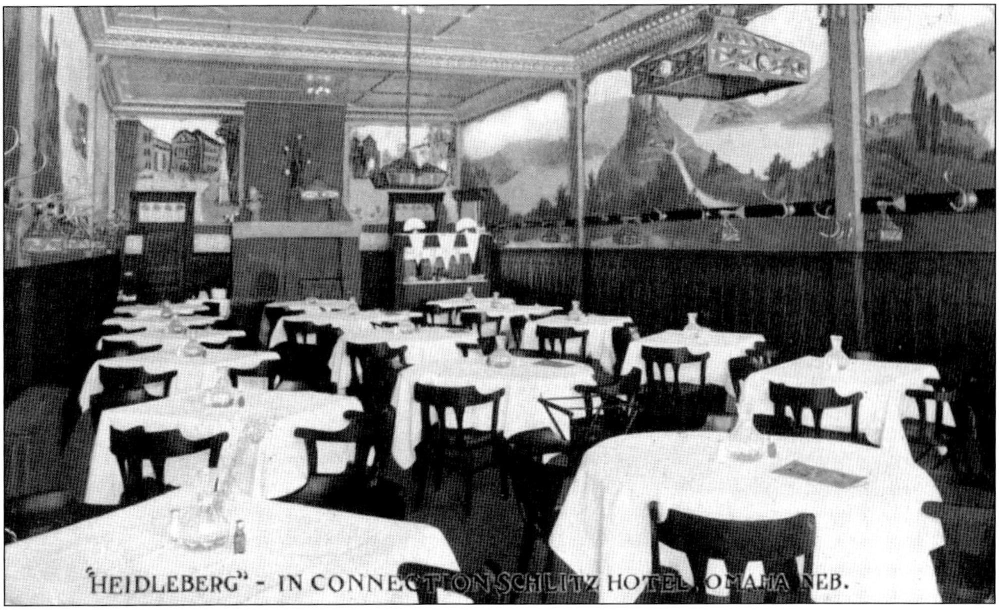

INSIDE THE SCHLITZ HOTEL. "It is the intention to make this café second to none in the United States," stated Mr. Lieven, the manager, in the July 21, 1896, *Omaha Daily Bee*. White tablecloths, glass water pitchers, captain's chairs, and ornate lamps attest that this is not a beer garden. Three walls were painted with mountain, lake, river, tree, and town scenes. The newly decorated Schlitz Roof Garden opened on April 30, 1898, to the accompaniment of Franz Adelman's orchestra. The hotel also had a Ladies' Café.

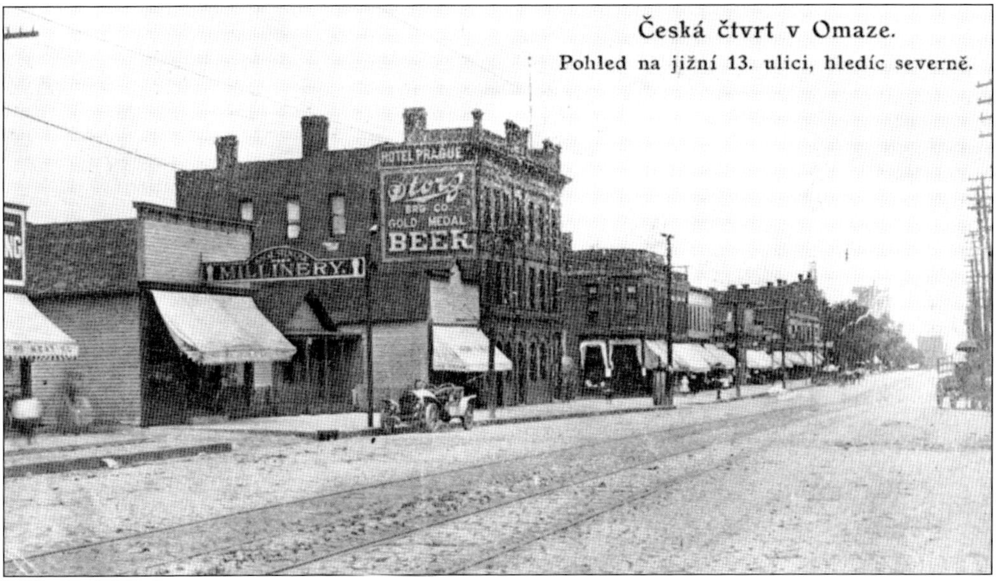

"THE CZECH QUARTER IN OMAHA." The 25-room Hotel Prague, designed by J.P. Guth and located at 1402 S. Thirteenth Street in South Omaha, opened in 1898. It catered to Czechs and Bohemians. The building has been converted to apartments. This scene contains a millinery store, Storz Beer wall sign, and streetcar tracks. Sokol Auditorium, located a half-mile away, opened in 1926. Other hotels serving South Omaha and the stockyards included the Exchange, Lee Hotel, and Reed. (Nebraska State Historical Society and Bruce Garver.)

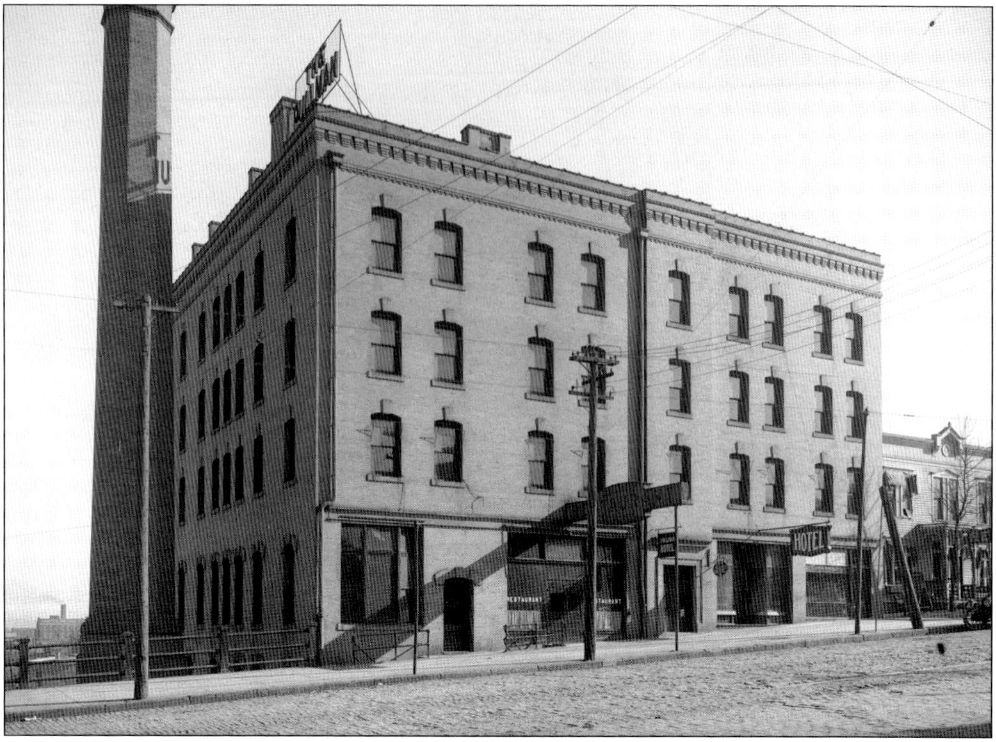

THE PULLMAN HOTEL. The Pullman, located at 1017 S. Tenth Street, just south of the Burlington station, had 55 rooms, 35 with private bath, two apartments, and a bar and café. It opened around 1900. It was the oldest hotel recommended in 1933 by the Chamber of Commerce (see pages 98–99). (Durham Museum, Bostwick-Frohardt Collection.)

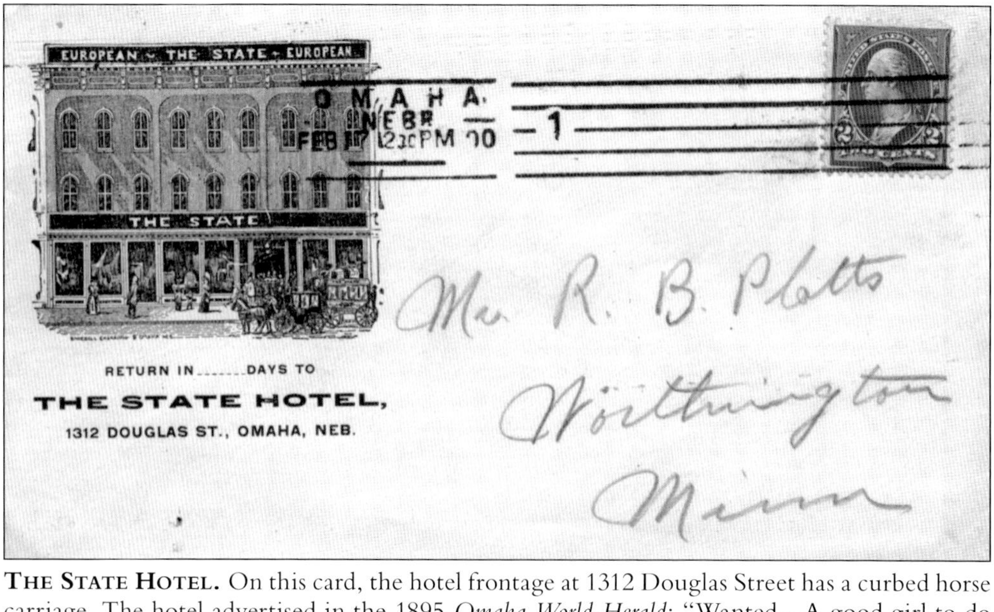

THE STATE HOTEL. On this card, the hotel frontage at 1312 Douglas Street has a curbed horse carriage. The hotel advertised in the 1895 *Omaha World-Herald*: "Wanted—A good girl to do cooking for a family and assist with chamber work at State Hotel." An explosion damaged it in 1932, and a 1938 "Morals Raid" labelled it an "ill governed house."

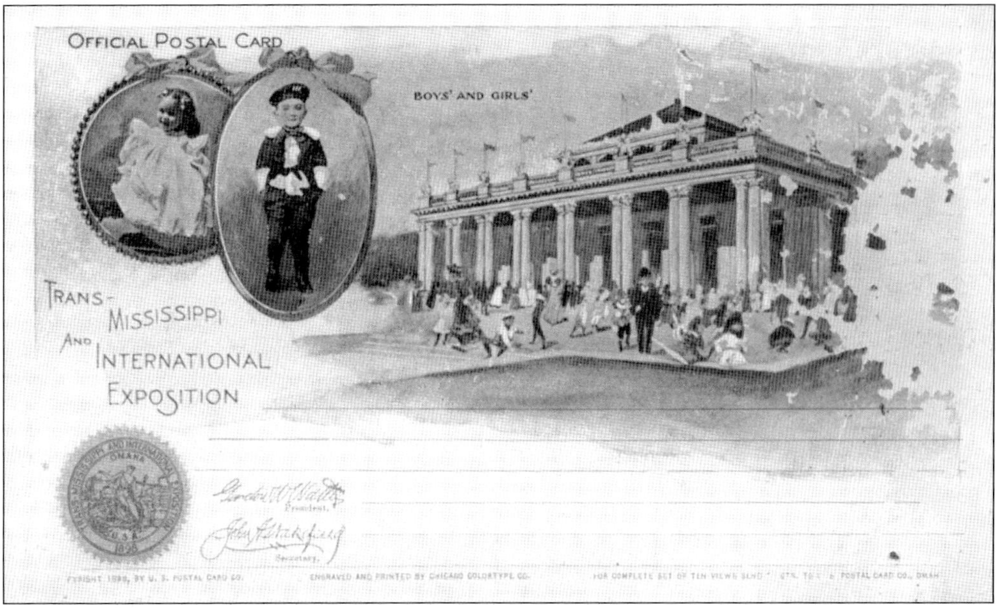

1898 TRANS-MISSISSIPPI INTERNATIONAL EXPOSITION. Exposition planning started in 1895. Thomas Rogers Kimball, the supervising architect, oversaw 20 architects who designed exhibition buildings, including Omaha architectural firms Walker & Kimball, Fisher & Laurie, Charles F. Beindorf, and John McDonald. Separate expo buildings displayed achievements in horticulture, liberal arts, machinery and electricity, mines and mining, manufacturing, government, and fine arts.

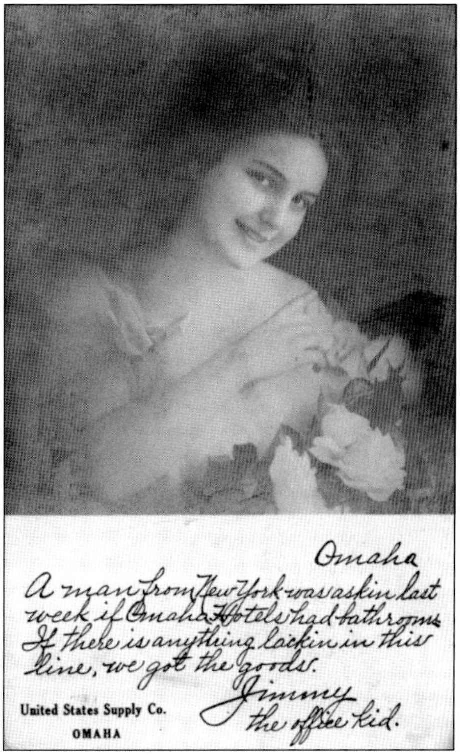

UNITED STATES SUPPLY CO. Improving streets, pavements, sewers, waterworks, and plumbing cost money and occurred slowly. This advertising postcard humorously attempts to dispel the notion of backwardness. The message pre-printed on this postcard read, "A man from New York was askin last week if Omaha Hotels had bathrooms. If there is anything lackin in this line, we got the goods." It was signed by "Jimmy the office kid." Located in a six-story building at Ninth and Farnam Streets, the company's motto stated: "The time to buy soil pipe—the U.S. kind."

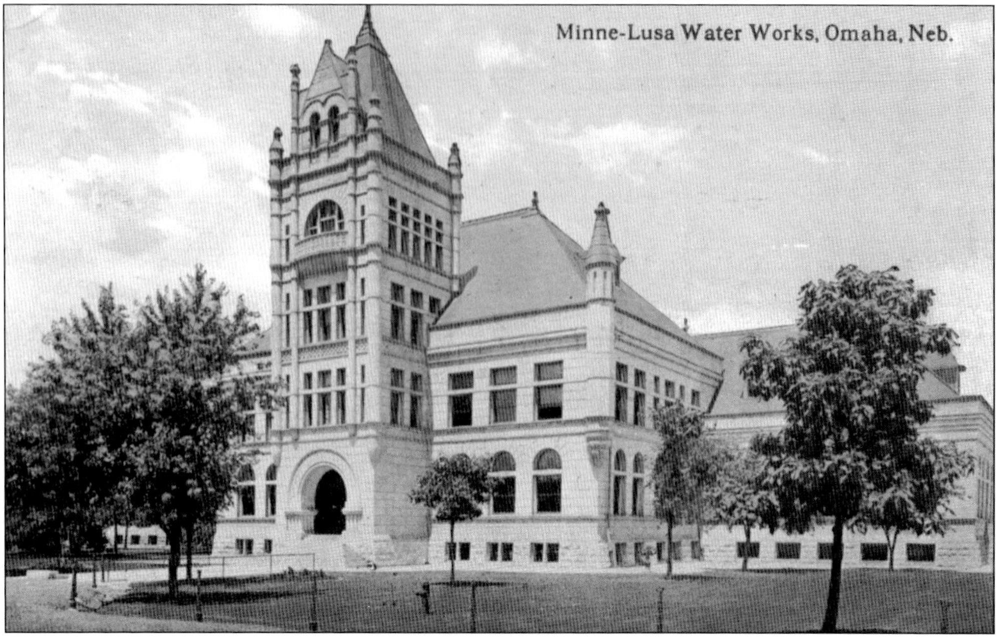

MINNE-LUSA WATER WORKS. This building was designed by Mendelssohn, Fisher and Lawrie in Florence, completed in 1889, and demolished in 1970. MUD (Metropolitan Utility District) still purifies Omaha's water on John J. Pershing Drive near this location.

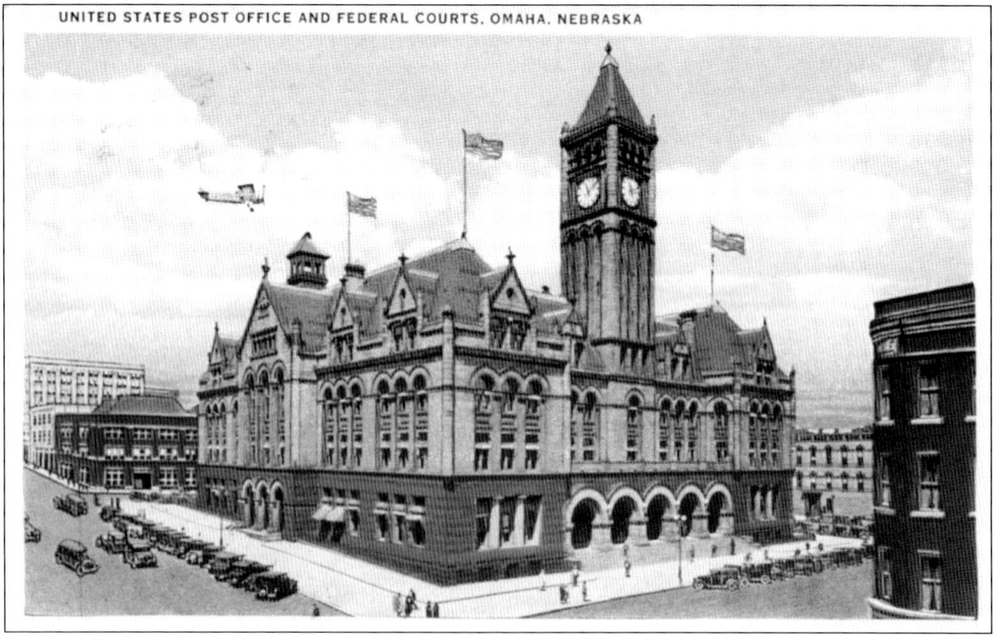

FEDERAL BUILDING AND POST OFFICE. This building was conceived in 1889, opened in 1898, completed in 1906, and demolished in 1966. John Latenser Sr. designed this $1.9-million Richardson Romanesque edifice at Sixteenth and Dodge Streets. Cheap, reliable postage democratized communications in the United States. Postal regulations in the first decade of the 20th century unleashed a torrent of postcard publishing, purchasing, writing, and mailing, inaugurating the great postcard age.

Three

Home Away from Home

The first half of the 20th century brought electrification, automobiles, airplanes, tragic wars, the passage and repeal of Prohibition, and the lighthearted Golden Age of Postcards.

Architects enhanced the city of Omaha. Brick and stone projected stability and permanence. Thomas Rogers Kimball designed Hotel Fontenelle and entered the Nebraska Hall of Fame in August 2017. John Latenser designed the Sanford Hotel and Omaha Athletic Club; John McDonald designed the Hill Hotel; Mendelssohn, Fisher and Lawrie designed Wellington Inn; Joseph P. Guth designed the Prague Hotel; George Prinz designed the Flatiron Building; and Alfred Dufrene designed the Burlington headquarters. Their names still resound. Tall buildings punctuated the skyline and housed hotels and corporate headquarters.

At least 30 postcard-worthy hospitality centers were built, opened, or renamed between 1900 and 1939: seven in the first decade; eighteen from 1910 to 1921, including the Fontenelle and Blackstone; and five in 1929 and 1930. The Great Depression brought an end to hotel construction.

The hotel industry responded to evolving consumer habits, the automobile, the rising motel industry, and the exodus from downtown. Cooperation was a survival strategy. The Hamilton, Wellington, Sanford, Keen, Delmar, Morris, Conant, Castle, Flatiron, and Neville, along with bus lines, advertised "Dollar for Dollar" in the *Omaha World-Herald*: "You will save money this winter by living in one of the downtown Omaha hotels. Special Low Rates for permanent guests are being made now." According to Jakle and Sculle, advertising budgets doubled during the Depression. Cost reductions meant layoffs, wage cuts, longer hours, and deferred maintenance.

Hoteliers, bonifaces, and "mine hosts" became familiar figures. The Kitchen brothers, Peter Goos, T.J. O'Brien, Rome Miller, Loyal Cohn, Mary and Harley Conant, Eugene C. Eppley, Bernard Schimmel, printer Irvin Medlar, real estate developer Harry A. Wolf, and ophthalmologist Dr. Harold Gifford would be in the Omaha Hotelier Hall of Fame if it existed. Eppley entered the Omaha Business Hall of Fame in 2000.

The Eppley, Blackstone, and Boss hotel chains fostered familiarity and loyalty. Guests always had a friendly place to stay with attractive and reliable restaurants, amenities, locations, prices, security, and comfort. By the middle of the 20th century, hotel and motel chains were becoming giants that marketed their inventory with teletype reservation systems. Sheraton started Reservatron in 1958 and free numbers in 1969. Holiday Inn introduced Holidex in 1965. Travelodge and Holiday Inn entered Omaha in 1961 and Hilton in 1970, writing new chapters in the history of Omaha's hospitality industry.

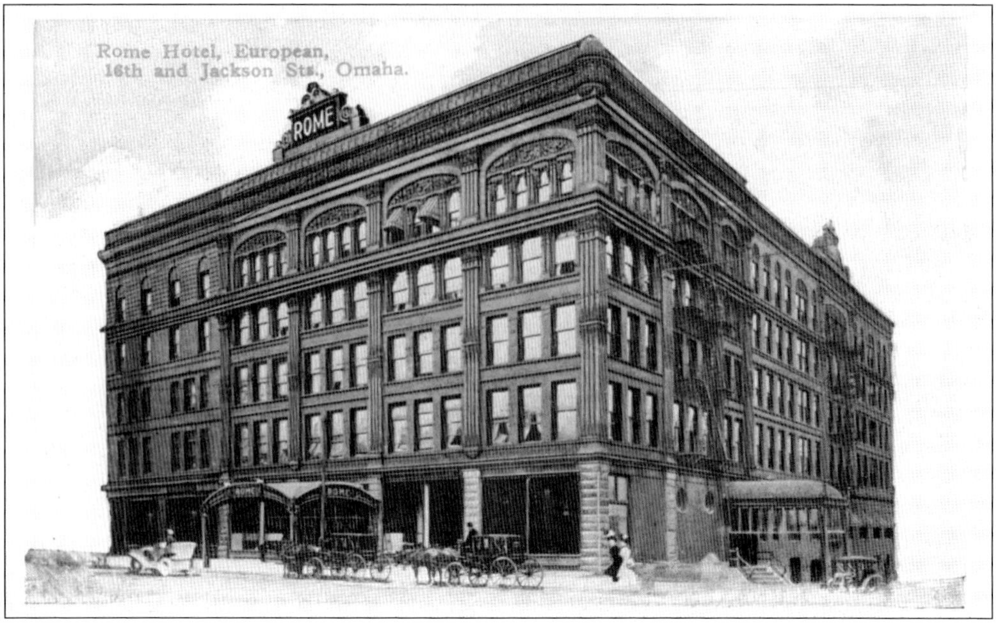

Rome Hotel at Sixteenth and Jackson Streets. This hotel opened in 1907 in the former Brunswick Hotel. At least 13 American cities are named Rome. Omaha's Rome Hotel is named after its owner, Rome Miller. Miller's hospitality enterprises, which operated from the 1880s until his retirement in 1920, included a Philippine restaurant at the Trans-Mississippi Exposition Midway. Nebraska's regiment served in the Spanish-American War.

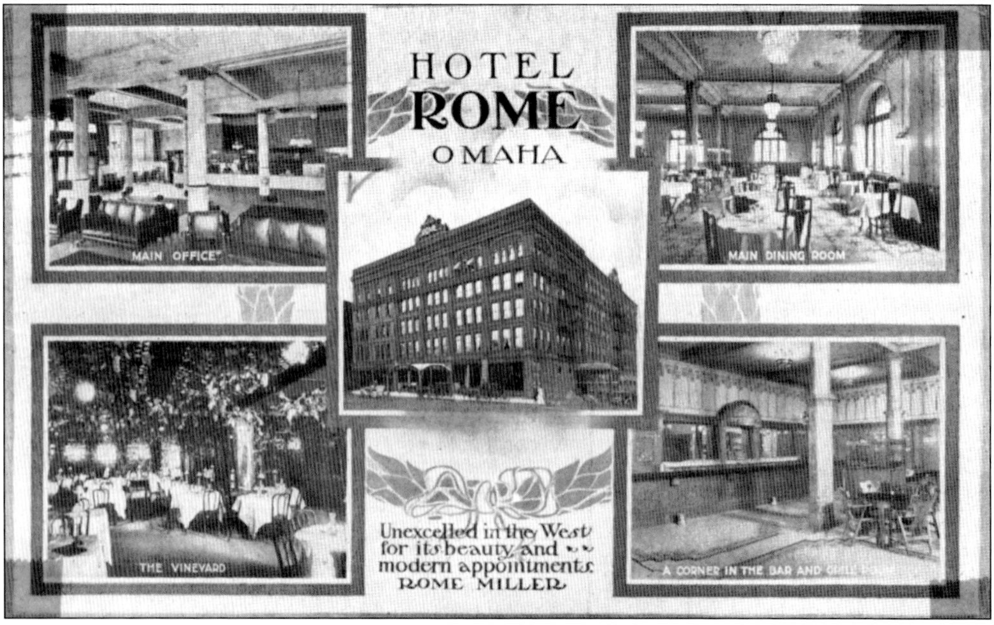

Rome Hotel Multiview. These five views include the hotel front, main office, main dining room, the Vineyard, and a corner in the bar and grill. This card is addressed to Eugene Warner in Buffalo, New York, and postmarked April 1910; the message reads, "This is the last postal you will receive on this trip. I hope to be with you in two more days. With lots of hugs and kisses to mother, father and you in which Grandpa joins in."

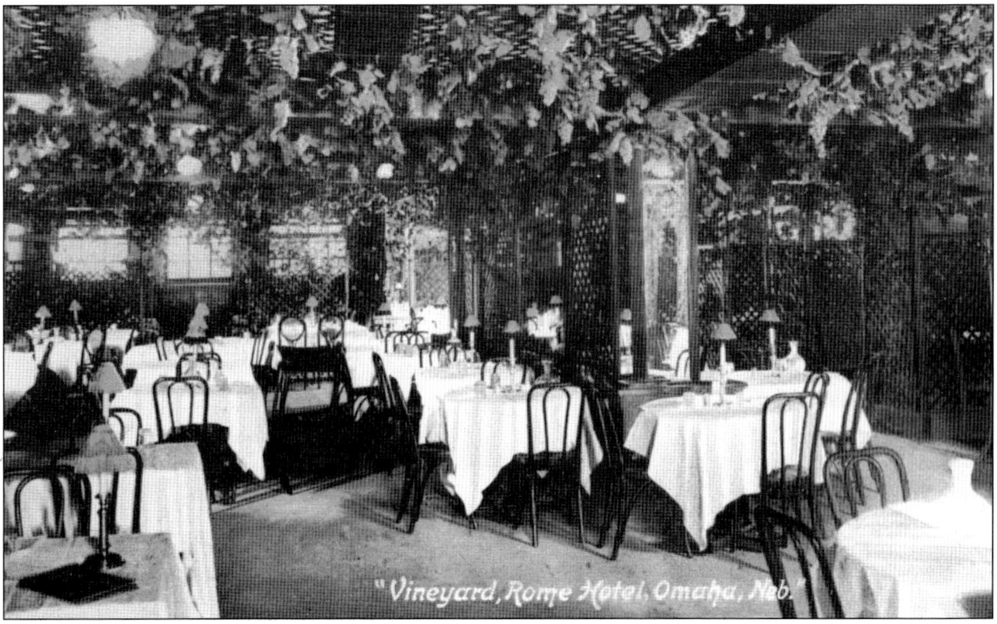

Vineyard Room. Rome Hotel offered elegant dining in an arbor-like atmosphere. In 1908, the Rome printed a colorful Thanksgiving menu with 12 dishes in Italian and two in English; Omaha had a substantial Sicilian population. Owner Rome Miller prepared typographically interesting menus. He advertised, "When in Omaha stop at the Hotel Rome." On this card, Susie wrote to Mrs. B. Kenyon in Iowa Falls in June 1912: "How does this look for a cozy corner for lunch on a hot day. We girls are having a great time."

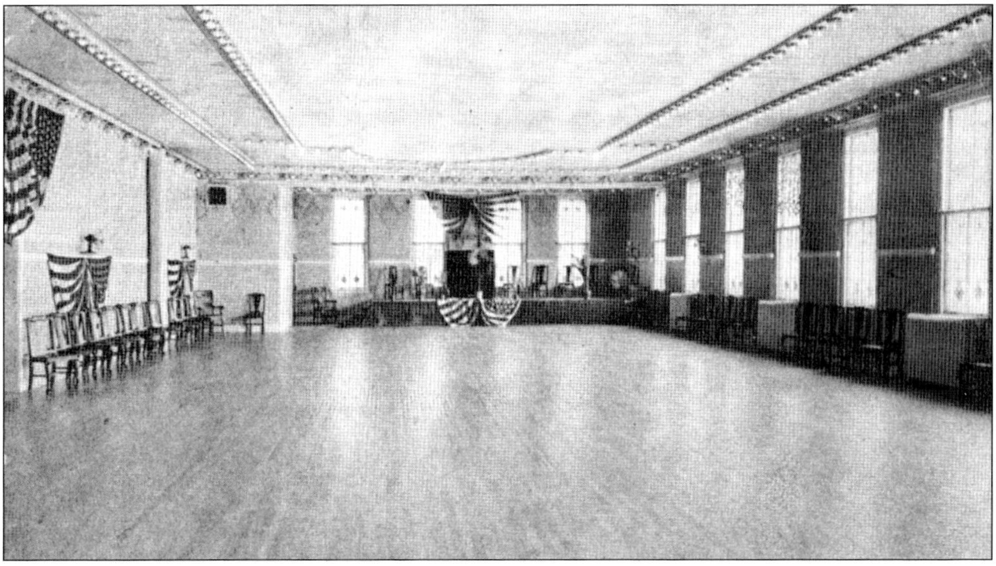

Assembly Room, Rome Hotel. The patriotic bunting perhaps suggests a political speech. The dais has chairs, so perhaps they were preparing to host a band and a Fourth of July dance. On January 2, 1913, the sender wrote to her sister May in Gallipolis, Ohio: "Hello Sis—Just received your picture. It was just the thing I wanted for Xmas but it is nothing like you. Glad all had a good time. You have got my letter now so I send this card. Love to all. Send Emmas' add." Postcards did not replace letters. (Omaha Public Library.)

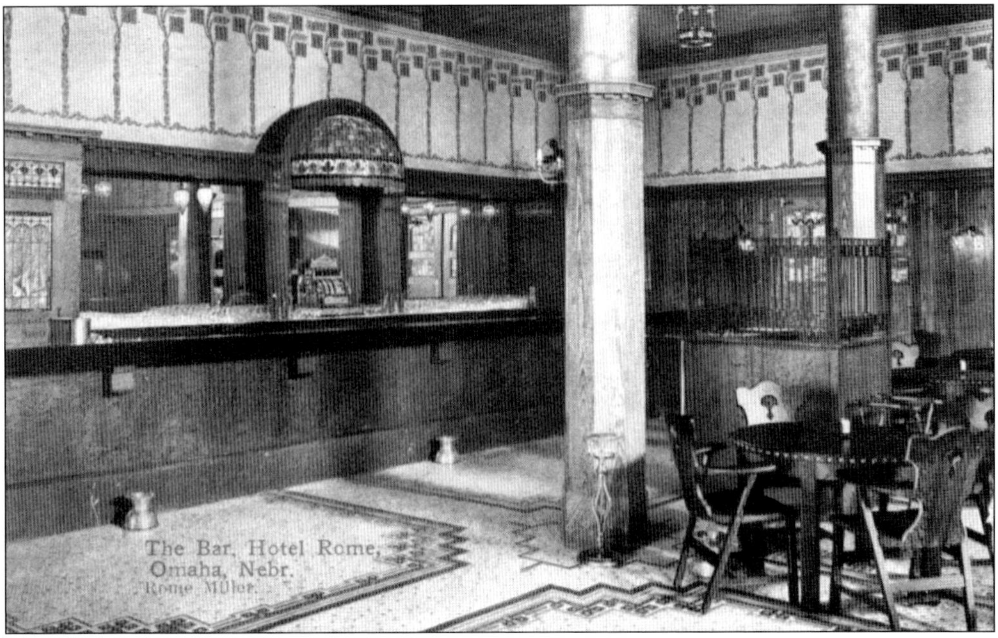

THE BAR AT HOTEL ROME. Local breweries offered Falstaff, Krug, Metz, Storz, and Willow Springs. Prohibition disrupted libations, socialization, celebration, business deals, and seduction at dives and opulent watering holes alike.

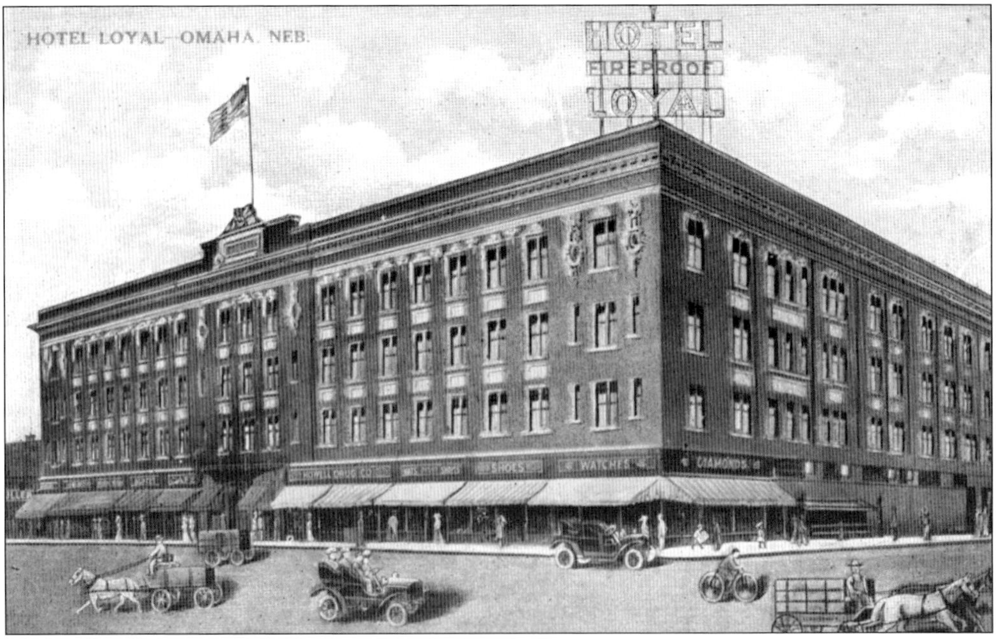

HOTEL LOYAL. This four-story hotel opened in 1907 at 211 North Sixteenth Street. The back states, "Omaha . . . is the gateway for the west. All the leading trunk lines pass through the city. It contains railroad shops, smelters, stock yards, and over 2,500 retail firms." Hotel Loyal commissioned the most varied postcards in Omaha. The hotel was named after owner Herman Cohn's son Loyal, the grandson of department store founder J.L. Brandeis. Herman was murdered early Sunday morning on March 26, 1911, during a robbery. The killer was never found.

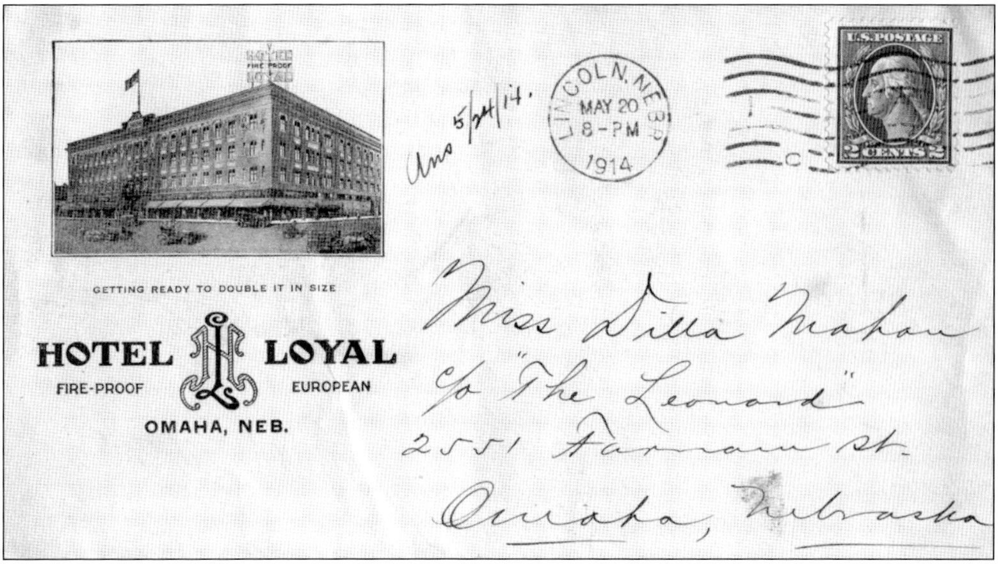

Hotel Loyal Envelope (above) and Expanded Hotel (below). This 1914 envelope has the same image as the previous postcard, a marketing and branding strategy, as is the elaborate calligraphic logo that also appears on the "Six Short Stories" card on page 62. The envelope states, "Getting ready to double it in size." Merchant signage on the first floor includes Buffet, Café, Howell Drug Company, and more. It housed Kieser's, a longtime Omaha bookstore. Buildings were frequently constructed with substantial foundations and the capacity to expand upward if necessary. Annexes and lateral expansion also solved some space needs. The Herndon and Millard Hotel had built upward, as did the Brandeis department store, and the Henshaw expanded sideways. Hotel Loyal, according to the envelope's claims, added a fifth story—or did it? When there was a fire in 1973 and the hotel was demolished in 1976, it had four stories.

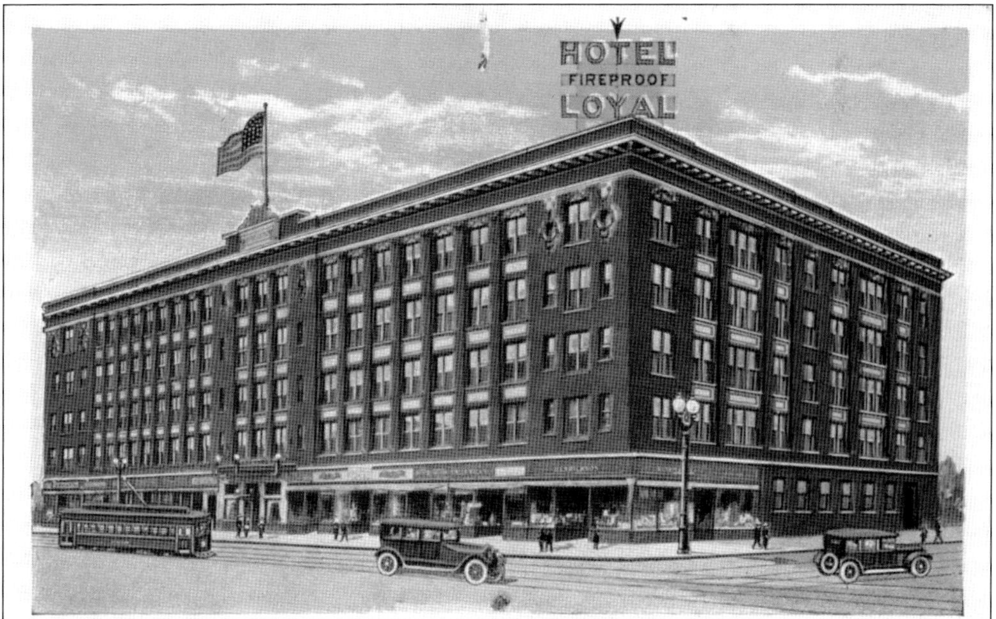

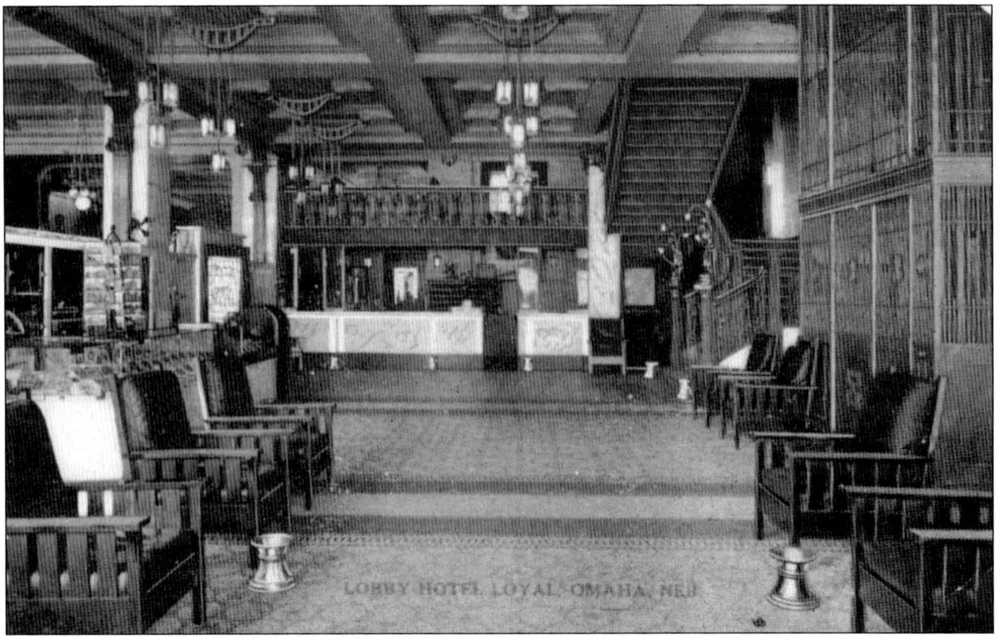

LOBBY (ABOVE) AND CAFÉ (BELOW) AT HOTEL LOYAL. Hotel Loyal owner Herman Cohn wanted a lobby that "will rival any west of Chicago." Mission or Arts and Crafts furniture fills the lobby, along with brass spittoons. The gift shop or souvenir counter on the left appears to have a rack of postcards. The leaded window is Tiffany-style. There is a mezzanine, Erte lamps, and a stairway. In the café, candlelit tables were invitingly set with white tablecloths and glasses in this Victorian atmosphere. Hotel owner Herman Cohn planned that the "cuisine will be unsurpassed by any in the entire west." The 1908 Fourth of July Dinner De Luxe cost $1, and the 1912 Thanksgiving dinner cost $1.50. In August 1913, the hotel suggested, "Sunday Dinners at home are a mistake. It's much more sensible to have your Sunday Dinner at the Hotel Loyal," where "a dozen oscillating electric fans keep the café cool." They boasted of "The best dinner west of Broadway." The Loyal also had a women's tea room.

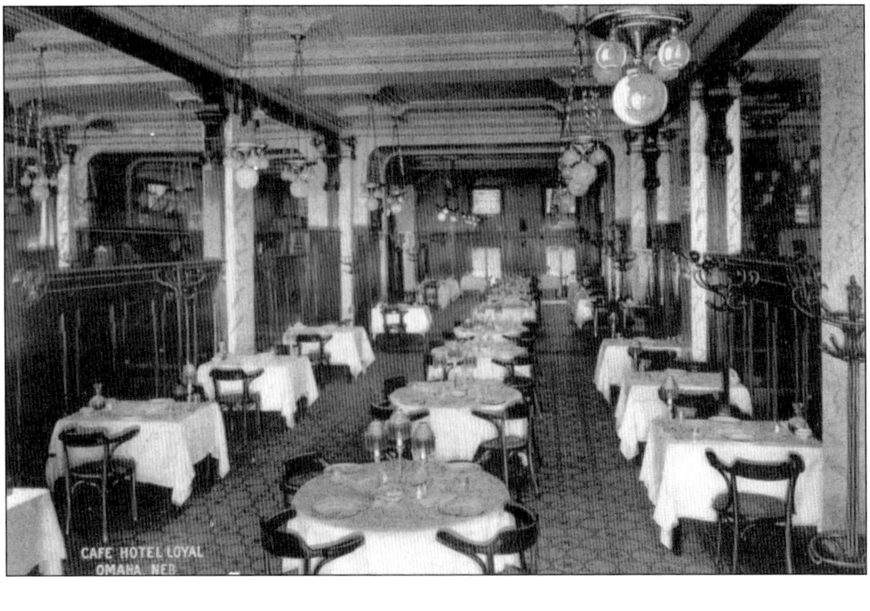

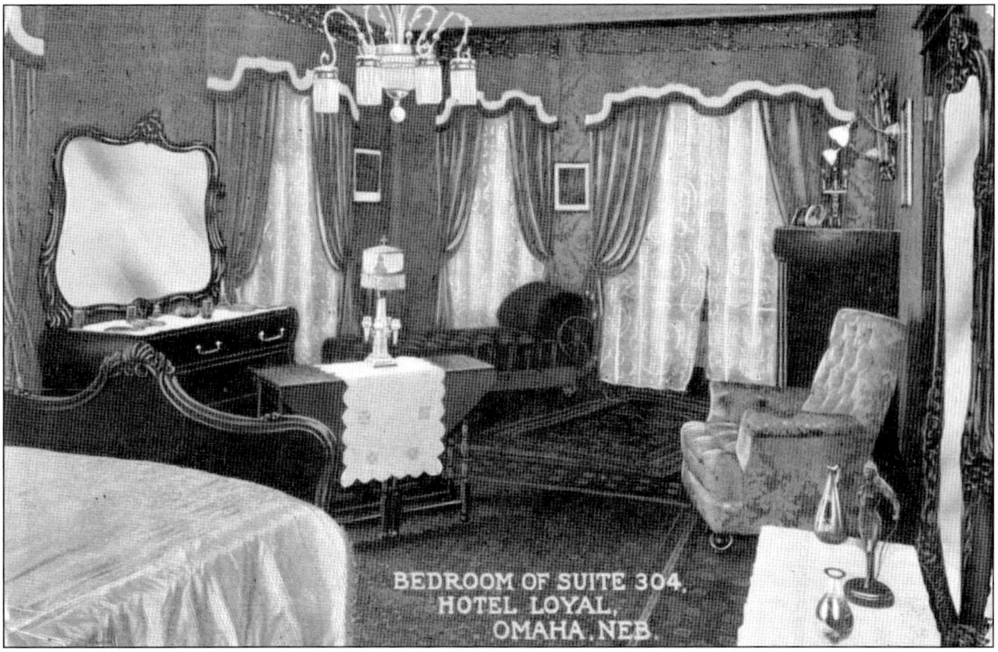

Bedroom of Suite 304, Hotel Loyal. This is made to look like a respectable home and suggests bourgeois opulence. Compare this and the following image to the cleaner, less cluttered lines of more modern rooms; this seems like a museum installation or furniture store display.

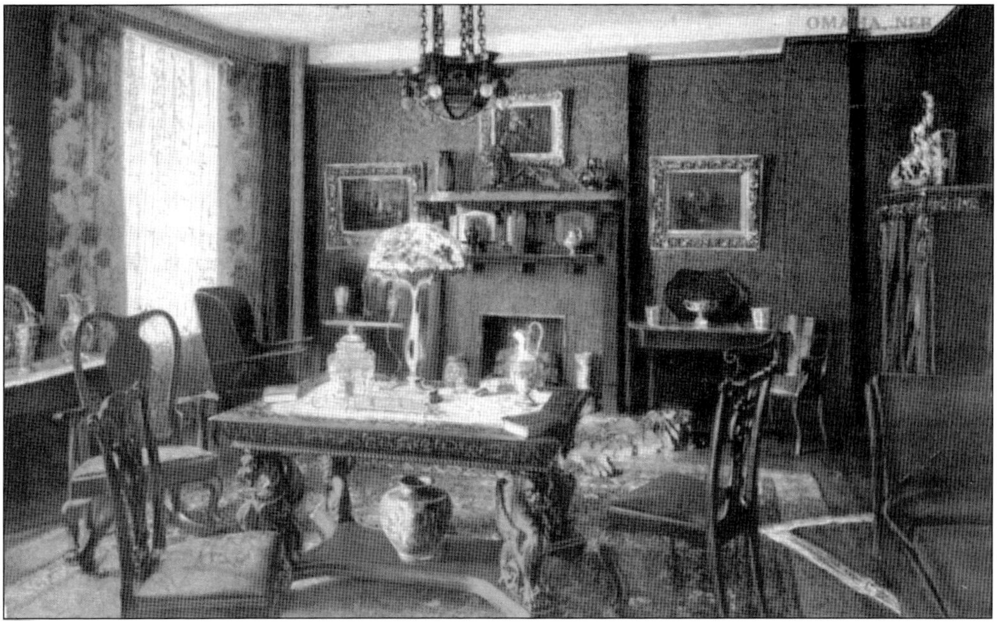

Living Room and Suite 308, Hotel Loyal. Lighting, ornate framed paintings on the wall, pottery, urns, carpet, throw rugs, two tables, seating for six, figurines, glassware, a fireplace with mantle and sconces, and perhaps a tiger skin emphasize ornateness. Sizzie in Benson wrote to Alwina in Florence, Nebraska, in 1910: "You must think I'm an awful kid for never writing, but that's a job I don't relish very well." Sizzie planned to visit on Sunday, "so then we'll have time to make up again."

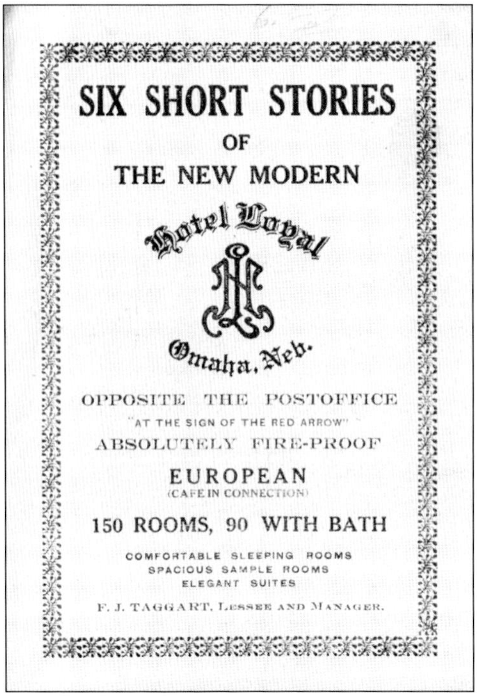

SIX SHORT STORIES OF THE NEW MODERN HOTEL LOYAL. Contained in this folder are six one-sided foldout postcards for guests to mail. They extol the fireproof hotel's qualities, sample room, lobby, café, well-furnished rooms, and the hotel visage. This was not a "penny dreadful," popular at the time—it was a marketing strategy. (Omaha Public Library.)

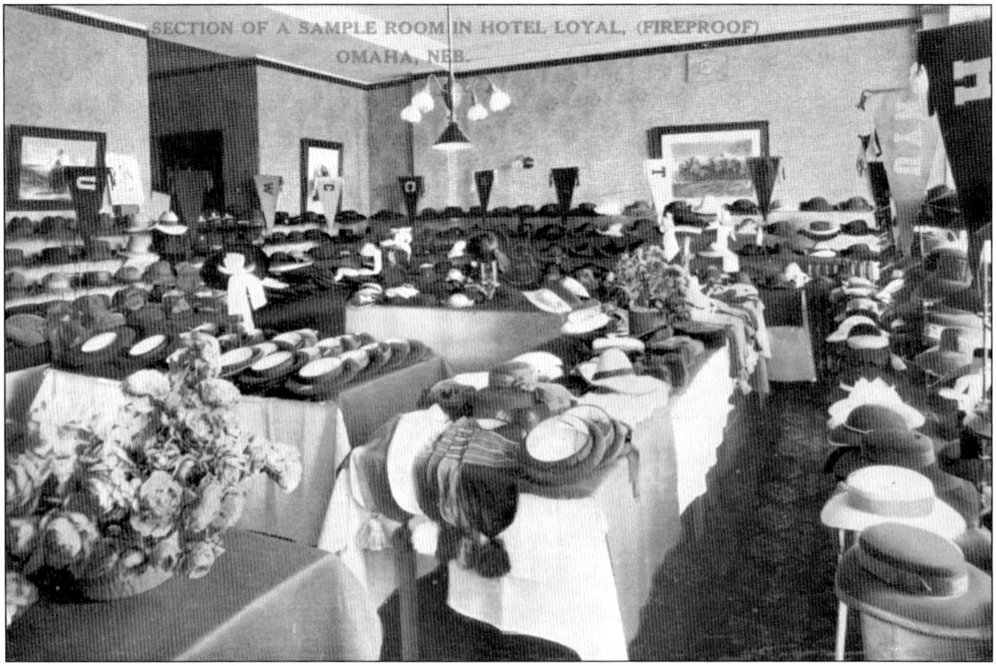

SECTION OF A SAMPLE ROOM IN HOTEL LOYAL. Salesmen displayed their wares in sample rooms, including labor-saving devices and women's and men's fashions from New York and Paris. They advertised the dates they would be in the sample room. This millinery display contains over 100 hats. According to Jakle and Sculle, in 1907, there were some 400,000 traveling salespeople. They competed with nearby J.L. Brandeis and Sons department store and the innovative Sears, Roebuck and Company mail-order catalogues. (Omaha Public Library.)

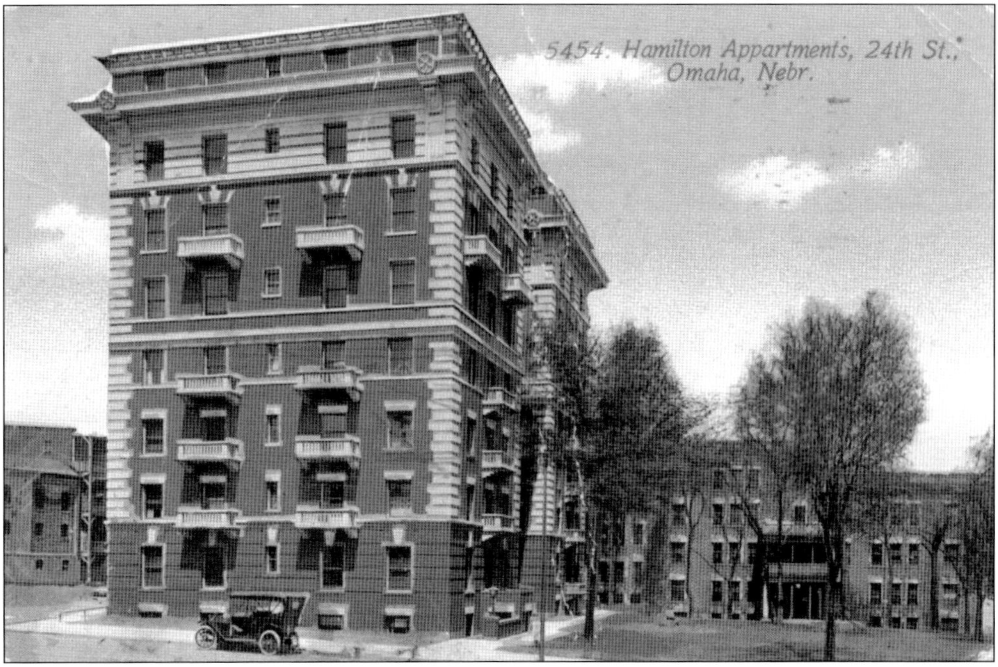

HAMILTON APARTMENTS. According to the "Adventures in Omaha History" blog, this property at Twenty-fourth and Farnam Streets started around 1904. Over time, it appears to have expanded. The manifestation on this postcard, postmarked August 1911, shows a seven-story building. The New Arcade, Hunter Inn, Hamilton, and Blackstone were a combination of long-term apartment residences and a hotel for transients. For many, living in a one-room downtown hotel became a way of life.

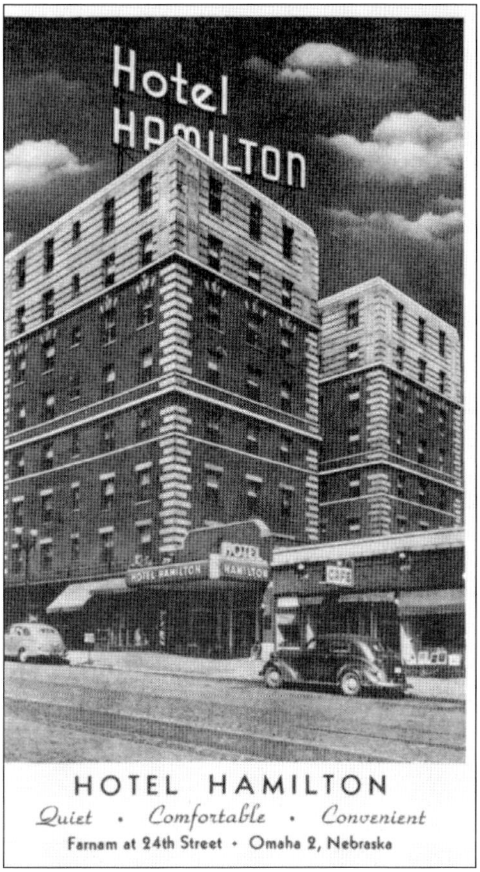

HOTEL HAMILTON REPURPOSED. Upon its reopening in 1921 with eight stories, Hotel Hamilton advised prospective tenants to "make your selection of a room at once before the choicest are taken." Hamilton became one of 11 hotels in the Host Inc. chain, with properties in eight states, then the Warren, Gisch, and Host Masters organization. This building was razed in 1977. The disappearance of low-end housing displaced the poor. The 1910 Colonial Hotel at Thirty-eighth and Farnam Streets fell into disrepair. Investors, aided by tax credits, gentrified it by reducing its 110 rooms to 40 and raising rents, which created controversy in 2017.

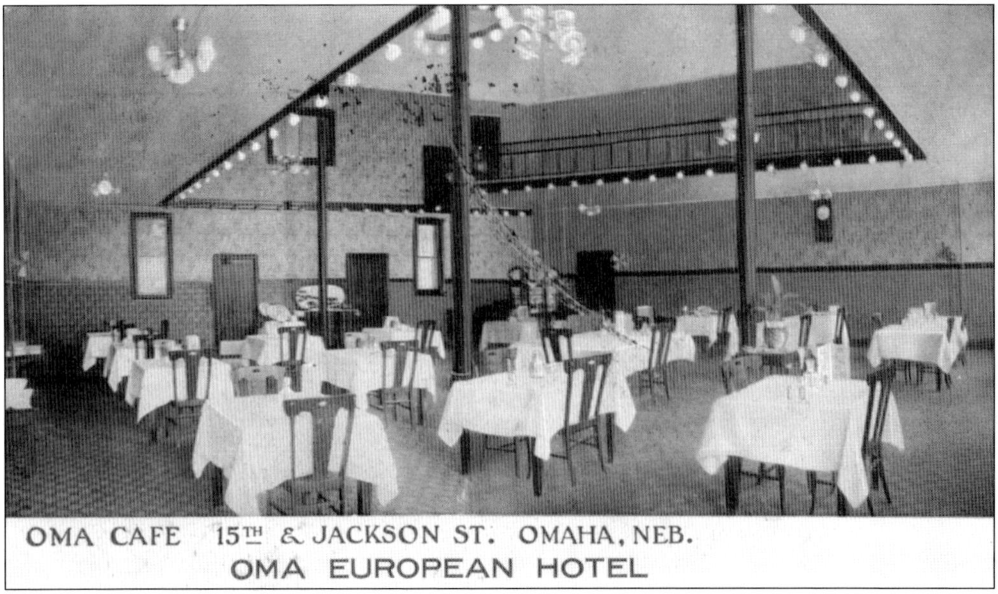

OMA CAFÉ AND EUROPEAN HOTEL. This unusually colorful, descriptive, and inviting card is for the establishment at Fifteenth and Jackson Streets. From 1908 to 1909, it advertised for a busboy, cook, serving girls, waiters, a woman to cook, and two dining room girls. A 1908 letter to Miss Annie Littler in Painesville, Ohio, reads, "This is the café where I took all my meals while in Omaha."

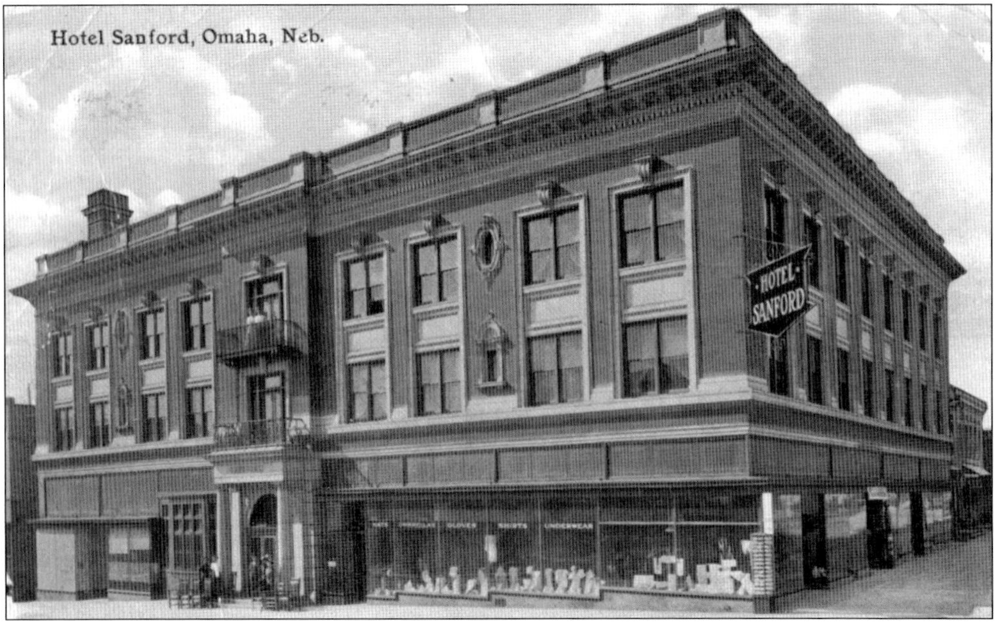

HOTEL SANFORD, AN OMAHA CHAIN. In the 1890s, Mary H. Conant ran a 10-room house, moved to 15 rooms at Dodge and Eighteenth Streets, and opened the 30-room Albany for the Trans-Mississippi Expo. Her son Harley started the Harley and Sanford. Mary, president of the Conant Hotel Company, and her son were adept at mergers and acquisitions. The letterhead on page 46 depicts the chain. The original three-story brick Hotel Sanford was built in 1910 at Nineteenth and Farnam Streets and had 60 rooms. Mary died in 1930 at age 70.

HOTEL SANFORD. The Conant Hotel Company holdings expanded. The seven-story Hotel Sanford at 1913 Farnam Street, built next to the 1910 three-story Sanford, opened in 1917. In 1939, the Regis purchased the original Conant at Sixteenth and Harney Streets. This Sanford became the Conant-Sanford in 1939. Owner and manager Harley Conant died in 1956 at age 81. It became simply the Conant in 1959. The Conant became City Pointe Apartments in 2014, with 57 apartments of 500–800 square feet.

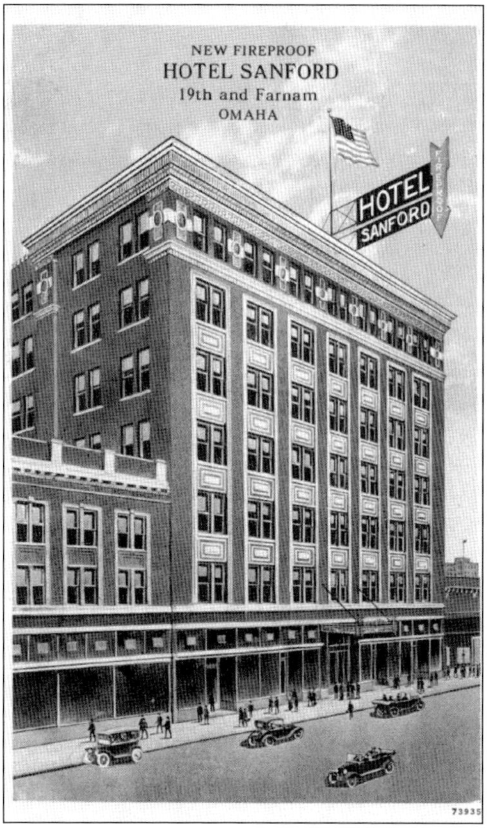

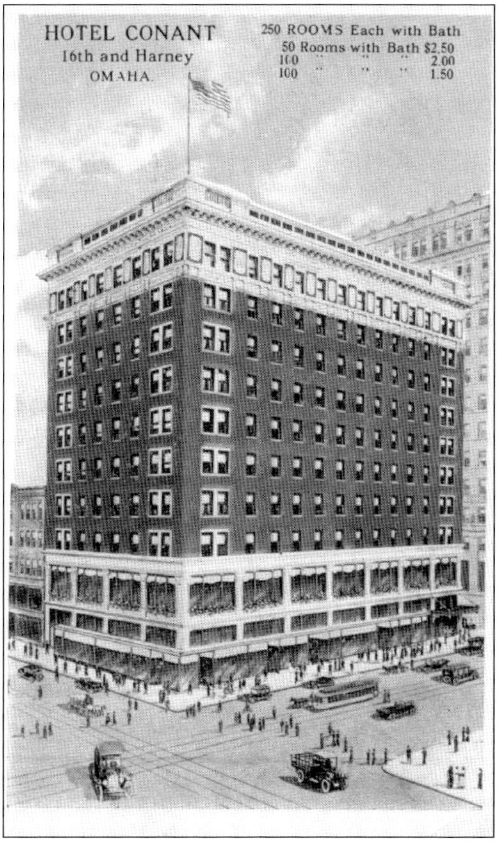

HOTEL CONANT AT SIXTEENTH AND HARNEY STREETS. This hotel opened in September 1918 with 250 rooms and 250 baths, satisfying Ellsworth Statler's slogan: "every room with a bath." Prices ranged from $1.50 to $2.50. Streetcars, horses and wagons, automobiles, trucks, and pedestrians fill the street. On September 4, 1922, Ray wrote on this postcard to Myron in Goodrich, Michigan: "We are staying over Sunday in Omaha. Some city. Everything fine. Nice trip."

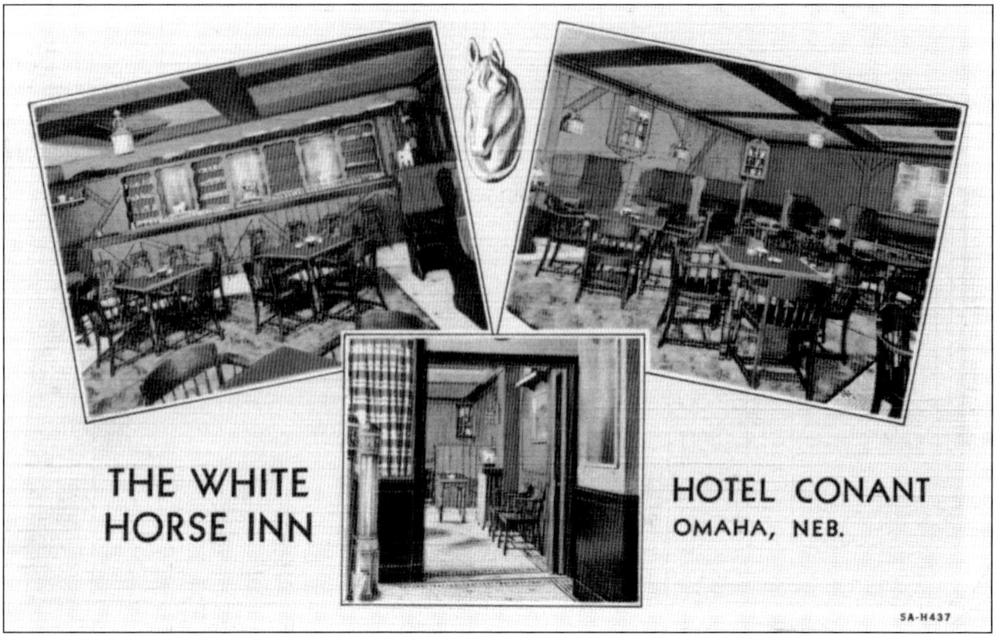

The White Horse Inn at Hotel Conant. Eating at hotel restaurants offered patrons reliable food and a chance to see and be seen. An August 1935 advertisement in the *Omaha World-Herald* reads: "Visit the White Horse Inn for a Long Cool Drink." It was summer, and Prohibition was only a bad memory. In June 1937, "Grand Pa Van" wrote to Robert in Rudd, Iowa: "Dear Bobby, I would like to see you."

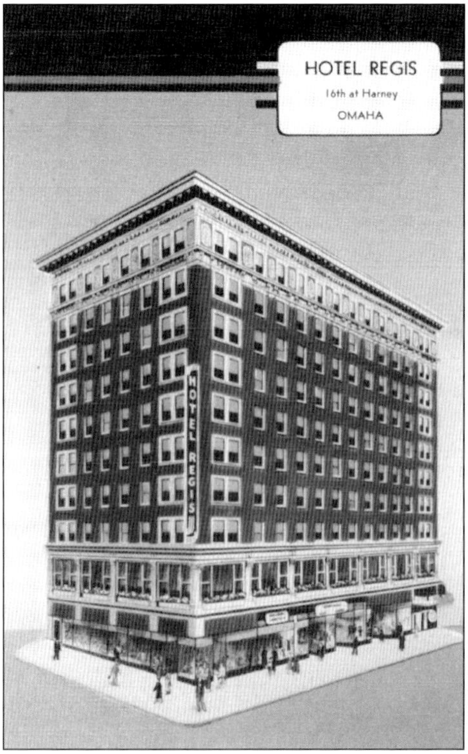

Hotel Regis. In 1939, Regis purchased the Hotel Conant at Sixteenth and Harney Streets. "In the heart of everything," the White Horse Inn and Diana Lounge remained. H.A. Wolf committed $25,000 to remodel, redecorate, and refurnish. A Regis guest wrote to Ethel in Bristol, Connecticut, in 1940: "Well, here I am in the town of A Relation and Two Exclamations. O-ma-ha! This is the last hotel, but the trip is a flop. I'll need to vacation when I get thru. Thanks for your pretty card." In 1984, this building became condominiums.

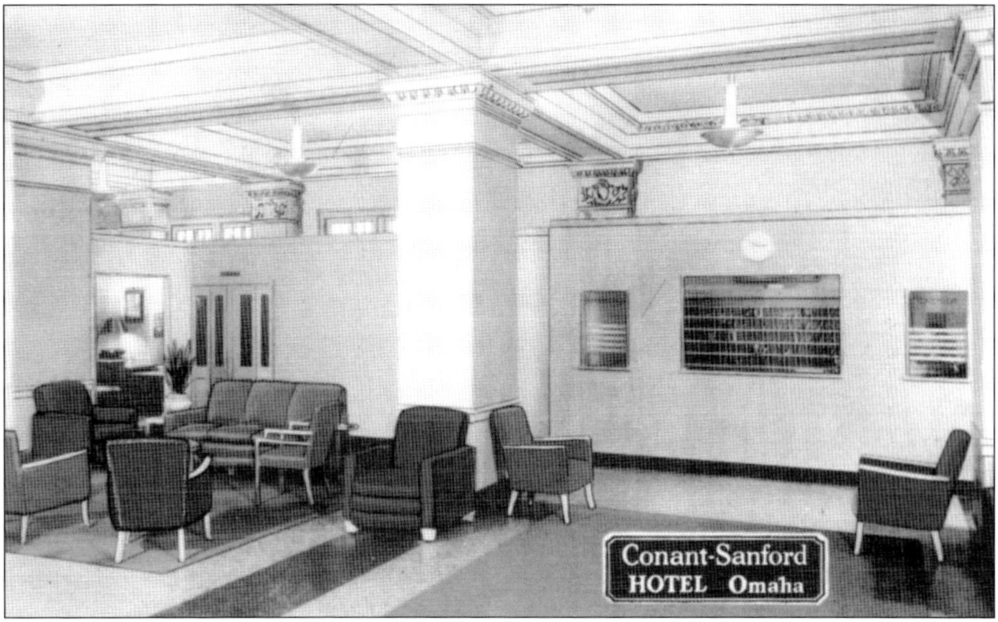

CONANT-SANFORD HOTEL. The Conant, like the Regis, underwent about $25,000 in refurbishment in 1939. Two postcards contained messages. Dad and Mom wrote to their daughter Anne in Minneapolis in September 1948: "Had a nice warm trip. Cooler today. Lots of fun renewing old friendships. A nice dinner party in our honor Saturday nite Athletic Club." In January 1950, K.O.T.W. [King of the World?] wrote to George in Chicago: "I got a whole bunch of free postcards from the Conant Hotel. Best wishes." "Sanford" was dropped from the hotel's name in 1959.

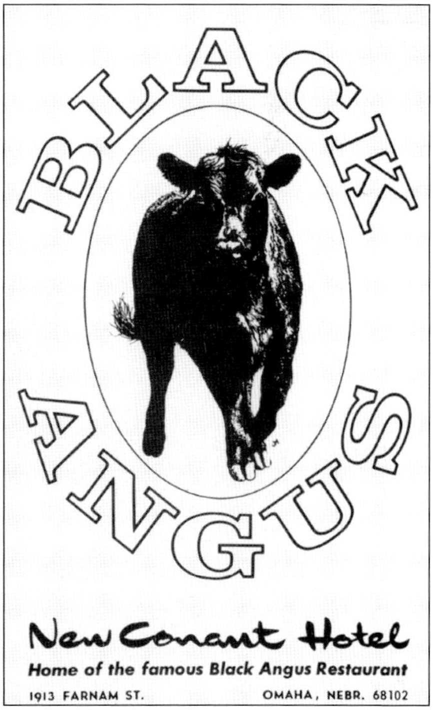

CONANT BLACK ANGUS, NEW CONANT HOTEL. Omaha has been called an "over-steaked town." Hotel restaurants had a built-in clientele (hotel guests) and also served local residents. Restaurants gave hotels more visibility. Nebraska, "the Beef State," is far from oceans and the gulf. Black Angus opened in the New Conant Hotel around 1959. The national franchise dates from 1964. Some seafood restaurants arrived in the Omaha area in the 1960s.

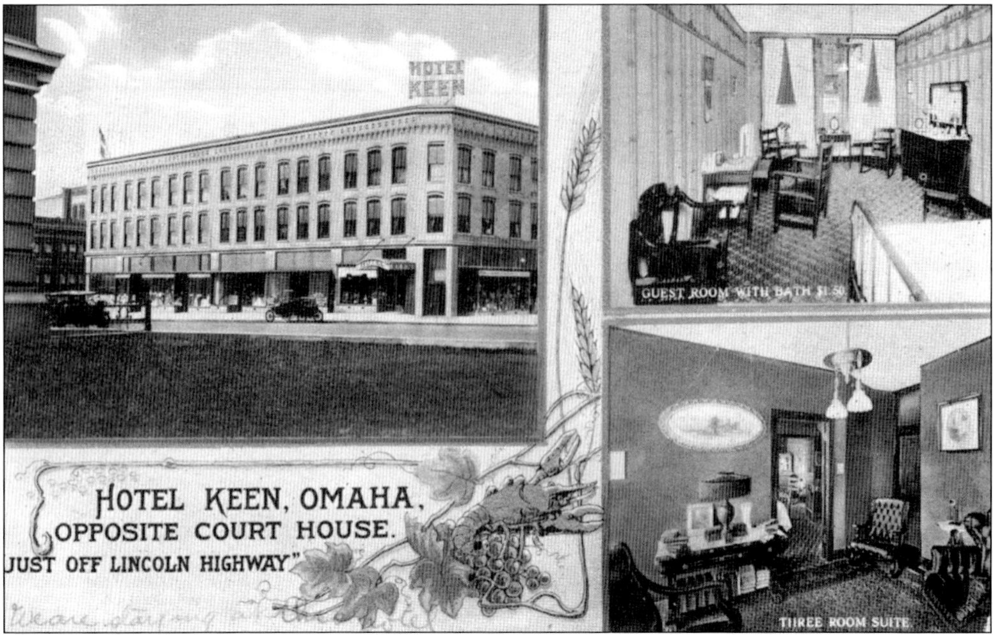

HOTEL KEEN. Built in 1911 opposite the Douglas County Courthouse, Hotel Keen opened in 1914. "Just off Lincoln Highway," it offered a guest room with bath for $1.50. Harry L. Keen, the proprietor, was a division manager for Royal Baking Powder Company. Keen served as the fifth vice president of the Nebraska Hotel Association in 1921. The courthouse corner is on the left. The hotel had "the widest sidewalk in the city, thirty feet," "[a] view of the court house lawn," and the " 'Welcome' sign half a block away."

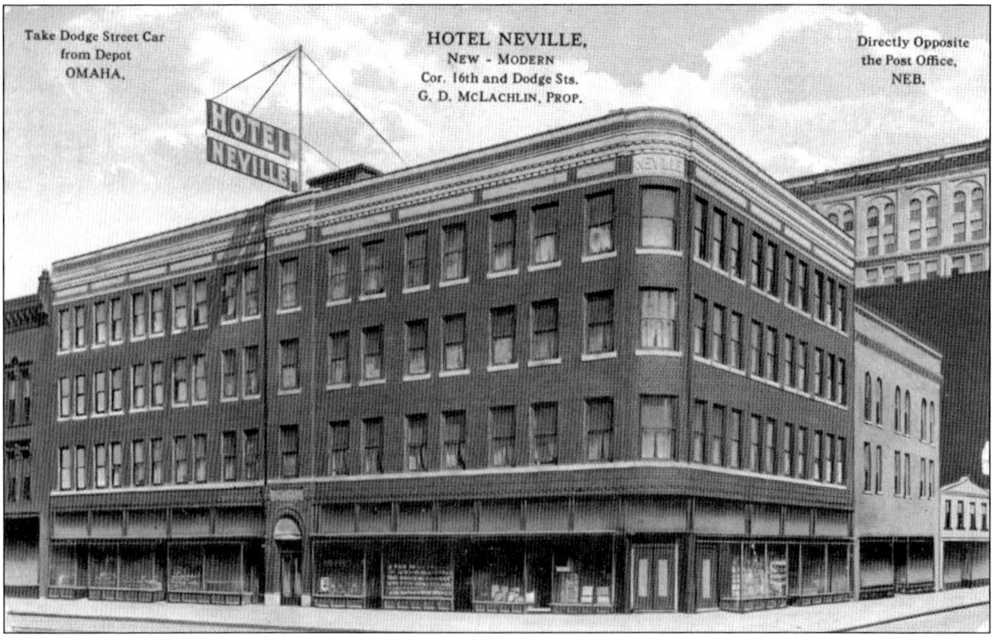

HOTEL NEVILLE. Judge James Neville built this four-story brick hotel at Sixteenth and Dodge Streets, opposite the post office, in 1913. It featured hot and cold running water, steam heat, electric lights, and a telephone in every room. The basement had billiards.

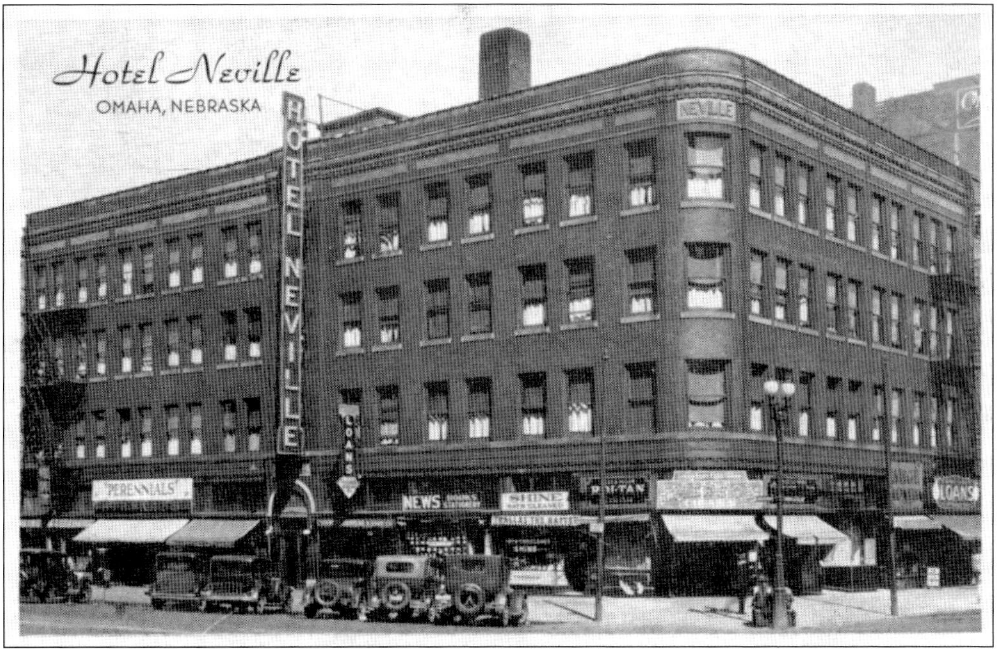

HOTEL NEVILLE WITH STOREFRONTS. Hotel Neville's ground floor housed a hat cleaner, Roi Tan cigar store, two loan offices, and a newsstand. Overland-Wolf Investment purchased the hotel in 1945 for $140,000, and it was razed in 1969 to make way for the Hilton Hotel and First National Bank parking.

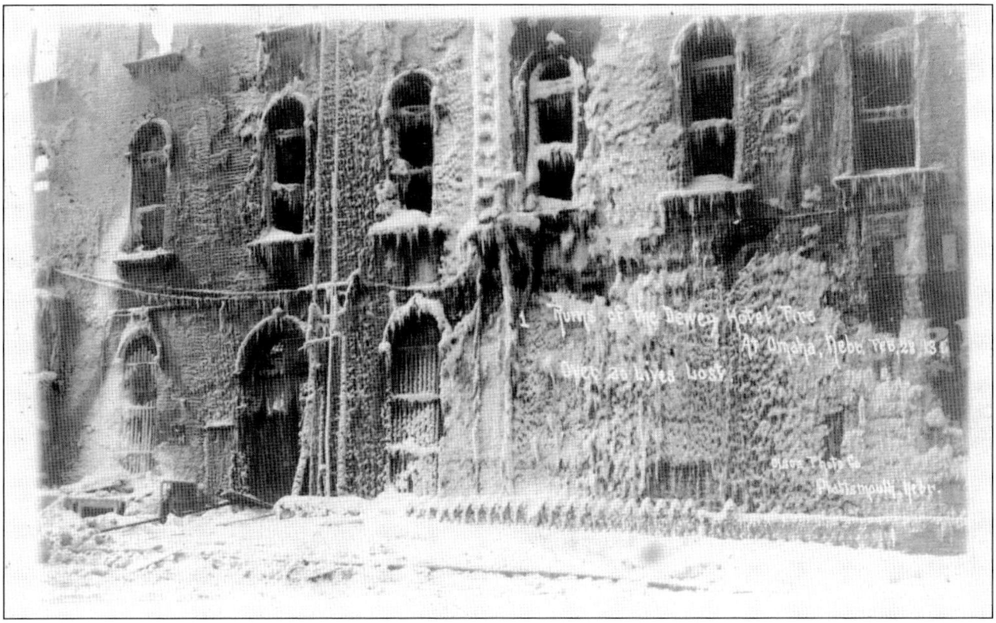

DEWEY HOTEL FIRE. The Dewey European Hotel did not have a postcard other than this one. The Dewey took over the Morehouse Hotel at Thirteenth and Farnam Streets in 1899. Fire consumed the Dewey in February 1913, and 20 people died. Fires in freezing weather result in eerie, distorted ice palaces. Dewey joined the Grand Central and Millard Hotels as tragic examples of loss of life and property.

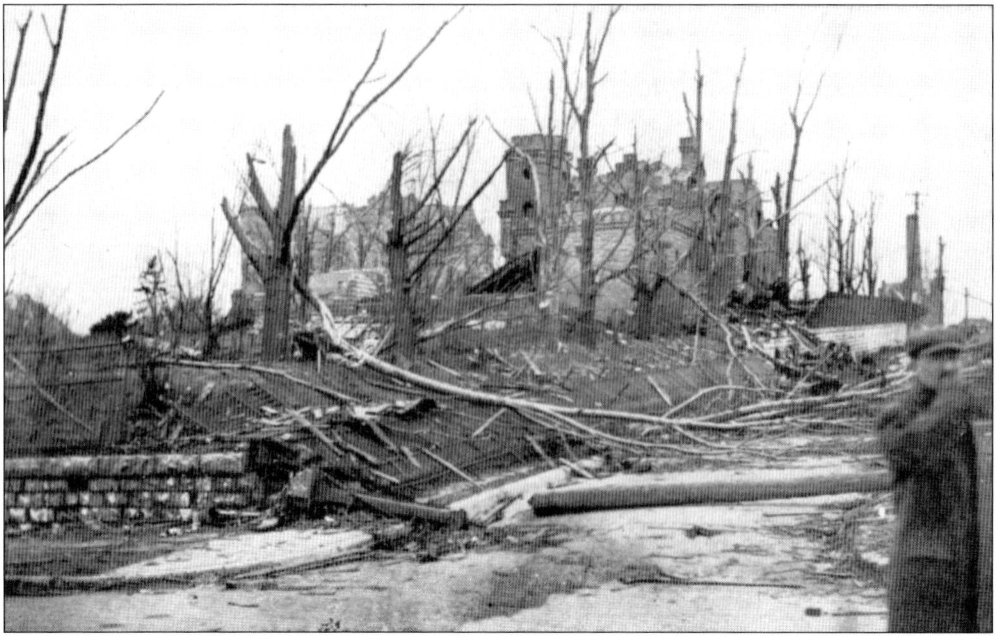

JOSLYN CASTLE. Two events in Omaha history—the uplifting 1898 Trans-Mississippi Exposition and the destructive Easter 1913 tornado—have resounded for over a century. The force-eight tornado had 120-mph winds and destroyed even the prestigious stone and brick home of newspaper entrepreneur George and Sarah Joslyn. The tornado resulted in 140 deaths, 1,250 destroyed homes, and 2,500 people made homeless. The Joslyns rebuilt the Castle; it served the Omaha Public Schools and is now a cultural center.

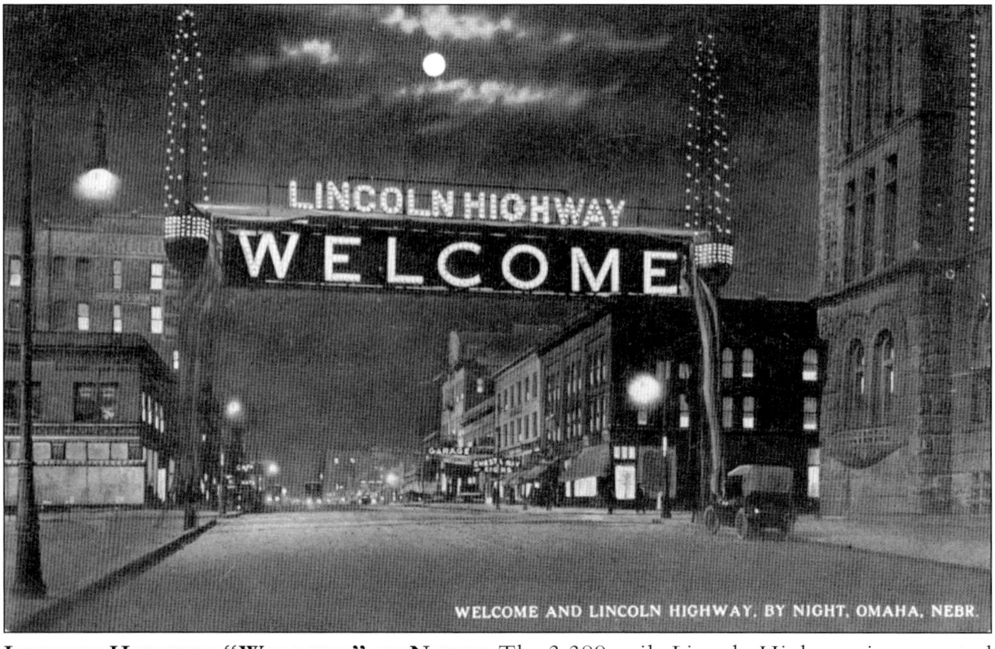

LINCOLN HIGHWAY "WELCOME" AT NIGHT. The 3,389-mile Lincoln Highway, inaugurated in 1913, starts in New York, runs through 14 states, and ends in San Francisco. Contrary to the depiction on this postcard, most of the highway was not lit at night.

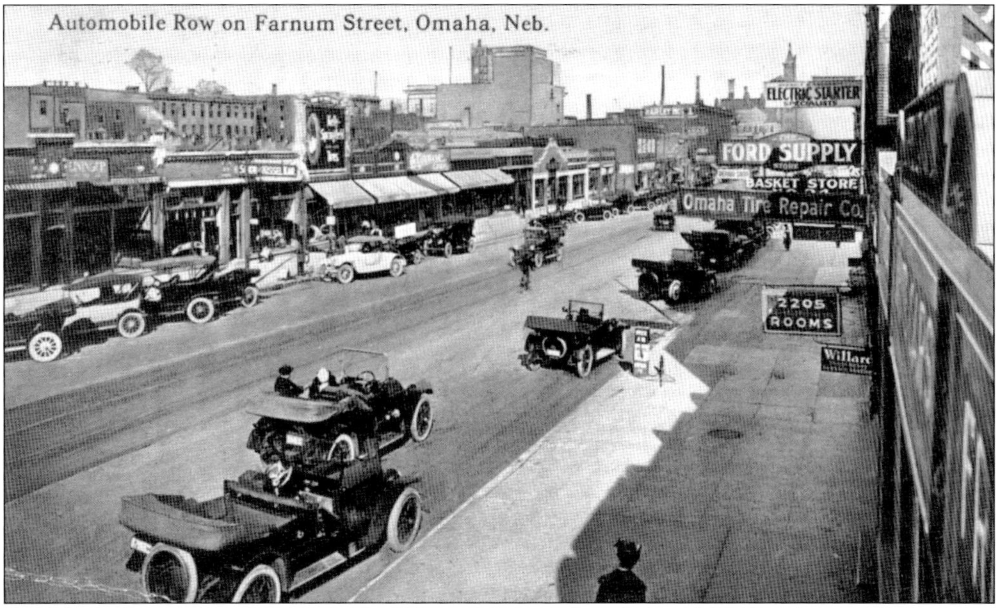

AUTOMOBILE ROW ON FARNUM [*SIC*] STREET. Useful technology spreads quickly. The American Automobile Association (AAA) was established in 1902. Car dealers and garages proliferated. Car and truck sales became a national economic index and an individual statement of independence and mobility. Signage includes Free Air at the curb, 2205 Rooms, Willard Battery, and Omaha Tire Repair Co. Basket Store, a Nebraska, Iowa, and Missouri grocery chain, went from one location in 1908 to 47, in 1921, and then went bankrupt. The Harley Hotel is on the left.

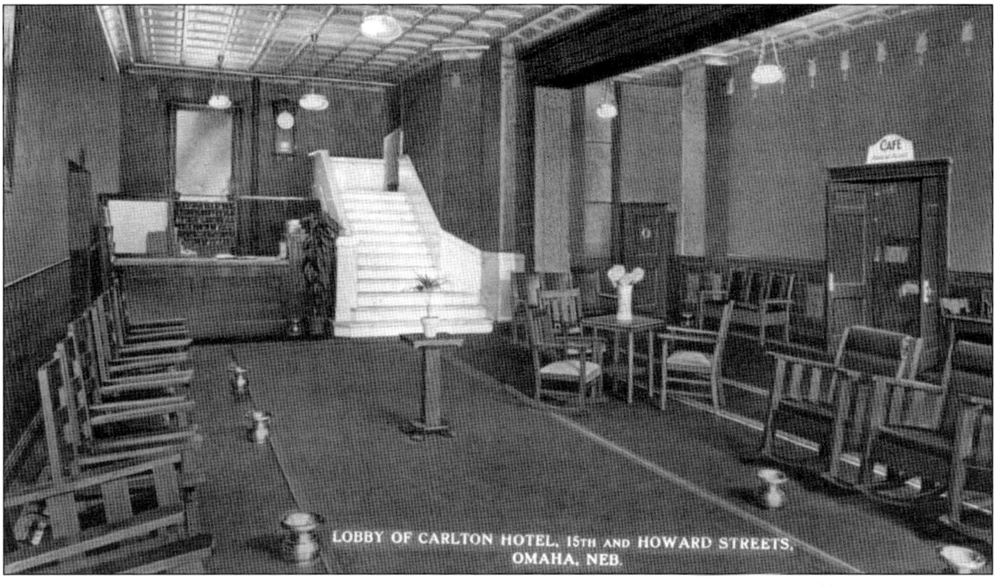

CARLTON HOTEL LOBBY. The Omaha Ice and Cold Storage Company had offices at Fifteenth and Howard Streets in the Shelly block since 1906. It moved in 1913 to the McCague building. Omaha Ice became the Carlton Hotel in 1913. In 1919, a hotelier with Millard and Neville Hotel interests purchased the Carlton. The lobby has carpet, marble stairs, tin ceiling, reception desk, five brass spittoons, pink carnations, about a dozen Mission or Craftsman chairs, and a café. A Carlton matchbook claims "Omaha's Biggest Bargain in Hotel Accommodations."

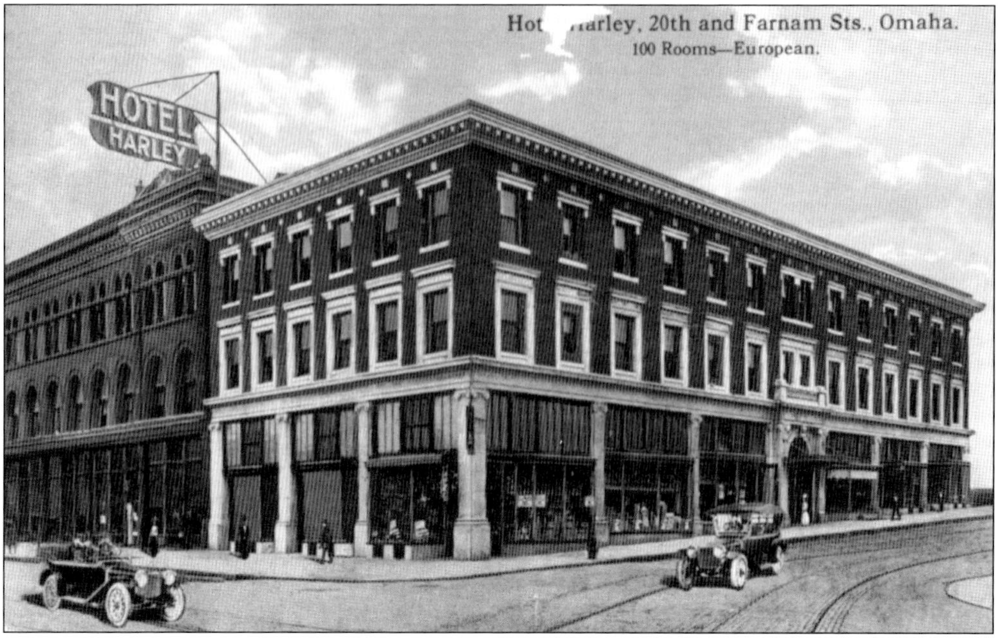

HOTEL HARLEY. Harley Conant purchased the three-story Bachelors' Quarters building at Twentieth and Farnam Streets in 1914 and renamed it the Harley Hotel. In 1898, Bachelors' Quarters had 60 rooms. It expanded to 100 rooms. Conant sold it in 1917 to the former Chatham manager. The Conant family also owned the Hotel Sanford. (Douglas County Historical Society.)

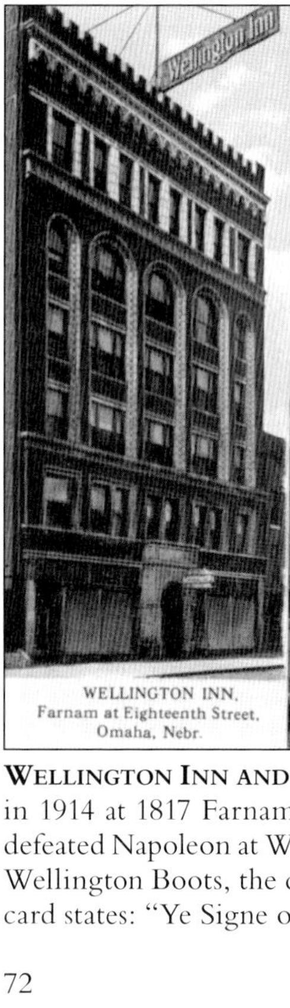

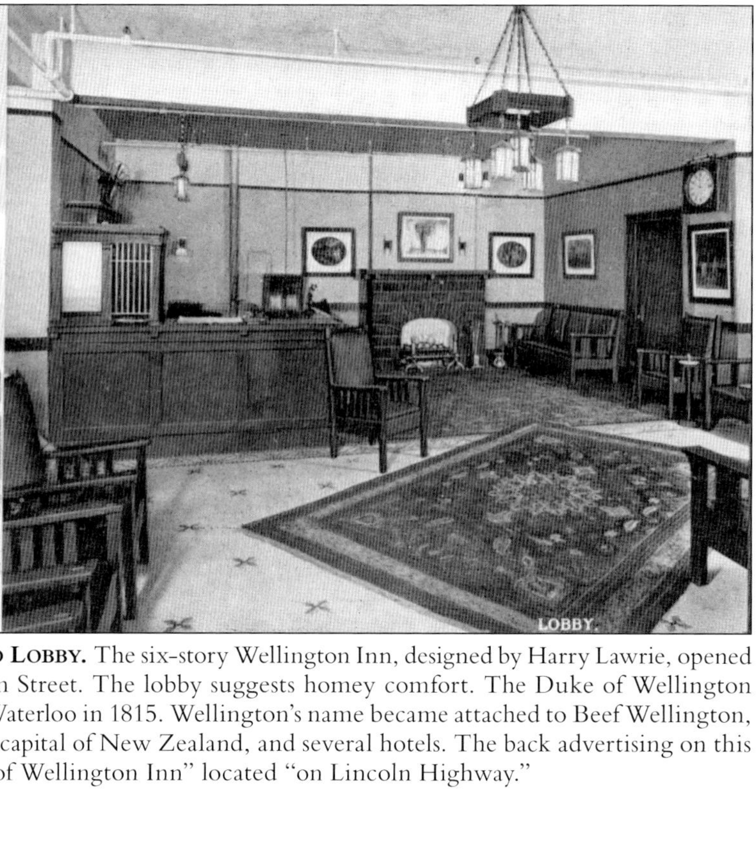

WELLINGTON INN AND LOBBY. The six-story Wellington Inn, designed by Harry Lawrie, opened in 1914 at 1817 Farnam Street. The lobby suggests homey comfort. The Duke of Wellington defeated Napoleon at Waterloo in 1815. Wellington's name became attached to Beef Wellington, Wellington Boots, the capital of New Zealand, and several hotels. The back advertising on this card states: "Ye Signe of Wellington Inn" located "on Lincoln Highway."

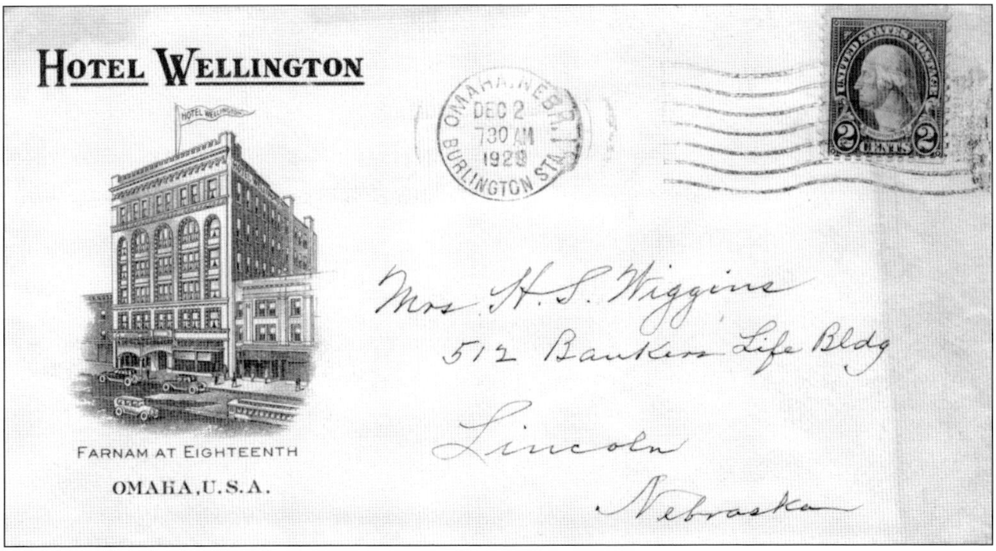

HOTEL WELLINGTON ENVELOPE. By 1920, Wellington Inn had become Hotel Wellington under new owners. A business college occupied the top two floors, which were soon converted to hotel rooms, raising capacity to 150 rooms. The Nebraska Federation of Labor held its fourth annual convention at the Wellington. The hotel maintained the Wellington Café and offered guests ink blotters and matchbooks. In 1969, the 59-year old building was demolished to make way for the new City-County Building.

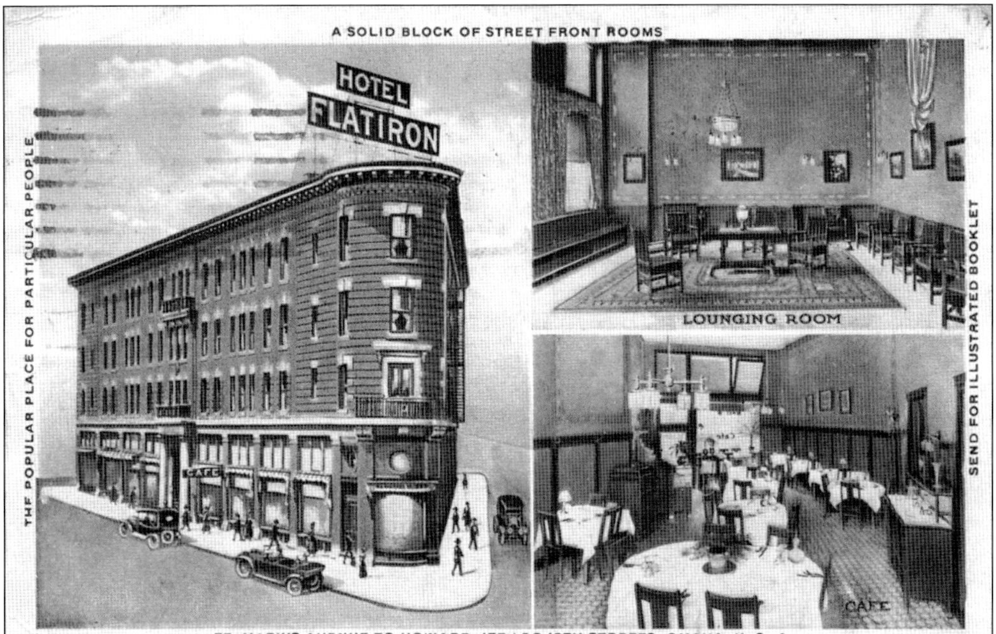

OMAHA'S FLATIRON BUILDING. Architect George B. Prinz's four-story design evokes New York's 22-story 1902 Flatiron Building. Ground was broken in 1911 for Bachelor Apartments. Ada S. Cook ran the New Flatiron Café; her 75¢ 1912 Thanksgiving Dinner was half the cost of the Hotel Loyal's. The Hotel Flatiron opened in 1914. The Flatiron building still exists but is no longer a hotel. (Omaha Public Library.)

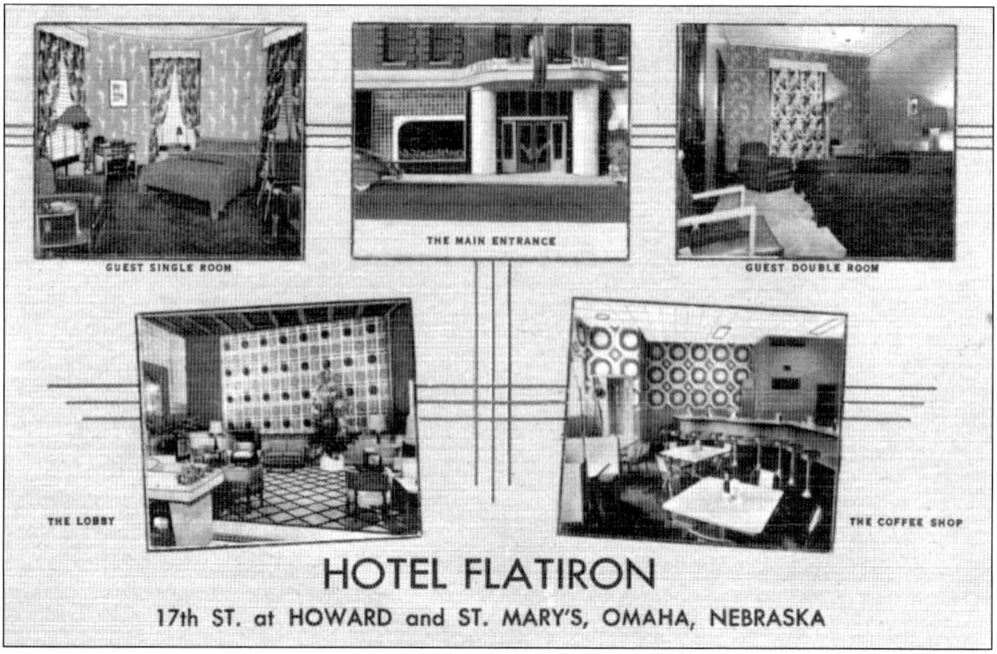

HOTEL FLATIRON MULTIVIEW. This postcard touts the Flatiron as "Omaha's most beautifully furnished Medium Priced Hotel. Attractive, Comfortable, Air-Conditioned rooms. Coffee Shop and Barber Shop. Only a block from the heart of Downtown Omaha." Daily rates were $2.25 to $3. It had handy parking across the street. The building currently houses one of Omaha's finest restaurants, frequented before and after theatrical events.

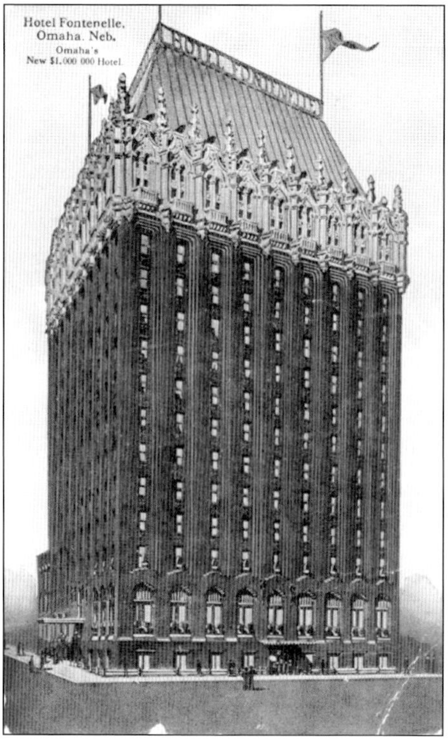

HOTEL FONTENELLE, OMAHA'S NEW $1 MILLION HOTEL. Thomas Rogers Kimball designed the Fontenelle. This card is postmarked April 23, 1914, but the hotel did not open until February 1915, so this is the architect's rendition. Hershel in Omaha wrote to H.L. West in Bassett, Nebraska: "Hope this reaches you before you start for Omaha. I will meet you Saturday on the morning train." A slightly later postcard placed the cost at $1,125,000. Another card read, "Built for your enjoyment by enterprising citizens of Omaha at a cost of $1,500,000."

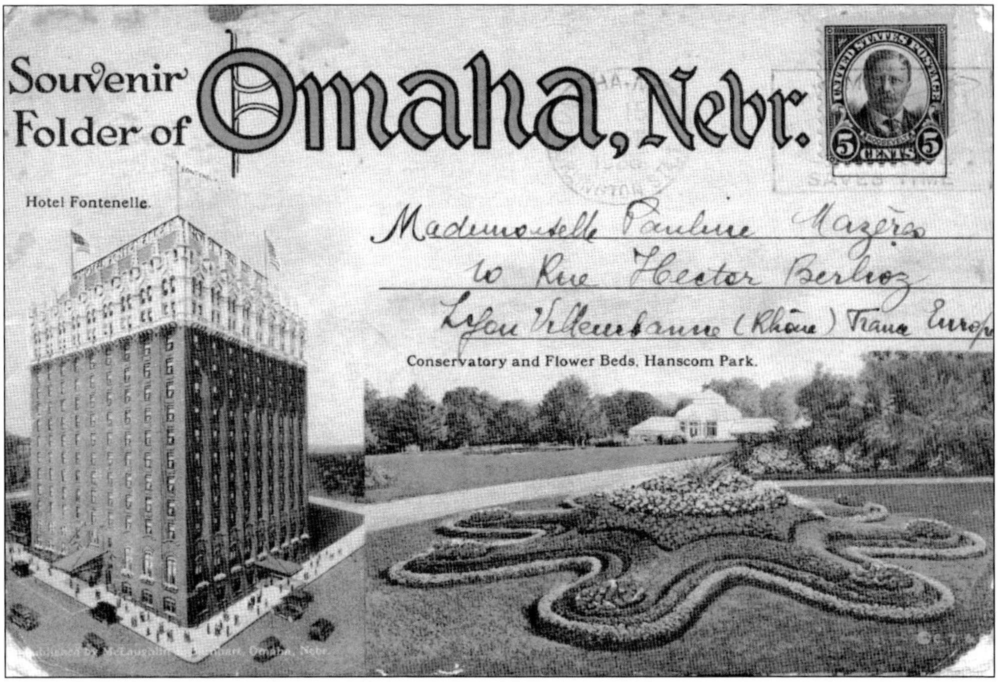

FONTENELLE HOTEL. This 16-story hotel with 350 rooms with baths opened in February 1915. This 1916 souvenir folder provided additional publicity. Hotelier Eugene C. Eppley acquired the hotel in 1921. He lived in the building and sold it to Sheraton in 1956. The Fontenelle was Omaha's iconic image of gracious hospitality. The Fontenelle closed abruptly in 1971, leaving planned conventions scrambling to find alternative venues, and was demolished in 1983. The approximately 15 souvenir folders published between 1910 and 1975 illustrate Omaha's development.

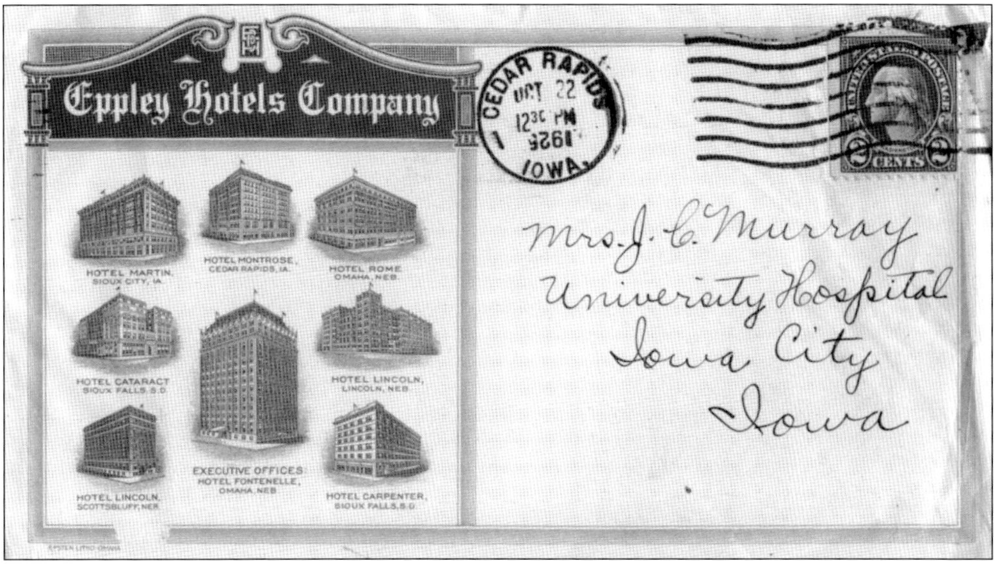

EPPLEY HOTELS. Eugene Eppley may have been the greatest American hotelier of his age. This envelope reveals his 1926 four-state, eight-hotel inventory, including Omaha's Hotel Rome. He also had hotels in Pittsburgh, Kentucky, Missouri, and Los Angeles, hence the motto, "from Pittsburgh to Los Angeles." The Fontenelle claimed to be "Omaha's welcome to the world."

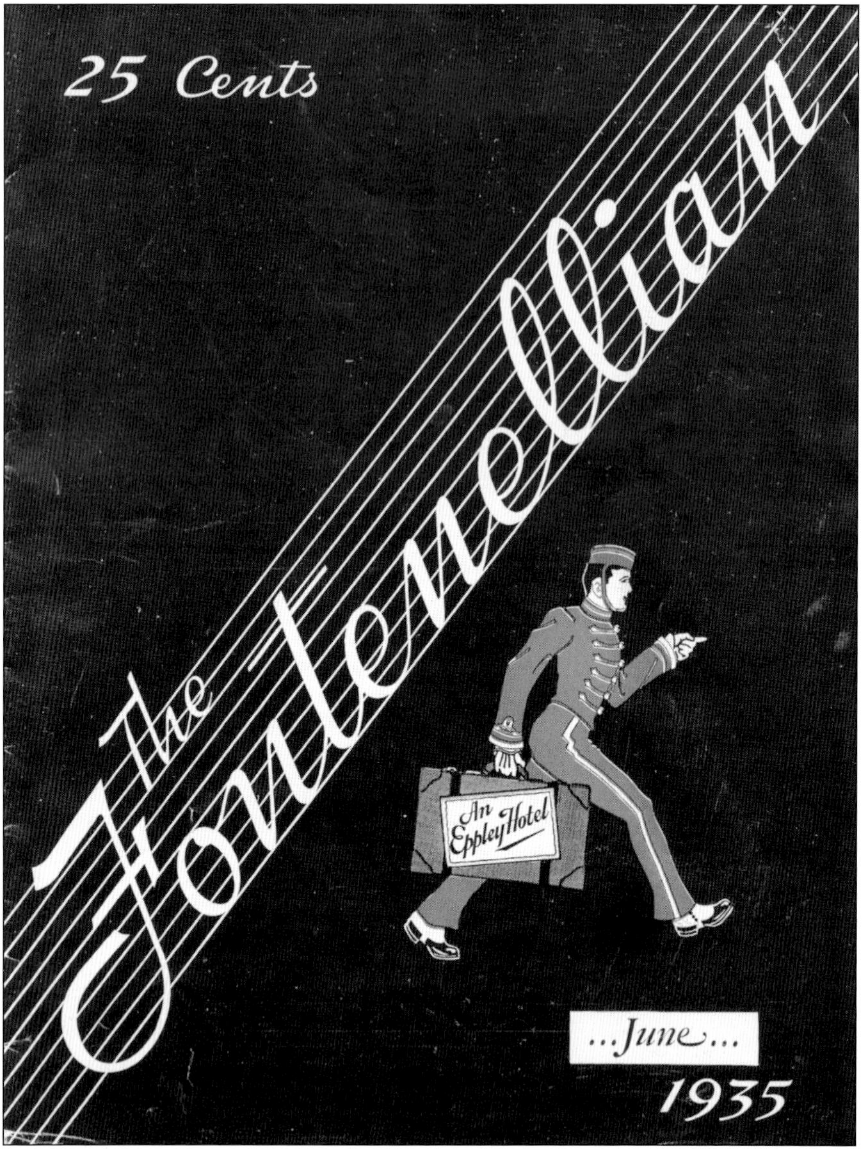

THE FONTENELLIAN. This promotional magazine extols the Fontenelle Hotel amenities and details owner Eugene C. Eppley's 13 other hotels across five states. Guests dined at the King Cole Room, Amber Room coffee shop, Black Mirror Room, and Bombay Room. Available services included a cigar shop and newsstand, barbershop, liquor store, drugstore, public stenographer, and a notary public. The Fontenelle provided a congenial place for the well-off to celebrate engagements, weddings, anniversaries, significant milestones, retirements, convention events, banquets, and testimonials. Eppley pioneered hotel empire–building. He purchased the El-Beudor Apartments, built in 1919 at Eighteenth and Dodge Streets, in 1927 at a referee's sale for $464,000. He renamed it Logan for Logan Fontenelle, who served as an interpreter for the Omaha Indian tribe. The Logan became Logan Motor Inn in 1962, and was known as the Sherwyn for most of the 1960s. The name "Eppley" commemorates the civic minded philanthropist and appears on the University of Nebraska at Omaha Administration Building, Eppley Airport, and the University of Nebraska Medical Center, among other buildings. Sheraton purchased this property in 1956 for $30 million, and it became the Sheraton Fontenelle.

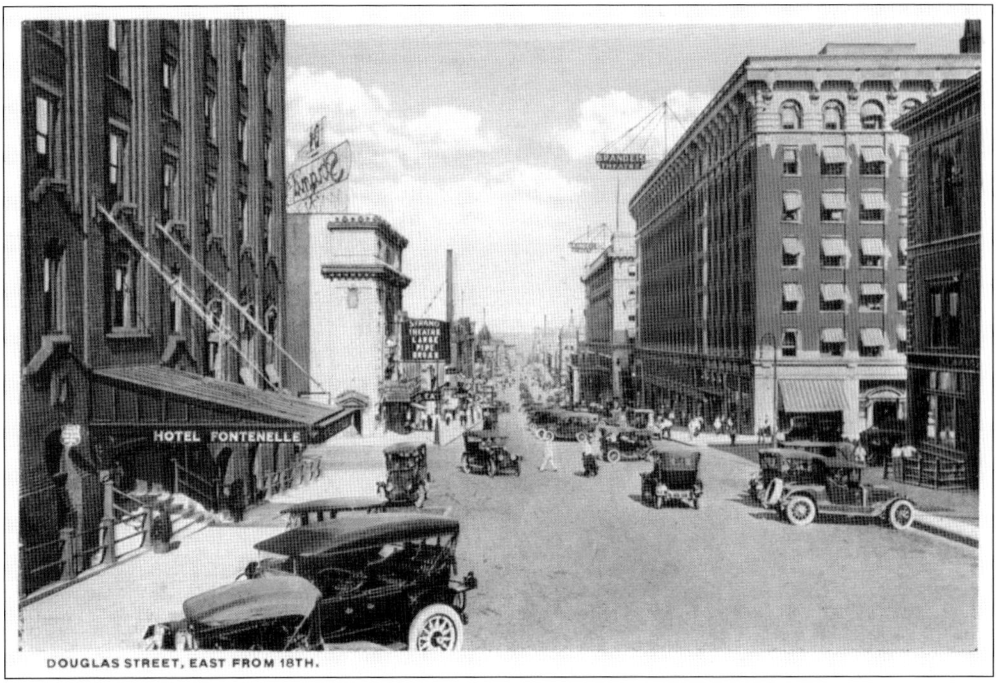

DOUGLAS STREET LOOKING EAST FROM EIGHTEENTH STREET. This view from a 1920 souvenir folder depicts Hotel Fontenelle's location in the heart of the fashion and theater district. From the Fontenelle entrance, guests could see the Strand Theatre, which had a large pipe organ in the age of silent film. The Brandeis Theatre and Brandeis Store (the Midwest's classiest department store) as well as a café and a drugstore line a street filled with pedestrians and automobiles.

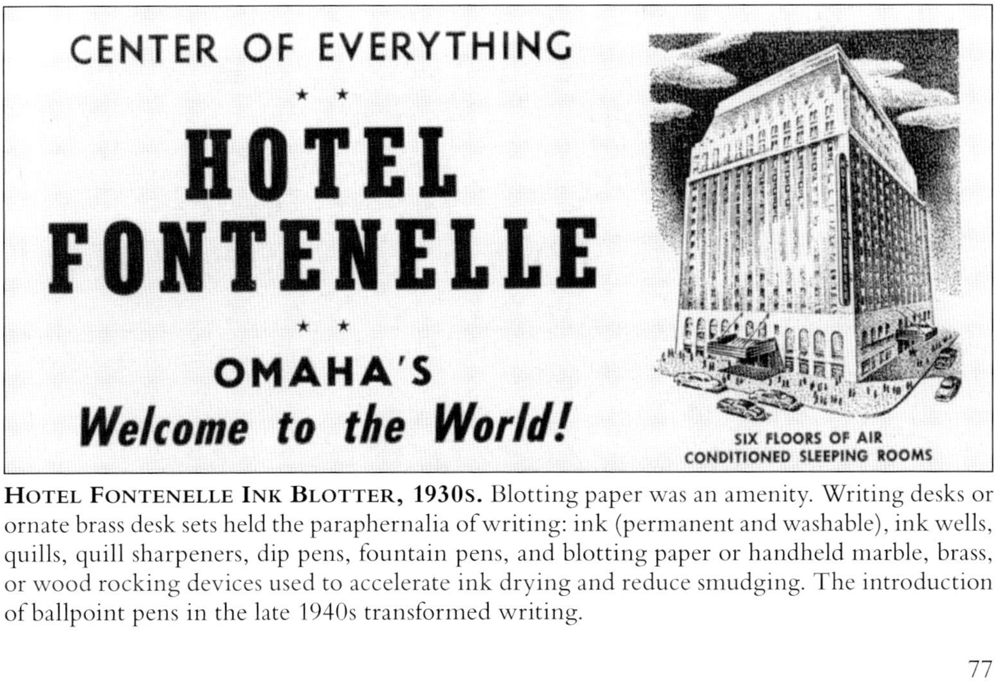

HOTEL FONTENELLE INK BLOTTER, 1930S. Blotting paper was an amenity. Writing desks or ornate brass desk sets held the paraphernalia of writing: ink (permanent and washable), ink wells, quills, quill sharpeners, dip pens, fountain pens, and blotting paper or handheld marble, brass, or wood rocking devices used to accelerate ink drying and reduce smudging. The introduction of ballpoint pens in the late 1940s transformed writing.

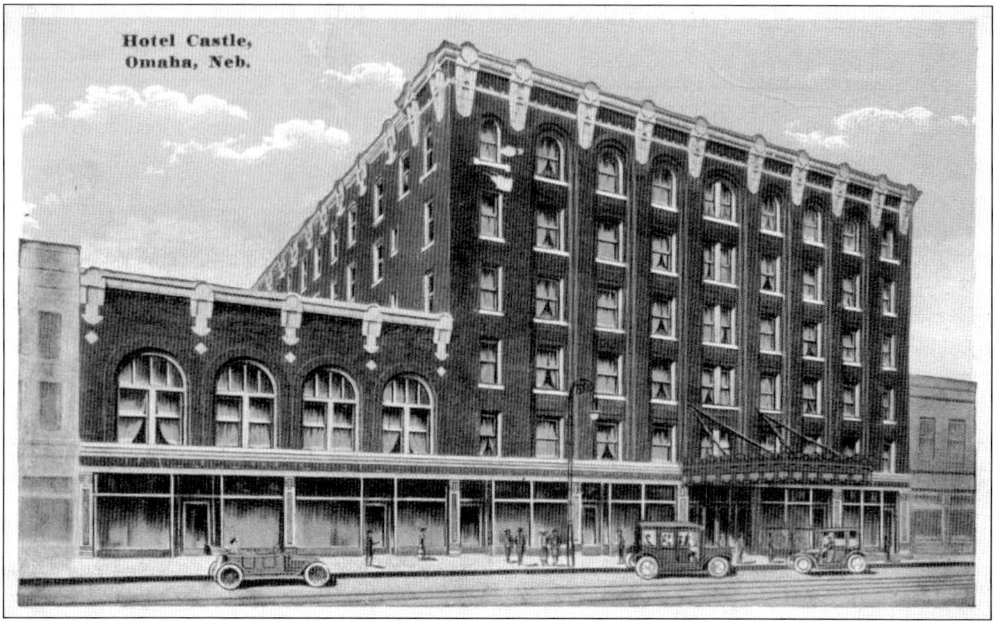

CASTLE HOTEL. Dr. Harold Gifford started construction in June 1914 at Sixteenth and Jones Streets. The hotel, named for its first operator, Fred Castle, opened in March 1915 with 300 fireproof rooms. A 1916 photograph shows Eckman Chemical Company and Basket Store No. 27 occupying two bays in the two-story annex. A convention hall or ballroom was on the second floor. By 1950, the main floor bays housed Castle Garage.

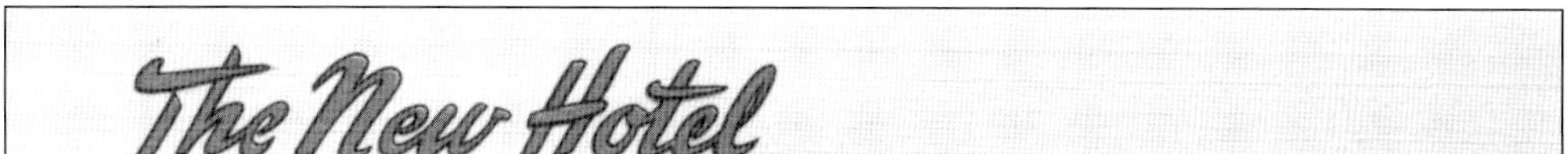

NEW HOTEL CASTLE LARGE-LETTER POSTCARD. The letters incorporate the lobby, building front, and bar with stools. This is a genre card that a parent might send home to a child. At least 2,500 large-letter linen postcards were printed during their heyday from the 1930s through the 1950s. Large-letter Omaha postcards had cameo vignettes within five letters representing popular images. Urban multiviews with several images reflect city pride in a nutshell.

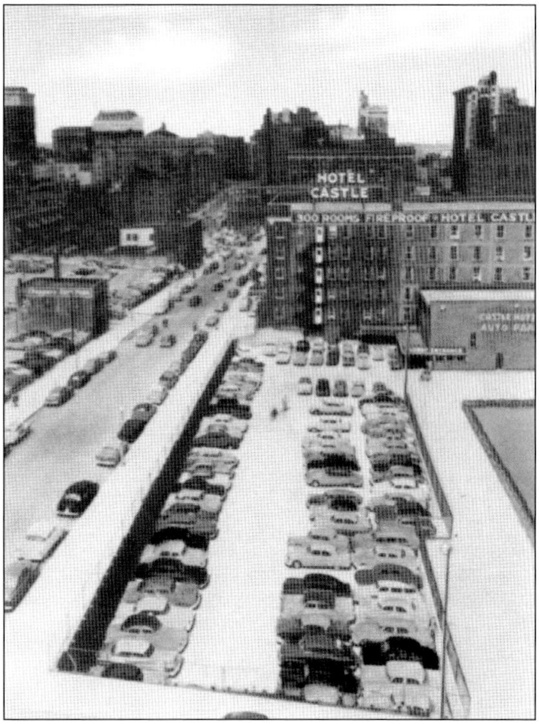

Hotel Castle—A Boss Hotel. Des Moines hotelier Edwin A. Boss, a contemporary of hotelier Eugene Eppley, had 15 hotels in Iowa, one each in Wisconsin and Illinois, and the ill-fated Pathfinder in Fremont. He acquired the Castle from the Gifford estate in 1937. The Castle Hotel Auto Park, full of colorful 1950s cars, was near the lobby entrance. The hotel was demolished in 1973 and became a parking lot.

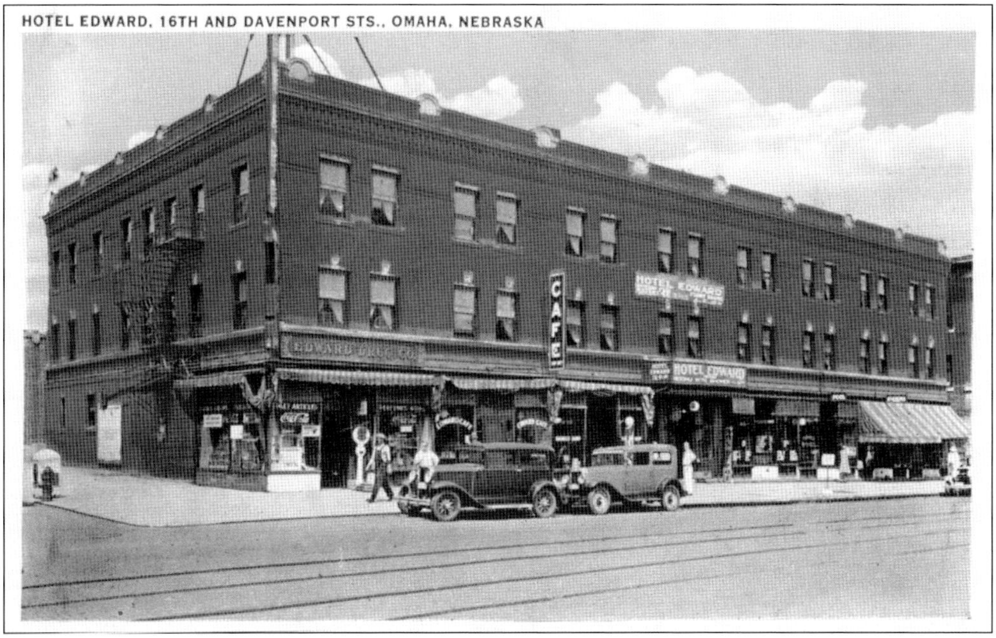

Hotel Edward. This hotel opened at Sixteenth and Davenport Streets (306 N. Sixteenth Street) in October 1915, as a bachelors' hotel with 130 rooms. Every room had a telephone, hot and cold running water, electric lights, and outside exposure (windows). It was named after Edward Sterricker, territorial pioneer and father of Major Sterricker, who also ran the St. James. Larson's Buffet managed the food. In 1960, it advertised as a "Discount Hotel" with rooms from $7 per week. Signs for pool, Coca-Cola, scales, and the Edward Café are clearly visible.

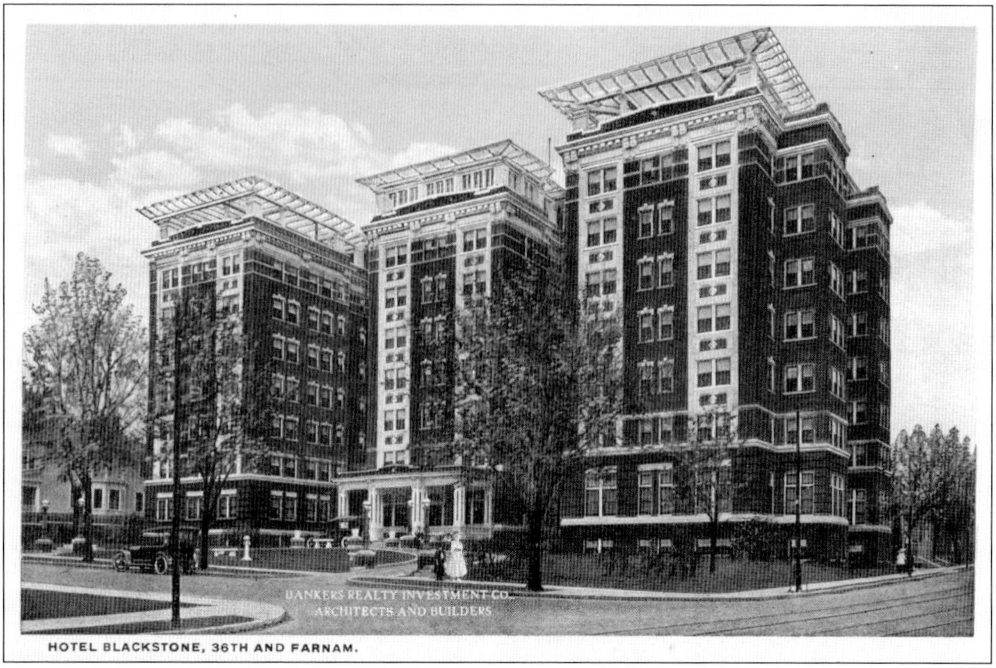

HOTEL BLACKSTONE AND OTHER BUSINESSES. Hotel Blackstone opened in 1916. This card advertises the hotel, realtor, architect, and builders. The Blackstone exuded Midwestern luxury and hospitality and had a dress code. Blackstone, noted for its cuisine, had several restaurants.

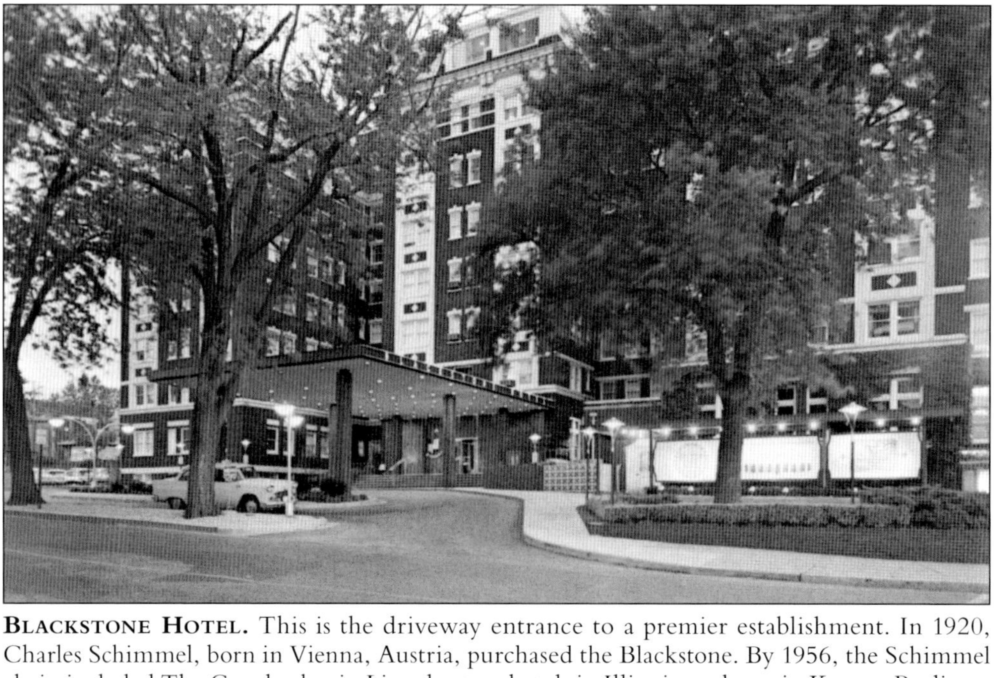

BLACKSTONE HOTEL. This is the driveway entrance to a premier establishment. In 1920, Charles Schimmel, born in Vienna, Austria, purchased the Blackstone. By 1956, the Schimmel chain included The Cornhusker in Lincoln, two hotels in Illinois, and two in Kansas. Radisson purchased Blackstone in 1968 and ran it until 1976. In 1984, it became Blackstone Center, an office complex. The Kiewit Corporation, headquartered across the street, purchased the Blackstone in 2007.

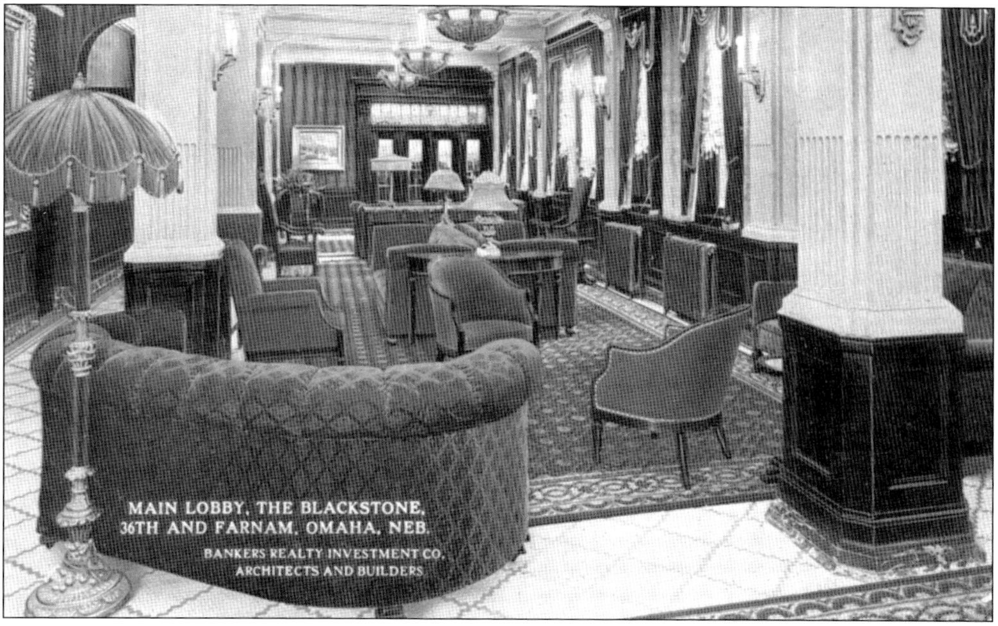

BLACKSTONE MAIN LOBBY. Does this look and feel like a lobby or like a private, overstuffed living room? This postcard shows radiators, chandeliers, floor and table lamps, fabric lampshades with fringes and tassels, carpet, couches and chairs upholstered with brocade and velour, a console table behind the couch, and paintings on the wall, creating a room that is stylish and ornate but not ostentatious, just comfortable. (Omaha Public Library.)

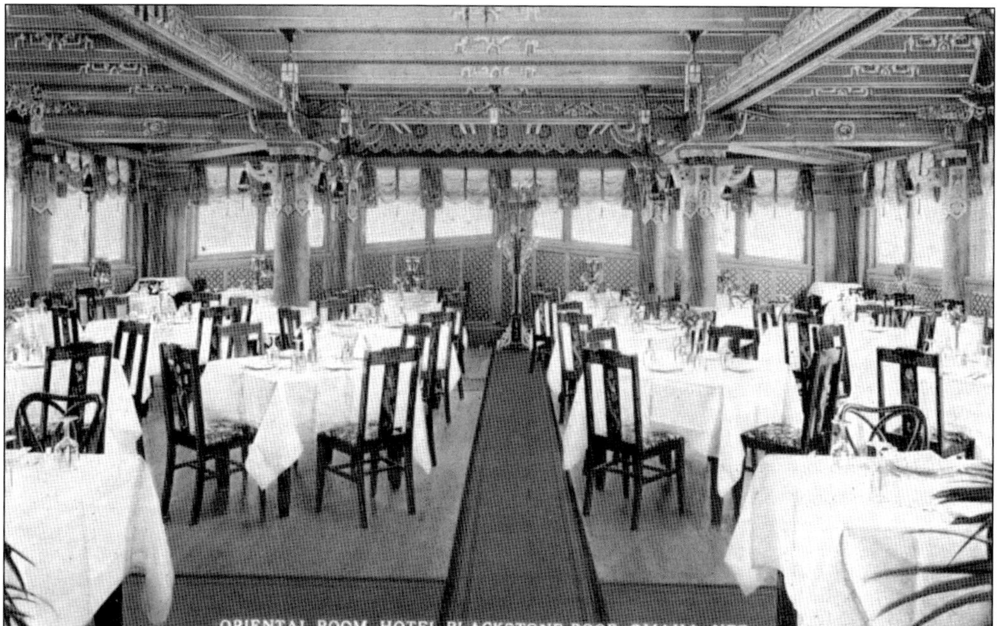

ORIENTAL ROOM, BLACKSTONE HOTEL. This room has hints of Japanese decor in the lighting and floral arrangements. The letter, dated September 6, 1918, mentions the war in Europe: "Mrs. Dawes just got Arts first letter since word he was wounded."

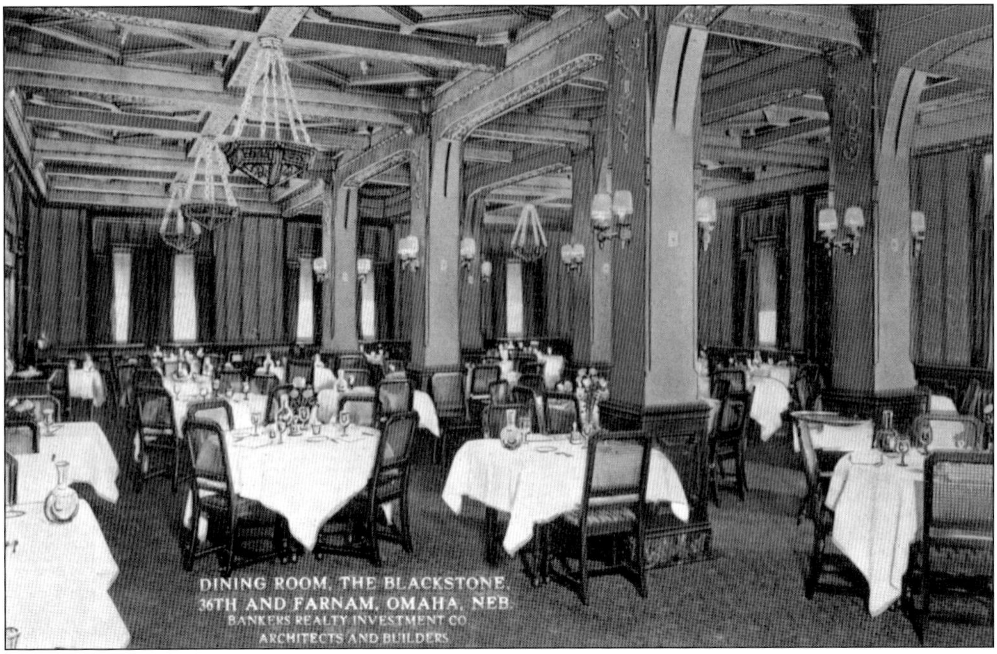

DINING ROOM, THE BLACKSTONE. Maybe a good meal set the tone for this advice to the writer's mother and father: "I don't think you will be able to settle yourselves down till you have a trip somewhere. I guess the gardens will keep you busy but I suppose it is healthy work. It seems to agree with Billy's mother. She has an acre to look after."

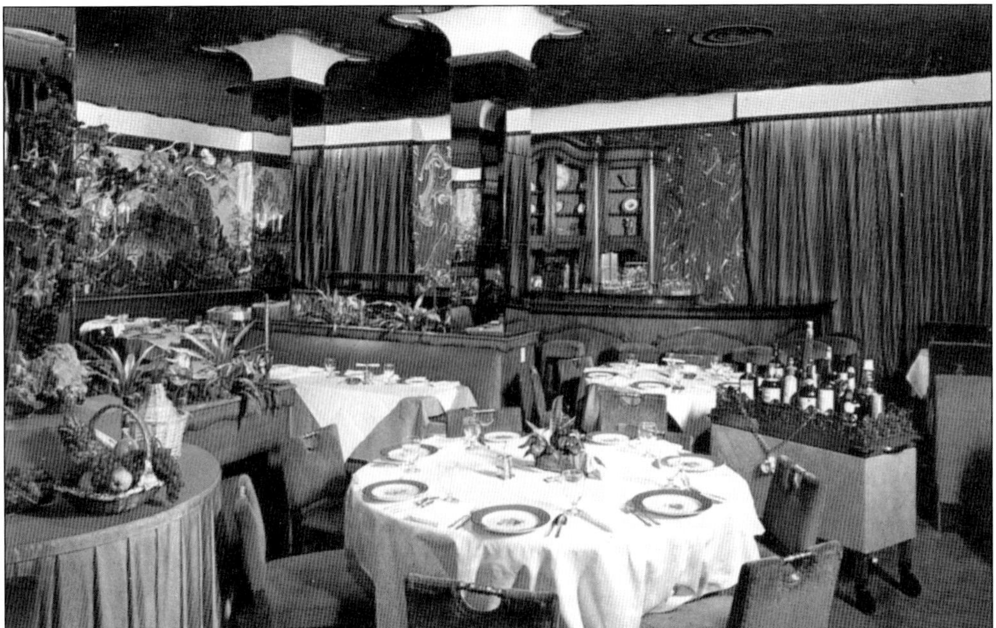

ORLEANS ROOM. The *Holiday* magazine award for excellence put this Blackstone restaurant on the gourmet map. Carts with choice cuts of meat, liquor, or tableside salads or flambés were typical at high-end restaurants. The Orleans Room had exquisite service. Orleans lived up to this postcard's hyperbole—"a truly memorable occasion."

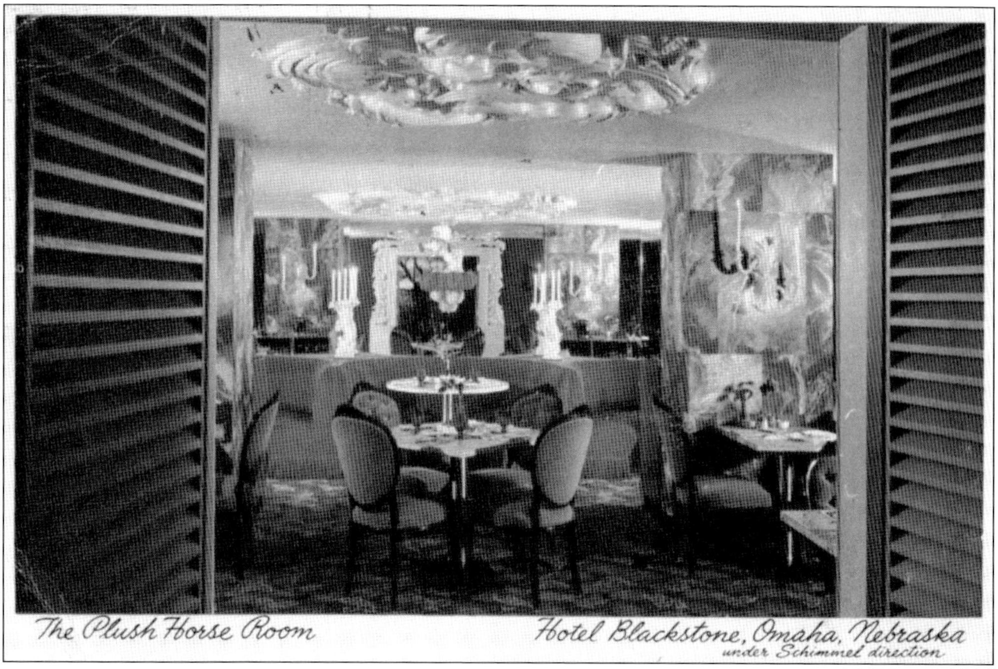

The Plush Horse Room. "The West's most beautiful cocktail lounge presents a translucent Photograph mural of a Missouri River Scene in natural color. You'll enjoy, too, a visit in the exotic Plush Horse Room." Hamilton wrote Francie and Marion in Hollywood in August 1948: "When you turned around after mailing the GONE card you no doubt found our letter. Sorry we were so negligent."

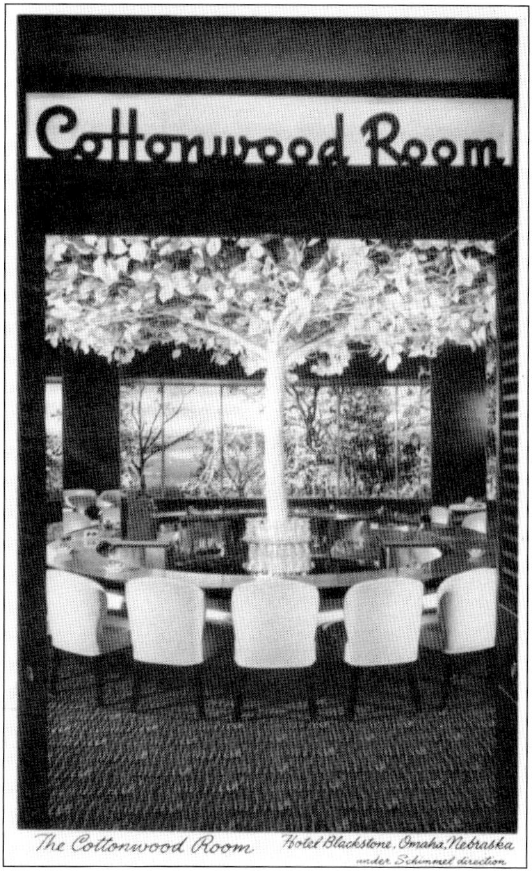

From the Cotton Club to the Cottonwood Room. Perhaps the name is a play on Harlem's Cotton Club. The Blackstonians, a six- or seven-piece orchestra, played in the Cottonwood Room and occasionally at the Rialto, Rome Hotel, Kel-Pine, and E. Oft's Hall in Bennington. Donna in Galesburg wrote to Mary in Detroit on November 26, 1944: "Hi Sis, Sis asked Jimmy what he wants for Christmas and so now I guess I'll ask you 'What do you want for Christmas.' Give these cards to Ruth."

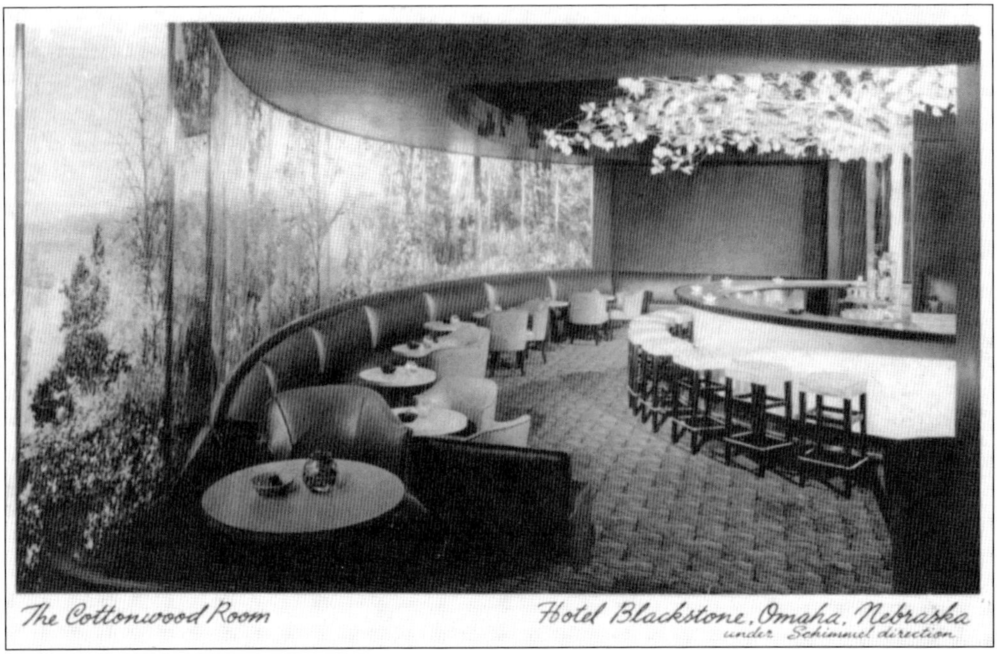

HANGING OUT AT THE COTTONWOOD ROOM. The Cottonwood was an elite hangout. Grace wrote to Sylvia Kaplan from Lincoln to Stockton, California, in June 1946: "Hi! I am in Lincoln. Came here for Jim's wedding. Will start back to Sacramento on the 3:30 am flight tomorrow morning. See you soon."

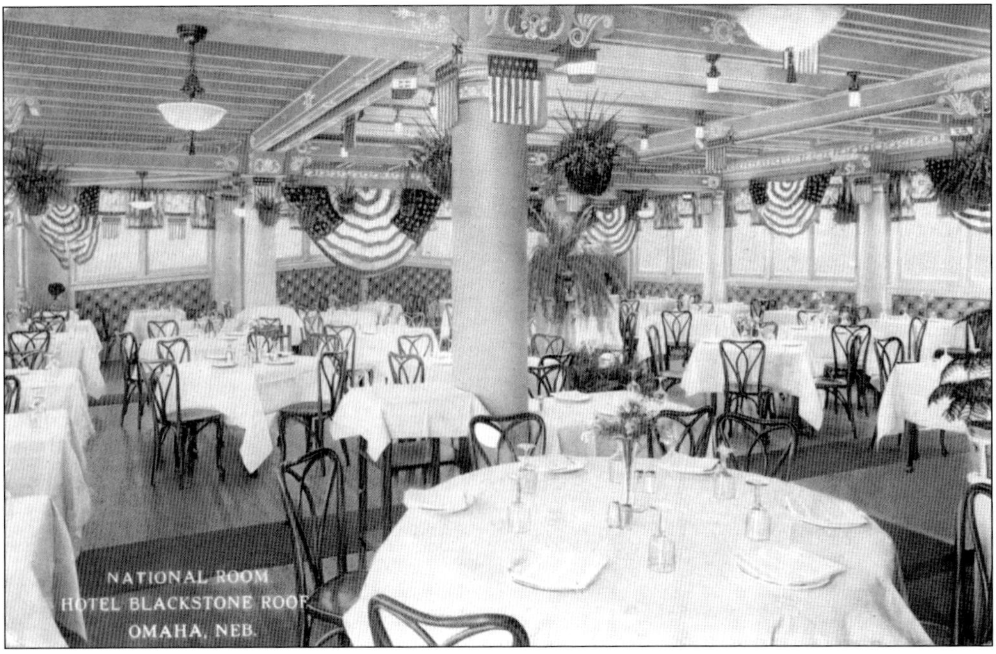

NATIONAL ROOM, HOTEL BLACKSTONE ROOF. The roof room is all dressed up in patriotic bunting. The decorations suggest speeches, fireworks, music—a fantastical evening. This room hosted formal dances, proms, recitals, and other events. The message sent to Minneapolis reads, "Having a fine time. Will stay in Kansas City near a week as they have some repairs on car."

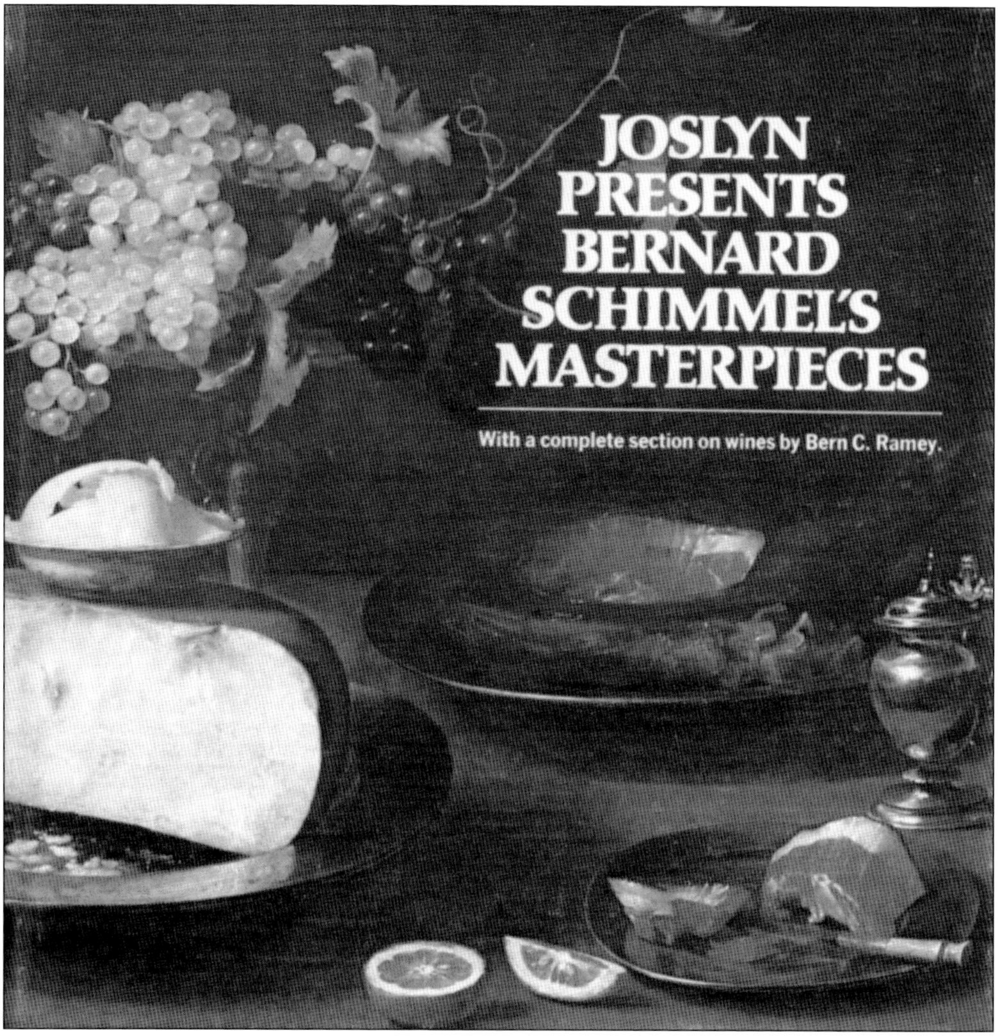

Bernard Schimmel 1976 Joslyn Cookbook. Today, celebrity chefs and restaurants publish cookbooks. This was not so common half a century ago. Schimmel, a third-generation hotelier and graduate of the Hotel School of Lausanne, Switzerland, served as the Blackstone's master chef. In 1976, the Joslyn Museum, which opened in 1931, published this cookbook as part of its fundraising efforts. Schimmel catered many Joslyn events. Eleven recipes bear Schimmel's name, including the Schimmelburger and Schimmel Reuben Sandwich. Recipes were mostly European fare—duck, goose, quail, two sweetbread recipes—and samplings from Senegal plus ten Cantonese and Mandarin and two Japanese recipes. The Oriental Salad recipe may have been served in the Oriental Room. The Joslyn provided 15 food-related illustrations, including this cover featuring *Still Life* by 17th-century Flemish painter Jacob Foppens van Es, a 1974 museum acquisition. Schimmel died in 1977. (Joslyn Art Museum.)

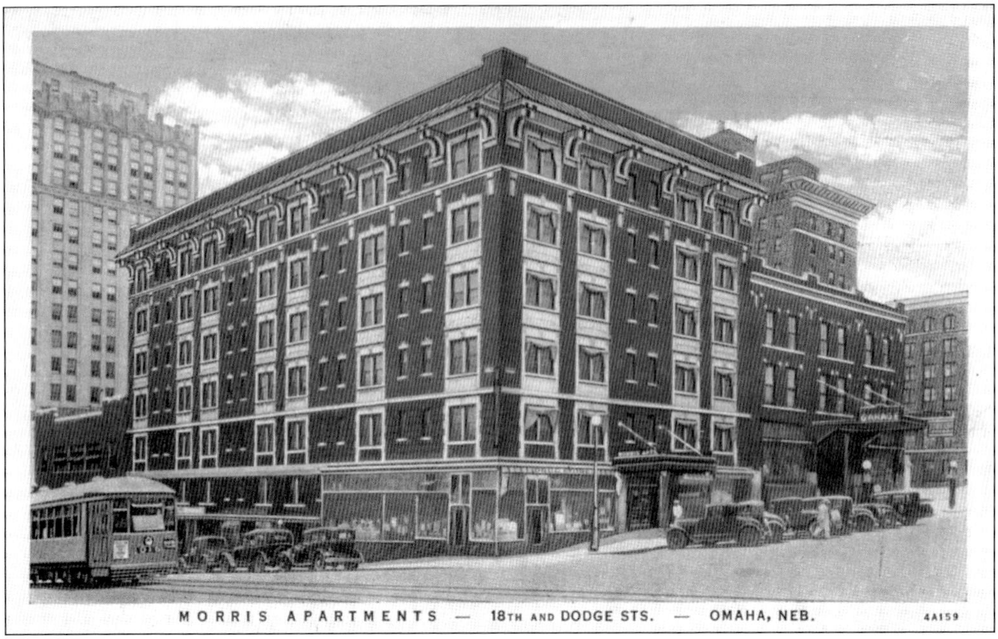

Morris Apartments. This structure was built in 1916 at 103 S. Eighteenth Street, diagonally across from the Fontenelle and on the same block as the new Omaha Athletic Club. The Morris presented itself as a downscale Blackstone. In 1917, the owners advertised for investors, offering a seven percent return. The corner enclosed retail establishments including the Morris coffee shop.

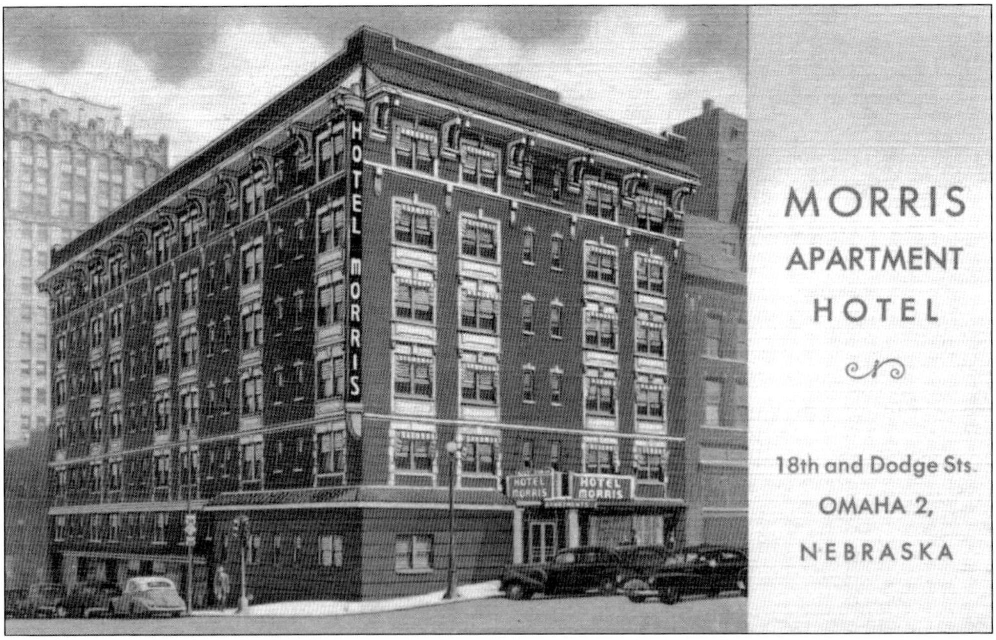

Morris Apartment Hotel. These elegantly appointed family apartments came with maid, janitor, bellboy service, and food for the refrigerator. One of the attractions of downtown living in the winter included proximity to many businesses—plus no lawn care or snow shoveling. Morris was a half-block from the post office and adjacent to five car lines. The Federal Reserve of Kansas City purchased the hotel in 1968; residents had 90 days to vacate.

HUNTER INN. James H. Hunter retired after working for 35 years at the Chicago Northwestern Railway. He had a realty company. He built the six-story Hunter Apartments at 2408 Dodge Street in 1910. By 1917, the Hunter Inn had 150 rooms that "combined the homeliness of the apartment house and the service of the hotel." The writer stated, "we find it very pleasant here," and drew arrows indicating where two friends lived. Woodmen of the World insurance acquired Hunter in 1937 and renamed it Commodore.

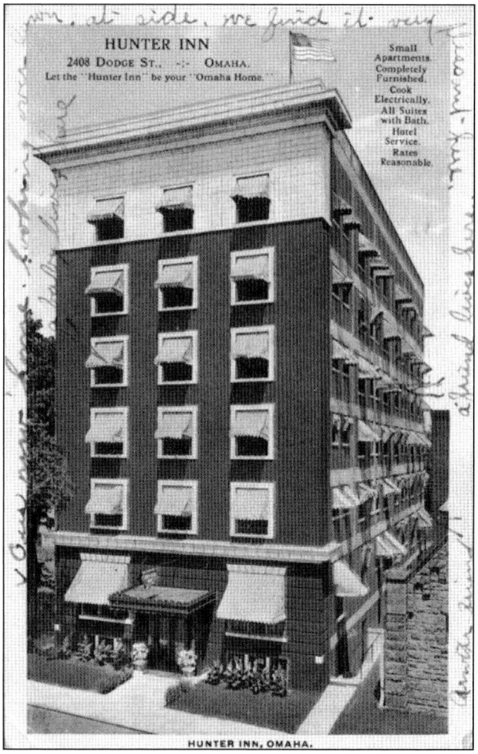

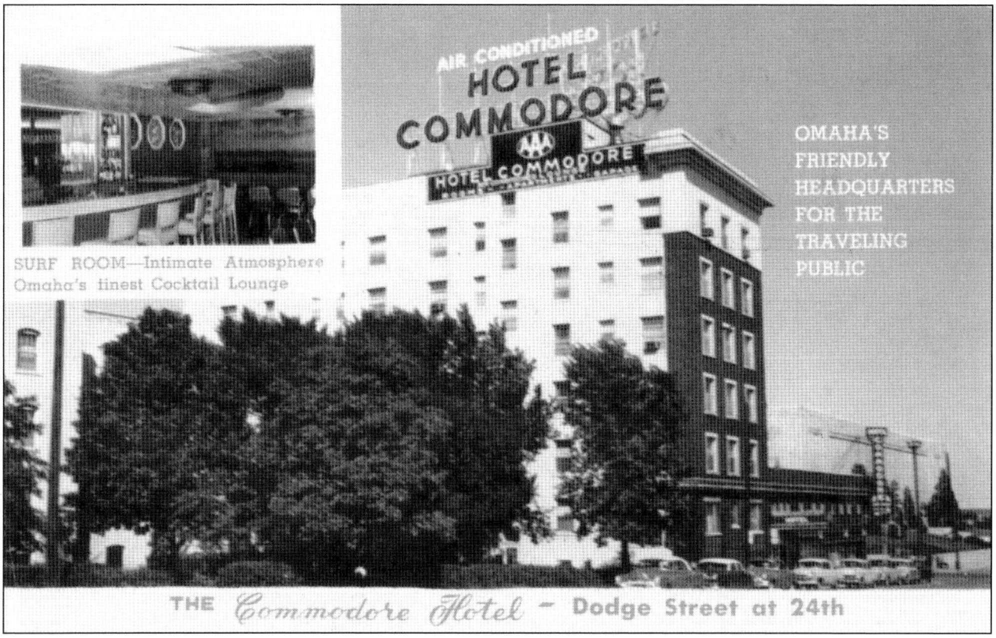

HOTEL COMMODORE. This hotel promoted itself as "Omaha's friendly headquarters for the traveling public." It featured "contemporary furnishings and tile-tub showers in every room." Friendliest, newest, and most modern were common superlatives. There was a garage entrance to the lobby, and the Commodore was AAA-recommended and a member of the American Hotel Association. The nautical theme carried over to the Surf Room (inset).

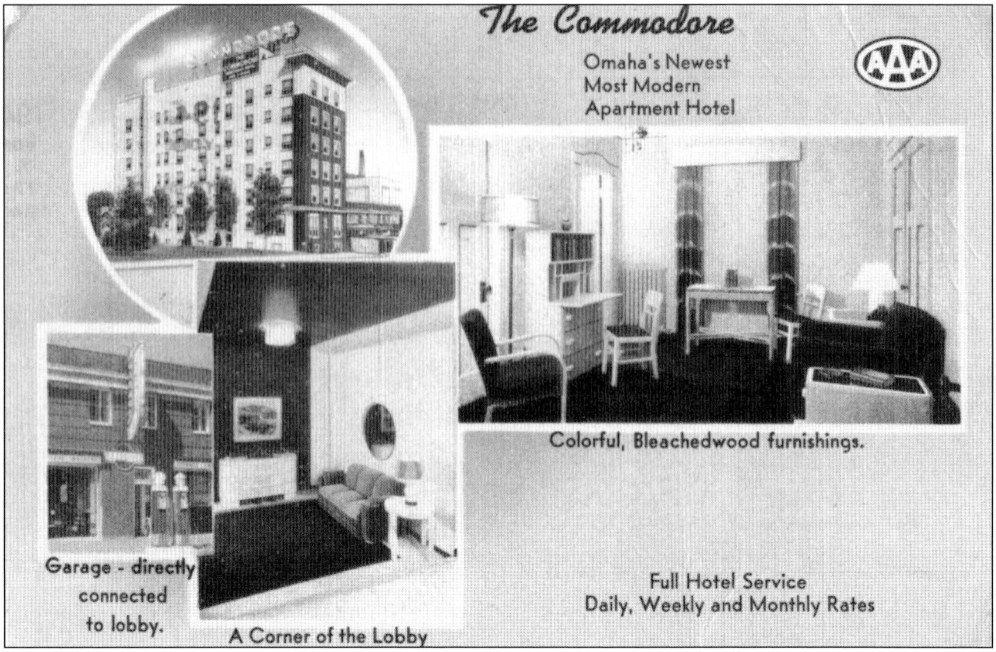

THE COMMODORE. Survival required adaptation. This multiview has four images. Bearing the AAA logo, one of the multiviews featured a garage—note the two gas pumps. The building sold in 1947. L wrote the Colvins in Washington, D.C., in April 1947: "Nice town—Could spend a few days here but of course we won't. Car's going fine now and Thelma's proud of a new wash job on it."

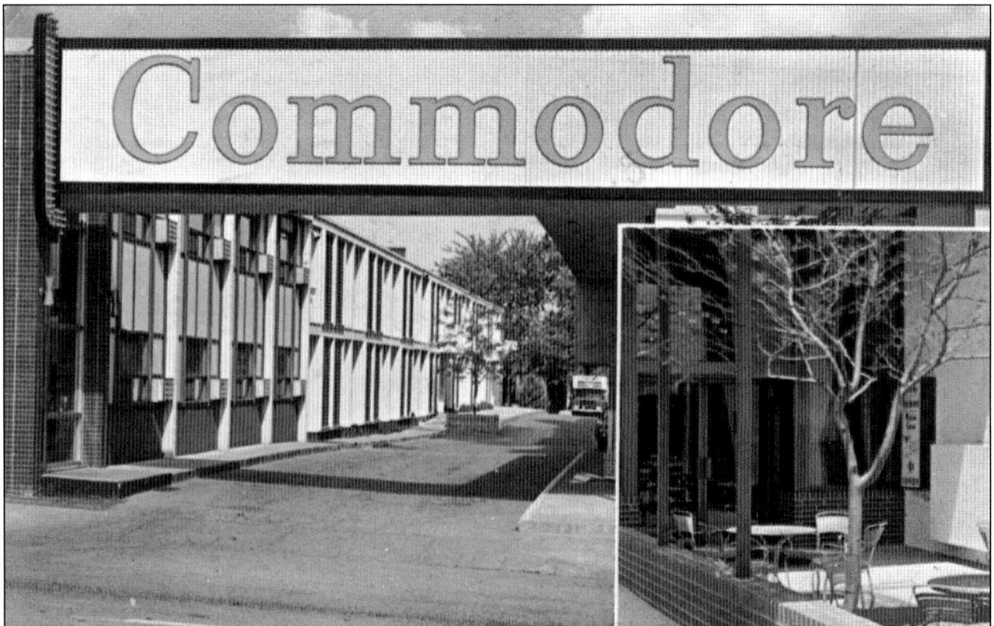

COMMODORE MOTOR INN. The Commodore transformed into a two-story motor inn that advertised 151 large units and the "famous Henry VIII Restaurant & Brewhouse."

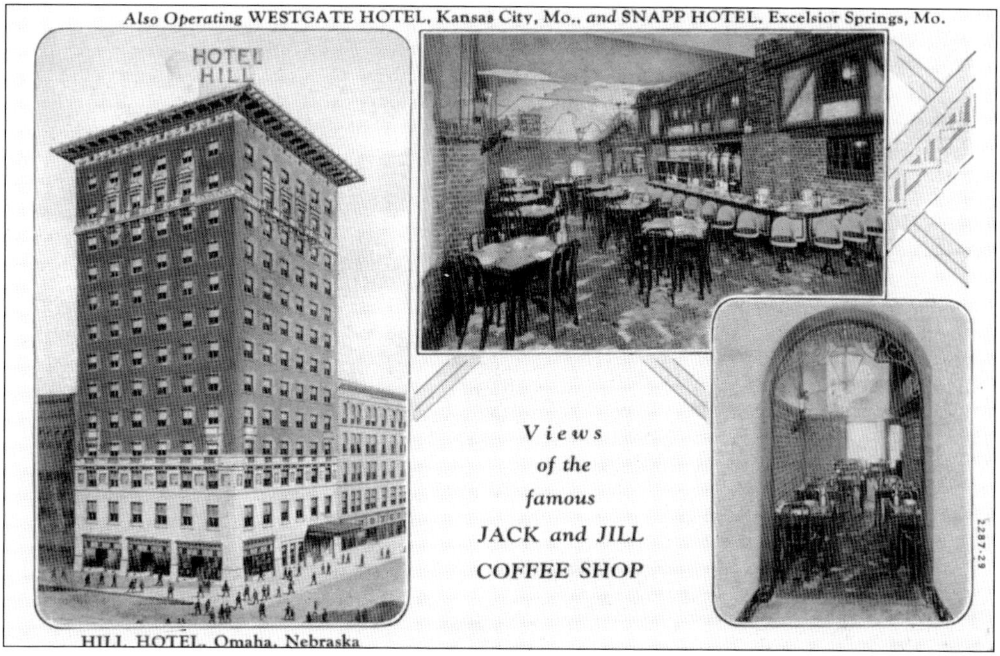

HILL HOTEL. The 13-story hotel with an extraordinary overhanging roof was built in 1919 at 505 S. Sixteenth Street and is named after brothers John and Lem Hill. It had affiliated hotels in Kansas City and Excelsior Springs, Missouri. The Jack and Jill Coffee Shop recalls the nursery rhyme; "quaintest place in town to dine" was inscribed above the entry door. It became the Kensington Tower Apartments in 1989.

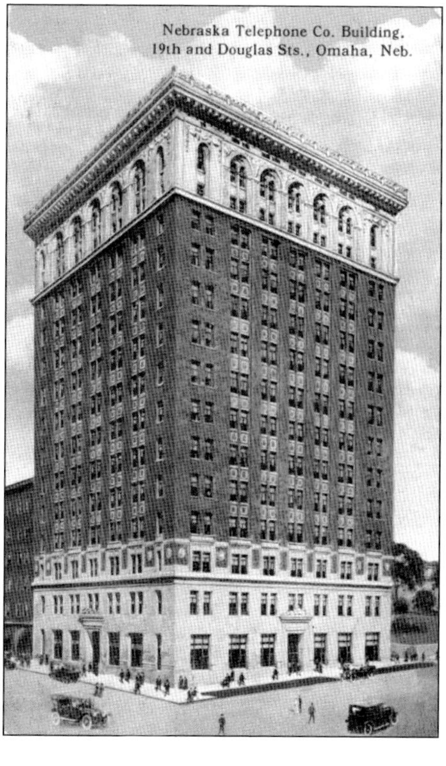

NEBRASKA TELEPHONE CO. BUILDING. The cover of this book features this 14-story building that was completed in 1919 at Nineteenth and Douglas Streets. Telephone companies were vital to 20th-century hotel operations. They supported local and long distance communications, teletype, and early online services. The Frank H. Woods Telephone Museum is in Lincoln, Nebraska. A wife wrote to her husband John in Clearmont, Wyoming, on September 2, 1919: "Dear Husband. I am at Omaha. Have got to wait till 4:20 arrived here at nine o'clock Tuesday. Meet at Clearmont. Good by."

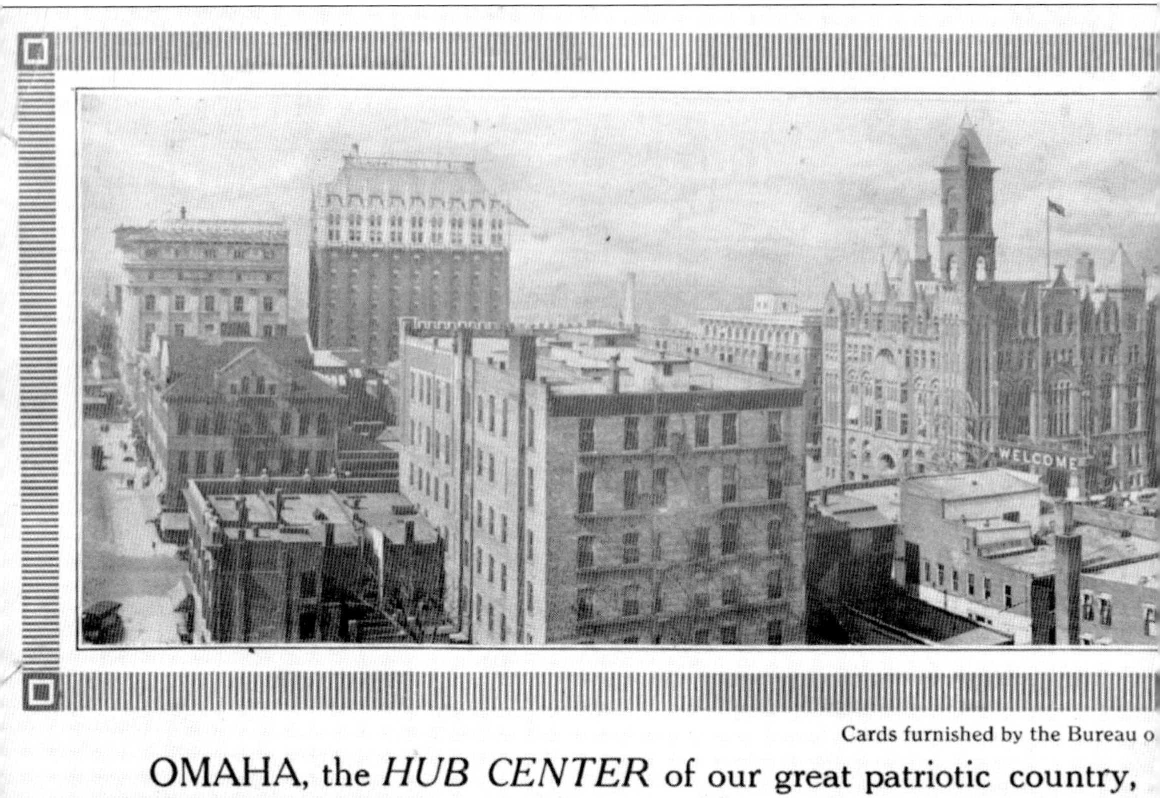

"GONE OVER THE TOP" ON EVERY PATRIOTIC DRIVE. This 1918 bi-fold panorama praises Omaha's war effort contributions. The United States entered World War I on April 6, 1917. On the left is the Fontenelle, with five flags flying, and the "WELCOME" in the center was by City Hall. Brandeis department store patriotically advertised: "Perfected. Overseas Service CONDUCTED WITHOUT PROFIT. For Your Boy. 'Over There.' " On the back of this bifold, a son wrote his mother about military life, riding the train, and mishaps in Omaha: "The Red

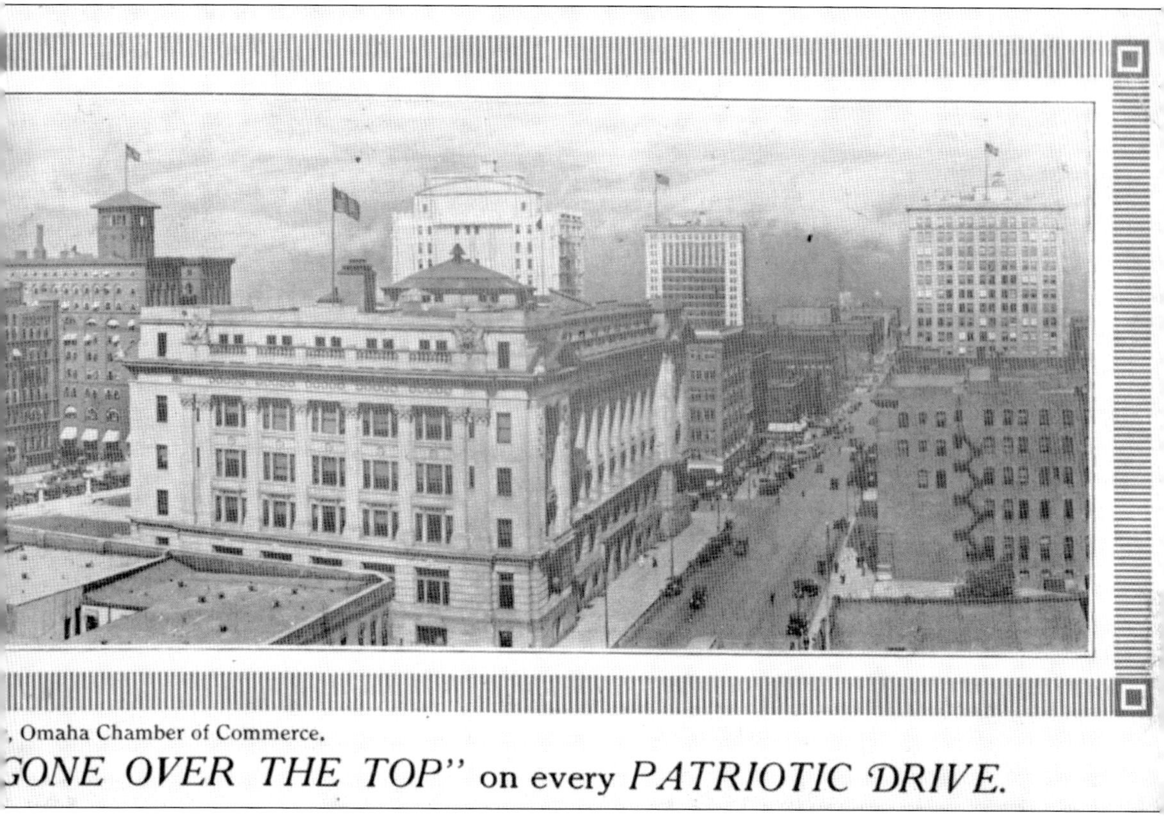

Cross canteen keeps us in cigarettes, chewing gum, matches and ice cream fruit & watermelon and also postcards." Kansas City is home to the National World War I Museum and Memorial. Monuments and memorials throughout the United States commemorate wars from the American Revolution to the present. The Grand Army of the Republic, American Legion, and Veterans of Foreign Wars provided camaraderie, lobbied, and honored the fallen at reunions.

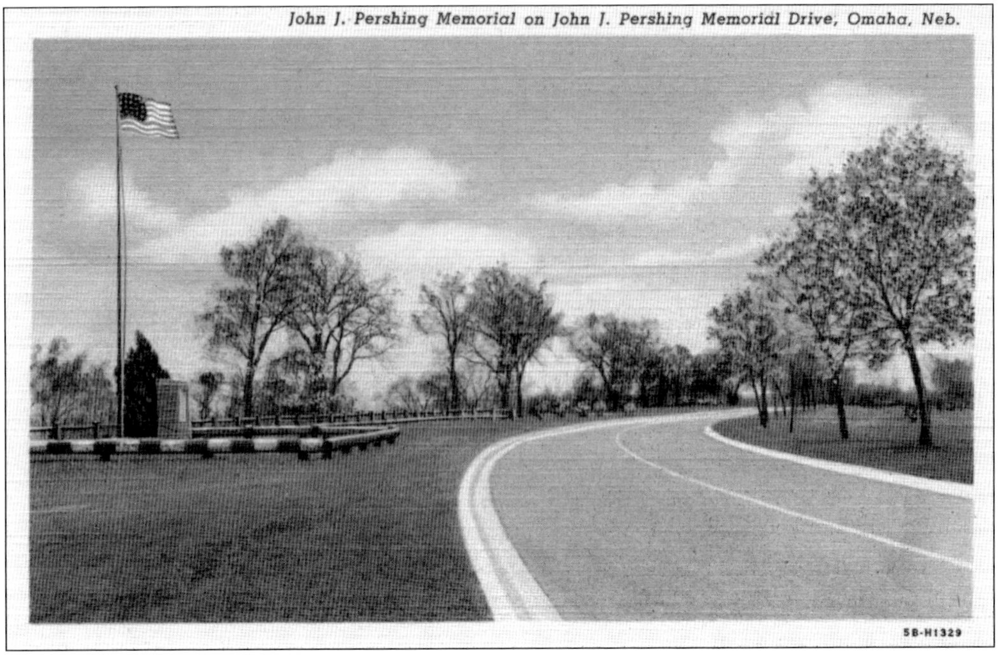

JOHN J. PERSHING MEMORIAL. Pershing, a West Point graduate, taught in Lincoln and commanded US forces in World War I. This memorial was established in 1940. Pershing's name is on five hotels, Lincoln's Pershing Auditorium, and Pershing Square in Los Angeles. Willa Cather won the 1923 Pulitzer Prize for fiction for her novel *One of Ours*, about Nebraskans fighting in France and Nebraska's anti-German sentiment. The patriotic effort on the home front included rallies, Four Minute fundraising speeches, and libraries collecting books for the troops.

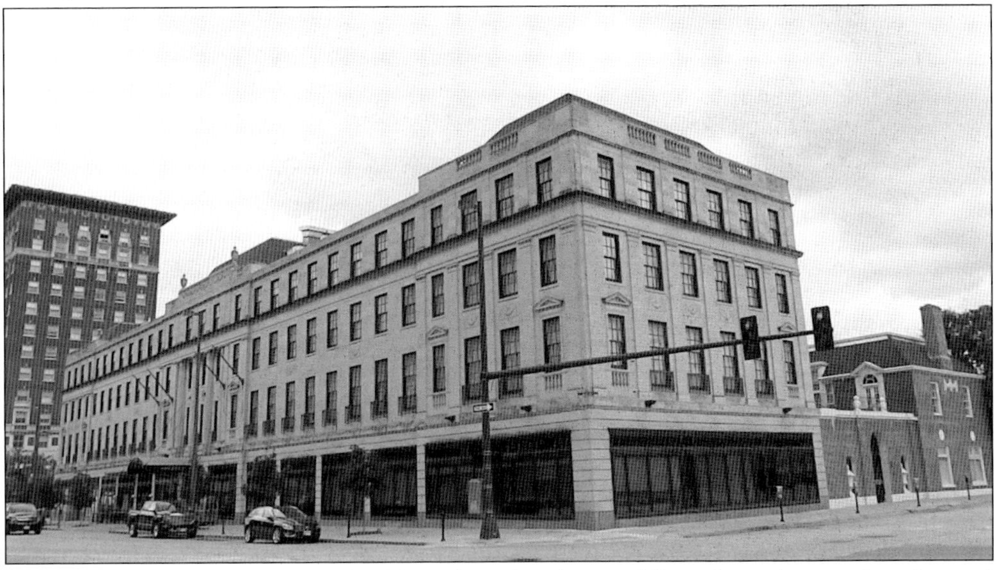

AQUILA COURT. Some Omaha buildings have lived several lives through reconfiguring and repurposing. A Chicago architecture firm designed the Aquila Court at 1615 Howard Street in 1923 as a block-long high-end office and residential complex with an interior court. Since the 1980s, the Aquila has been the Westin, Sheraton, and Magnolia hotel. The 1920s tenant signage list hangs on the wall. The Kensington Tower (formerly the Hill Hotel) is in the background.

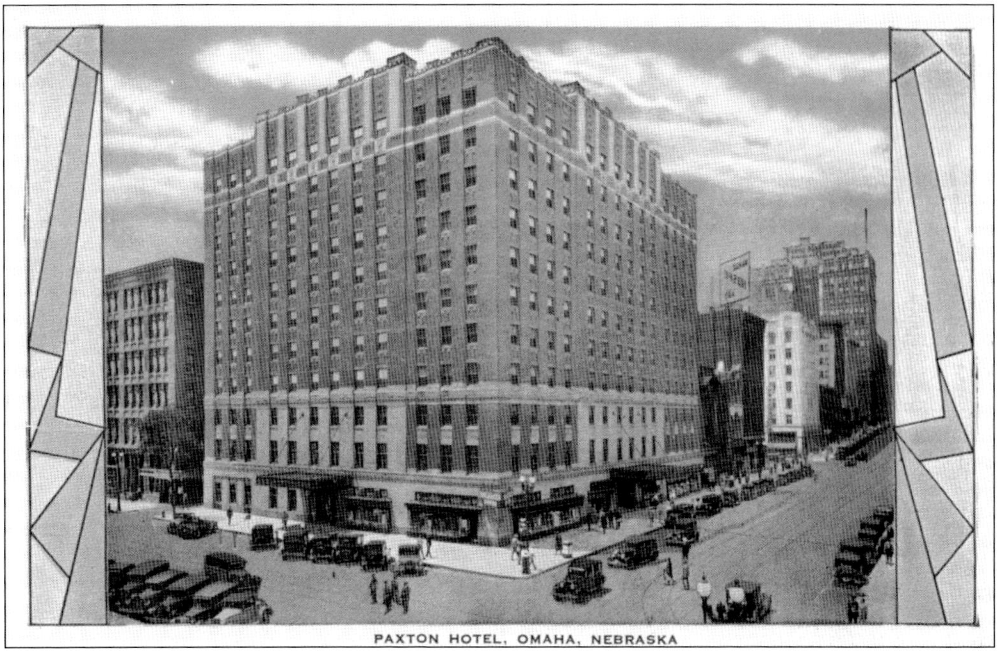

PAXTON HOTEL. In 1929, this Paxton Hotel at Fourteenth and Farnam Streets replaced the 1882 hotel. It took eight months and $1.5 million to build this 420-room hotel. This card is bordered with a yellow and gold art deco design. The back of the card states, "Ceiling fan in every room. Everything new but the name." Paxton later became part of Affiliated National Hotels, with 33 hotels in 10 states. This view shows the old Murray on the left and Hospe's Music and the 14-story First National Bank on the right.

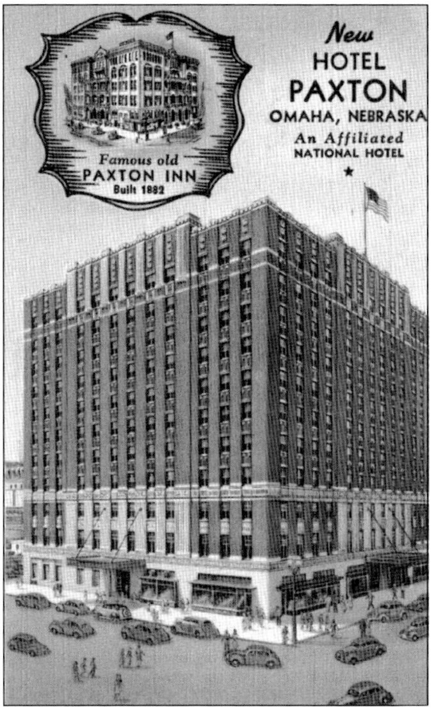

NEW HOTEL PAXTON. The 1882 Paxton Hotel is pictured here. The cars on the street are more recent than depicted on the previous card. The 50-word description on the back of this card mentions "Air-Conditioned" three times, as well as "Running Ice Water." It had a rooftop dog kennel. During the first College World Series, held in Omaha in 1950, the participating teams stayed at the Paxton.

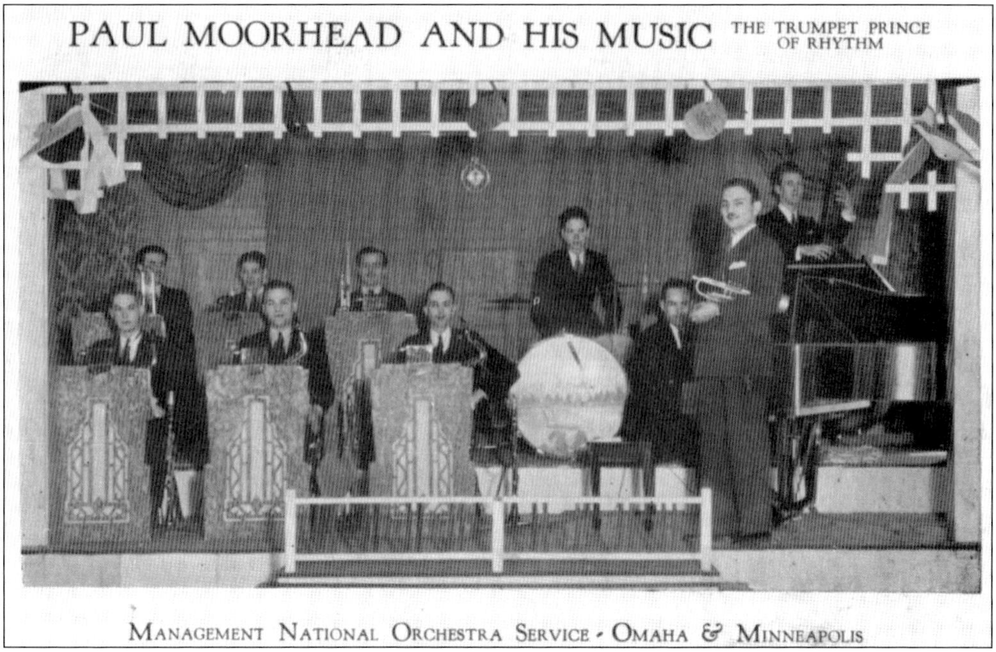

PAUL MOORHEAD AND HIS MUSIC. The National Orchestra Service operated from Omaha and Minneapolis from 1930 to 1960. Moorhead, from Grand Island, performed regularly at the Paxton Hotel during the 1930s and 1940s, and the performances were broadcast weekly from coast to coast. A performance of Moorhead and his orchestra playing the Omaha-themed "Golden Spike Days" on the Midnight Records label is on YouTube. Another territorial band, The Earl Gardner Orchestra, performed at Omaha venues such as Peony Park and Happy Hollow Club.

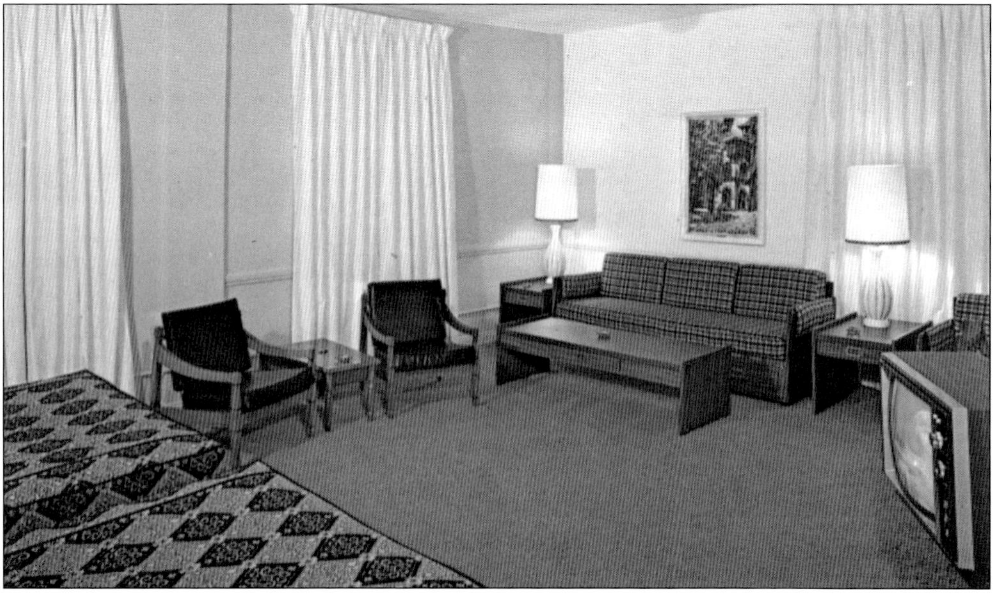

NEW PAXTON HOTEL. This 1971 card displays the comforts of mid-century Danish modern style and a color television. Other amenities included free overnight parking, free in-room coffee service, and free local telephone calls. The Pump Room offered fine dining at "coffee shop prices." "Moderate rates" suggested economy. (John D. Freeman Studios.)

Redick Tower. This 11-story high-rise art deco building at 1504 Harney Street is named for the Redick family, who came to Omaha in the 1850s. Their mansion became the main building at the University of Omaha in 1908. Omaha architect Joseph G. McArthur originally designed the tower to be used as commercial office space. It took one year to build, had a large garage, and opened in 1930. It has operated as a Radisson Hotel, Best Western, and Hotel Deco XV and has housed several restaurants.

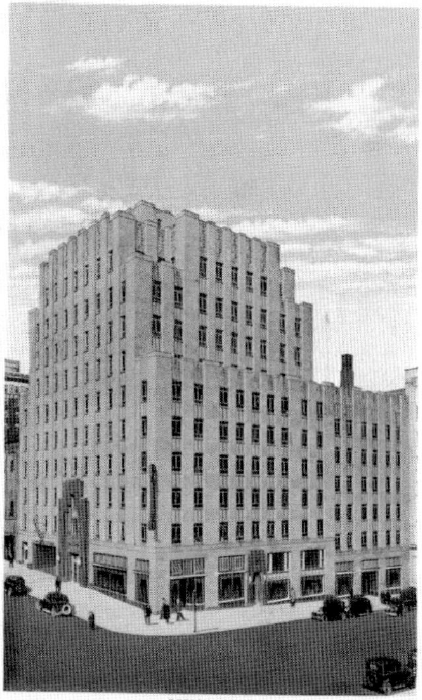

REDICK TOWER

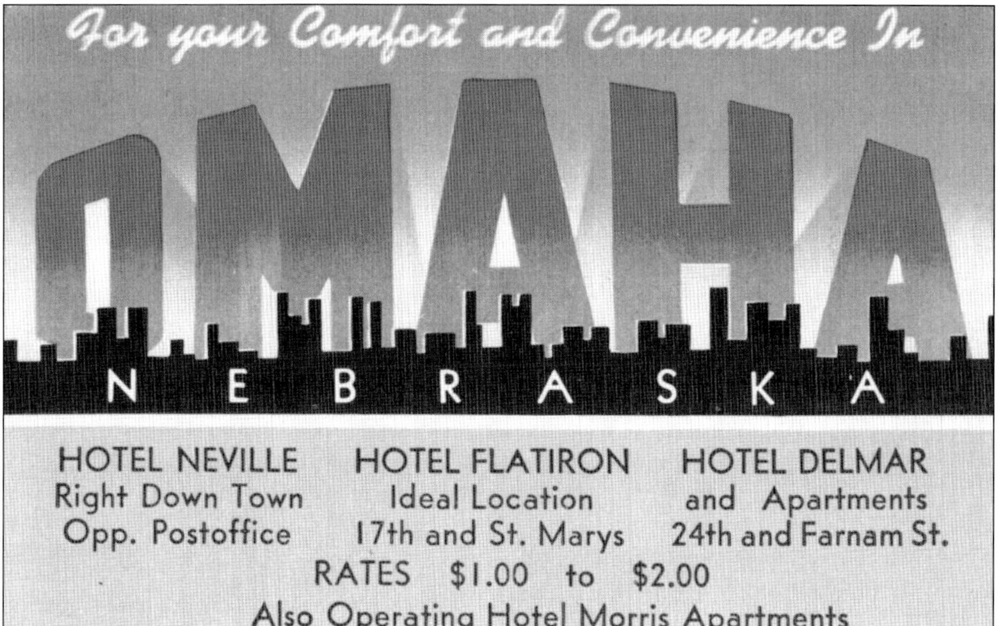

Joint Advertising. This card advertises four hotels: Neville, Flatiron, Delmar, and Morris. The January 19, 1942, postmark—the month following the Japanese attack on Pearl Harbor—reads: "BUY DEFENSE SAVINGS BONDS and STAMPS." The hotel was proud of its innerspring mattresses. Although the Neville advertised itself as "centrally located in shopping district," a mother wrote to her daughter Betty in Dover, Minnesota: "Well angel, I haven't seen anything you would want. Will be home." Did she not go to Brandeis?

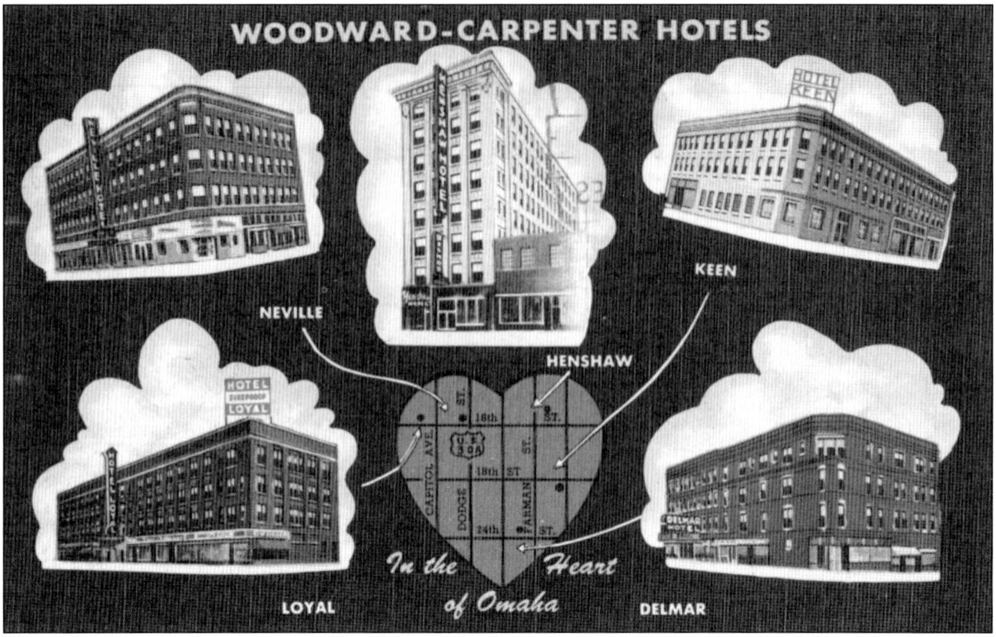

Joint Advertising: Woodward-Carpenter Hotels. This 1957 multiview with 600 rooms in the "heart" of Omaha includes Neville, Henshaw, Keen, Loyal, and the Delmar (built in 1916 at 213 S. Twenty-fourth Street). The desk clerk arranged for lodging down the road. Woodward-Carpenter's general offices were in Hotel Loyal. By the 1980s, Delmar provided low-rent housing for the elderly; it was torn down in 2001. Only the Henshaw survives today.

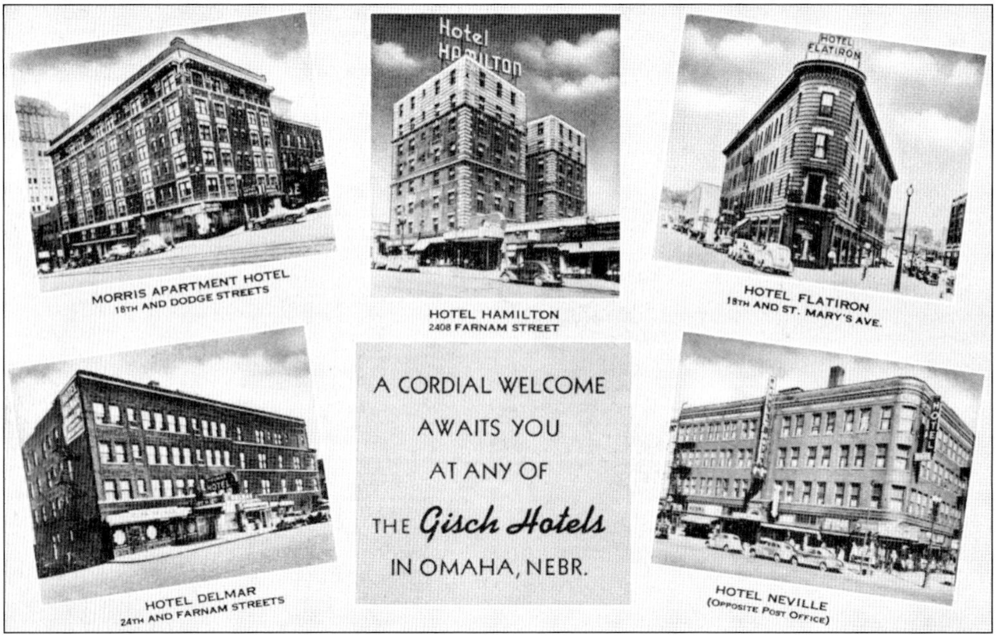

Joint Advertising: The Gisch Hotels. This card features a changing hotel inventory and showcases the Morris Apartment Hotel, Hotel Delmar, Hotel Hamilton, Hotel Flatiron, and Hotel Neville. Room charges and amenities differed, and this array catered to a "segmented market." A Gisch matchbook read: "Thank you, your patronage is appreciated." (Omaha Public Library.)

Chamber of Commerce Brochure. In 1893, 25 businessmen formed the Omaha Commercial Club, which became the Omaha Chamber of Commerce in 1919 and the Greater Omaha Chamber of Commerce in 1970. Its goal is recruiting new business and boosting investment and employment. It works to mobilize business, lobby the legislature, and support a business-friendly atmosphere. The chamber moved its headquarters from Eighteenth and Dodge Streets to Thirteenth and Harney Streets in 1982. To mark the centennial in 1993, the chamber created the Omaha Business Hall of Fame, a permanent exhibit at the Durham Museum. It includes several real estate developers and one hotelier (Eugene C. Eppley). The chamber opposed pool halls and minimum wage, assisted with relief for 1913 tornado victims, and supported the war efforts, improved race relations, and housing initiatives. (Greater Omaha Chamber of Commerce.)

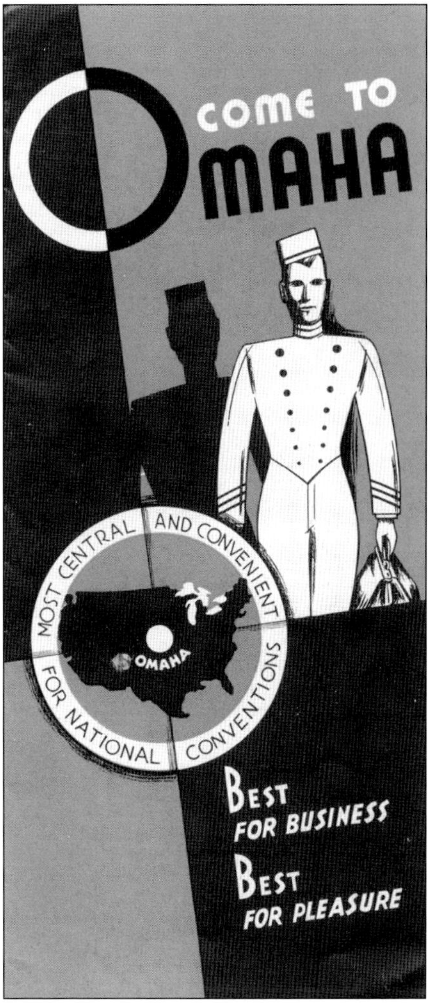

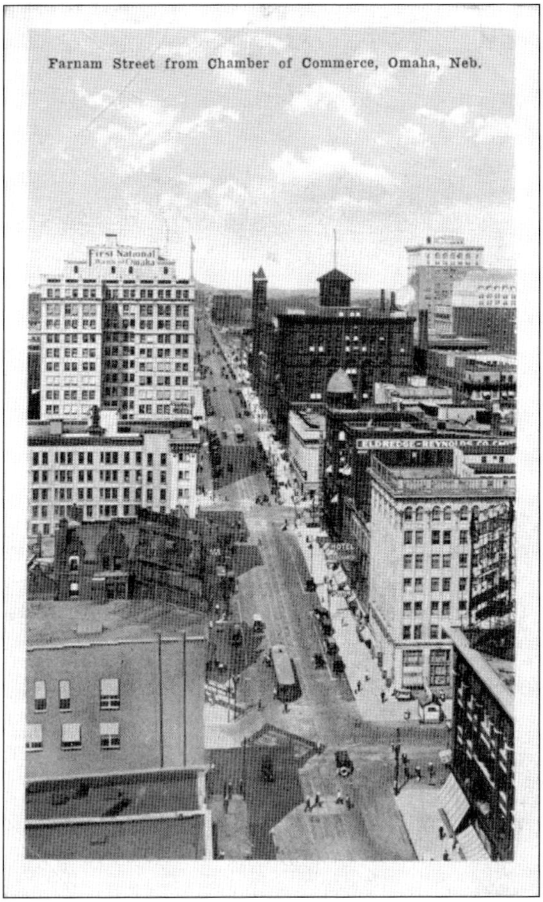

Farnam Street from the Chamber of Commerce. This is an allegorical postcard. Although viewers cannot see the building, they have a bird's-eye view of the chamber's mission: commerce in Omaha.

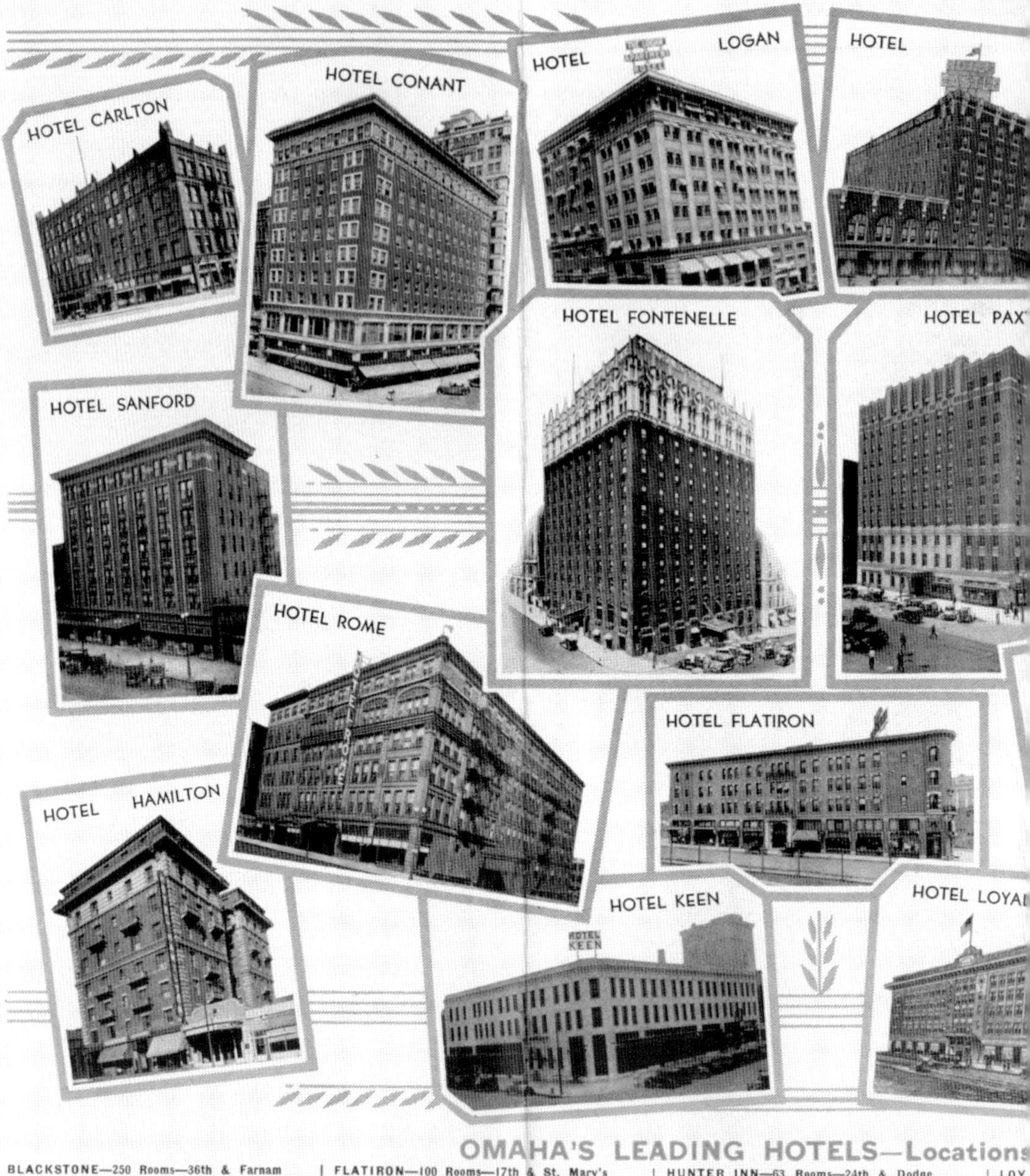

OMAHA'S LEADING HOTELS—Locations

BLACKSTONE—250 Rooms—36th & Farnam
1 Person —With Bath, $2.50 and Up
2 Persons—With Bath, $3.50 and Up

CARLTON—125 Rooms—15th & Howard
1 Person —With Bath, $1.50
2 Persons—With Bath, $2.00
1 Person —Without Bath, $1.00
2 Persons—Without Bath, $1.50

CASTLE—275 Rooms—16th & Jones
1 Person —With Bath, $1.50 to $2.50
2 Persons—With Bath, $2.50 to $3.50
1 Person —Without Bath, $1.00
2 Persons—Without Bath, $1.50 & $2.00

CONANT—250 Rooms—16th & Harney
1 Person —With Bath, $2.00 to $3.00
2 Persons—With Bath, $3.00 to $4.00

FLATIRON—100 Rooms—17th & St. Mary's
1 Person —With Bath, $1.75 & $2.50
2 Persons—With Bath, $2.50 & $3.50
1 Person —Withiut Bath, $1.00 & $1.50
2 Persons—Without Bath, $1.50 & $2.50

FONTENELLE—400 Rooms—18th & Douglas
1 Person —With Bath, $2.50 to $5.00
2 Persons—With Bath, $4.00 to $7.50

HAMILTON—125 Rooms—24th & Farnam
1 Person —With Bath, $1.50 to $2.00
2 Persons—With Bath, $2.00 to $3.00

HILL—200 Rooms—16th & Howard
1 Person —With Bath, $2.00 to $3.50
2 Persons—With Bath, $3.00 to $5.00
1 Person —Without Bath, $1.50-$1.75
2 Persons—Without Bath, $2.50-$3.00

HUNTER INN—63 Rooms—24th & Dodge
1 Person —With Bath, $1.50 and Up
2 Persons—With Bath, $2.50
Hotel Apartments with Kitchenette

KEEN—100 Rooms—18th & Harney
1 Person —With Bath, $1.50 to $2.50
2 Persons—With Bath, $2.50 to $3.50
1 Person —Without Bath, $1.25 to $1.50
2 Persons—Without Bath, $2.00 to $2.50

LOGAN HOTEL—18th & Dodge
1 Person —With Bath, $2.50 to $6.00
2 Persons—With Bath, $3.50 to $7.50

LOY

PAX

PUL

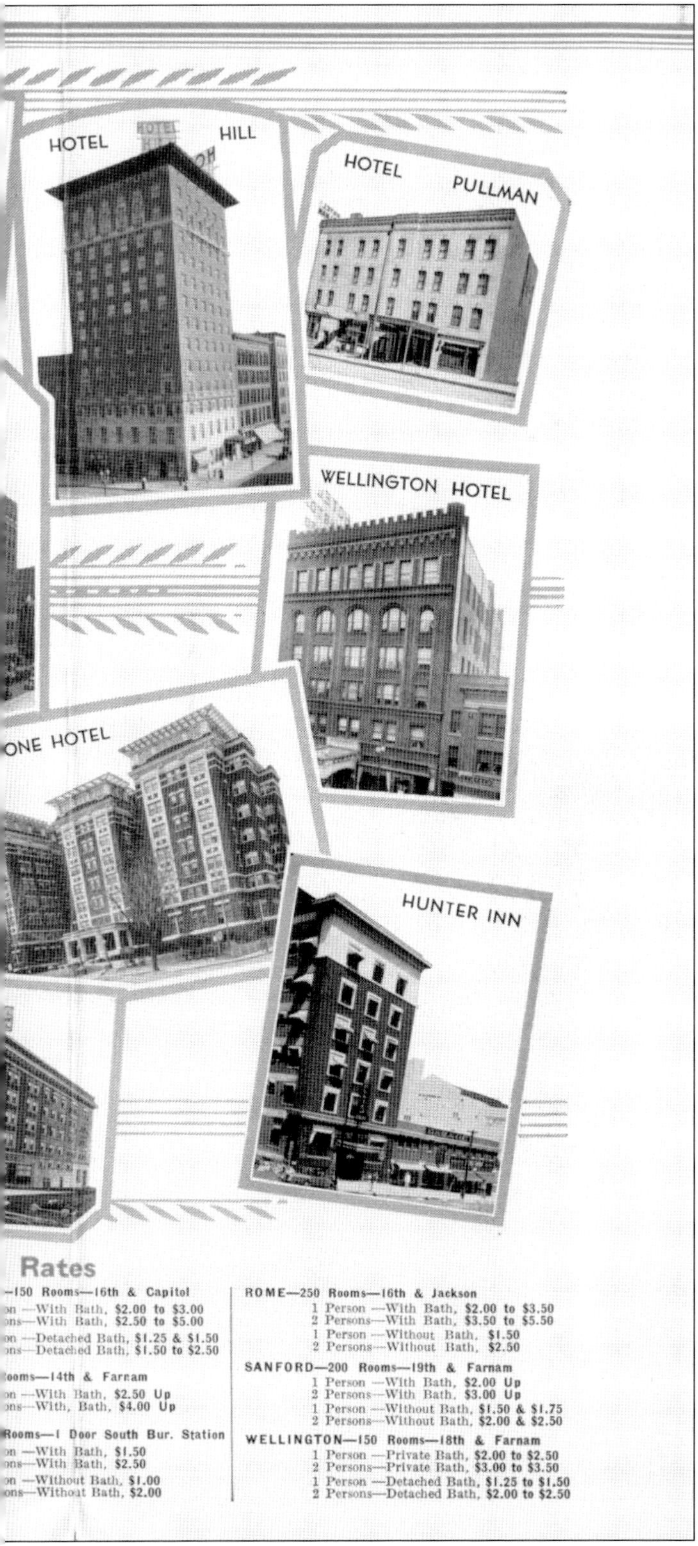

"Omaha's Leading Hotels." This illustration is from the "Come to Omaha" brochure. The Omaha Chamber of Commerce, visitor's bureaus, and hotel associations combined advertising resources to encourage recovery from the Great Depression by maximizing visitor revenue. Hotel advertising doubled during the Depression. This 1933 brochure created by the Omaha Chamber of Commerce publicity department extols Omaha's capacity to host conventions with thousands of attendees. Omaha was "Most central and Convenient for National Conventions." It was "Best for business, Best for pleasure." It contains pictures, room rates, and locations. The most expensive were the Blackstone, Fontenelle, Paxton, and Logan, all with rates starting at $2.50. The Flatiron started at $1 without a bath. The brochure gushes as it describes Omaha as the "Crossroads of the Nation—By Rail—By Auto—By Air . . . Only 12 hours from New York by air . . . a little longer from the west coast. Tourists and travelers of every description, more and more are going to or through Omaha, The City Surrounded by the United States." The brochure included 17 thumbnail hotel pictures, curiously excluding the Henshaw and showing the Loyal as having five stories. Only the Hotel Pullman dated from the 19th century. (Greater Omaha Chamber of Commerce.)

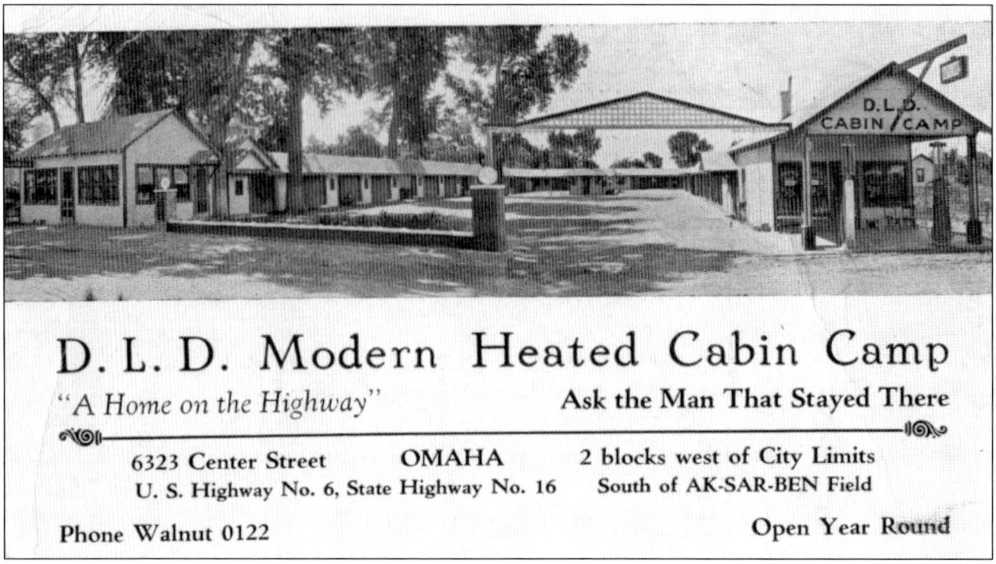

D.L.D. MODERN HEATED CABIN CAMP. The automobile fostered new types of lodging. During the 1920s, Elmwood Park maintained a tourist auto camp. This camp, located at 6323 Center Street, was part of the evolution of tourist villages, motor courts, and motels and has two gas pumps in front of the office. AK-SAR-BEN Field was a geographical icon. The language was direct and appealing: "A Home on the Highway—Ask the Man That Stayed There."

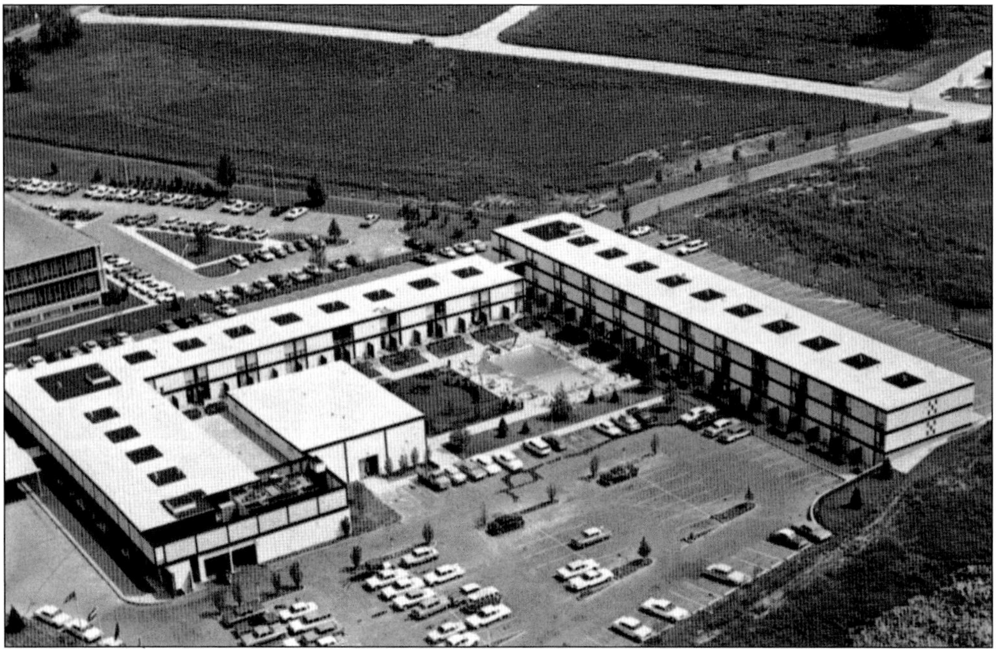

SCHIMMEL'S INDIAN HILLS INN. Blackstone's success and the rise of motels on city outskirts resulted in the building of a 206-room motel—advertised as "Newest and finest Midwest motor inn"—at 8501 West Dodge Road in 1962. Kavalier Restaurant and Lounge had a European touch. The Backstage Lounge had a turn-of-the-century theatrical setting. Methodist Hospital purchased it in 1968 to provide housing for nursing students. The nearby Indian Hills Cinerama Theater, built in 1962, was demolished in 2001 for a Nebraska Methodist Health parking lot.

Four

Membership and Exclusivity

Clubs supported members with both written and unspoken rules of exclusion. Race, gender, faith, ethnicity, and income fostered accommodations catering to unique clienteles. Single (unescorted) women seeking security and respectability went to the YWCA, the Scandinavian YWCA, or responded to advertisements for rooms above stores for "working girls." Scandinavians were among Omaha's three largest immigrant groups. Segregation and Jim Crow laws utilized in public accommodations became a target of the Civil Rights movement in the 1960s, as lunch counters and hotels were picketed.

Anatole France stated, "The law, in its majestic equality, forbids the rich as well as the poor to sleep under bridges, to bed in the streets, and to steal bread." Poverty creates its own club. Nebraska's weather extremes did not stop people from living on the street; they placed pressure on charities to minimize exposure to frostbite and worse. Workingmen's hotels, the Salvation Army, the Society of St. Vincent de Paul, settlement houses, old people's homes, and poorhouses catered to a distressed clientele.

The "undesirable classes"—Jews, Poles, Czechs, and African Americans—developed their own clubs and took pleasure in public parks. Jews formed the Metropolitan Club in 1883 and the Highland Country Club in 1922. The Metropolitan Club, located at 2203 Harney Street, closed in 1911, and the new tenant was the Omaha Women's Club.

Before the 1960s Civil Rights movement, African Americans faced humiliating discrimination throughout the United States, especially while traveling. In 1954, the black-run *Omaha Star* sought housing for a minister's convention. Amy H. Forss's *Black Print with a White Carnation: Mildred Brown and the* Omaha Star *Newspaper, 1938–1989* (2013) and Matt Holland's *Ahead of Their Time: The Story of the Omaha DePorres Club* (2014) describe racial discrimination in housing and employment. African Americans navigated the country with the help of *The Negro Travelers' Green Book*, a guide published from 1936 to 1966. In 1962, the Broadway Hotel, G.H. Ashby Tourist Home, L. Strawther Tourist Home, Payton's Hotel, and the Willis Hotel—all on the north side—catered to African Americans, although none had postcards (as far as the author can tell).

Some of the buildings in this chapter provided lodging for members. Others were friendship beacons for out-of-towners. Voluntary associations built headquarters and clubhouses, leased space, and had meeting halls and taverns. Downtown was home to the New Masonic Temple, Scottish Rite Masonic Center, Independent Order of Odd Fellows, International Order of Foresters, and Fraternal Order of Eagles.

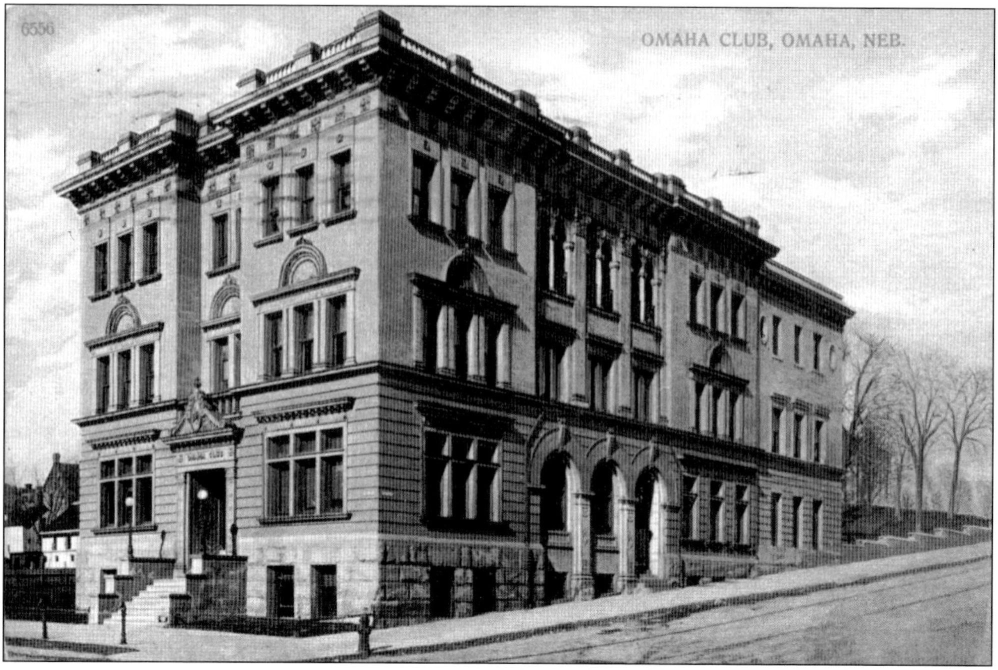

OMAHA CLUB. Founded on January 1, 1884, with 245 members, the Omaha Club built this clubhouse in 1894 at the northwest corner of Twentieth and Douglas Streets. This exclusive group comprised Omaha's business elite. In September 1908, Vesta wrote to Ethel in Creighton, Nebraska: "The Aksarben, (our annual carnival) begins today. Almost everybody has a great time during the ten days that it is here."

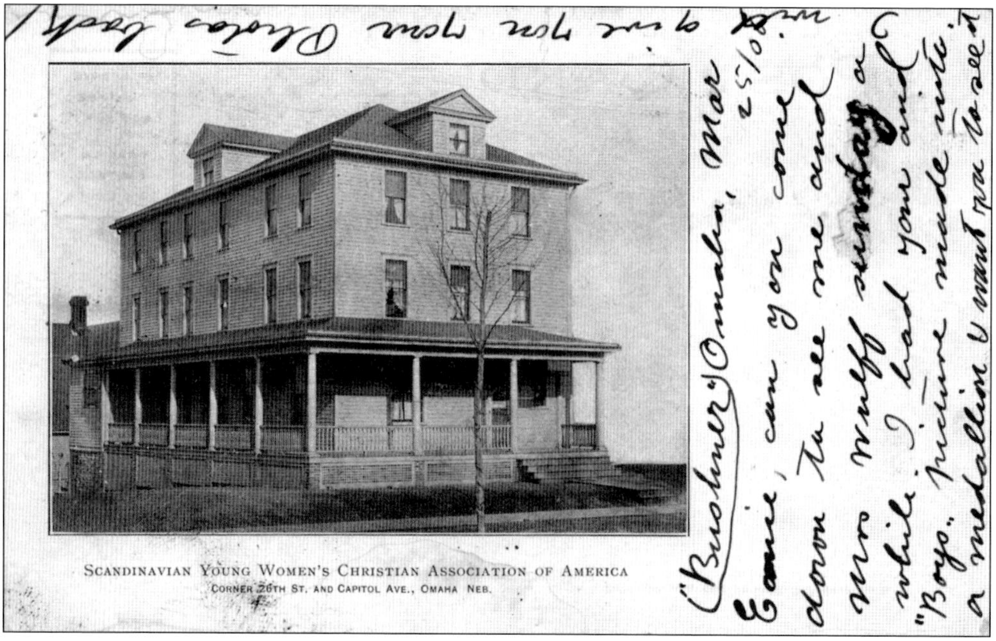

SCANDINAVIAN YWCA OF AMERICA. This organization, started in 1895 at 1813 Cass Street and continued at Twenty-sixth and Capitol Streets, provided housing for immigrant women. (Omaha Public Library.)

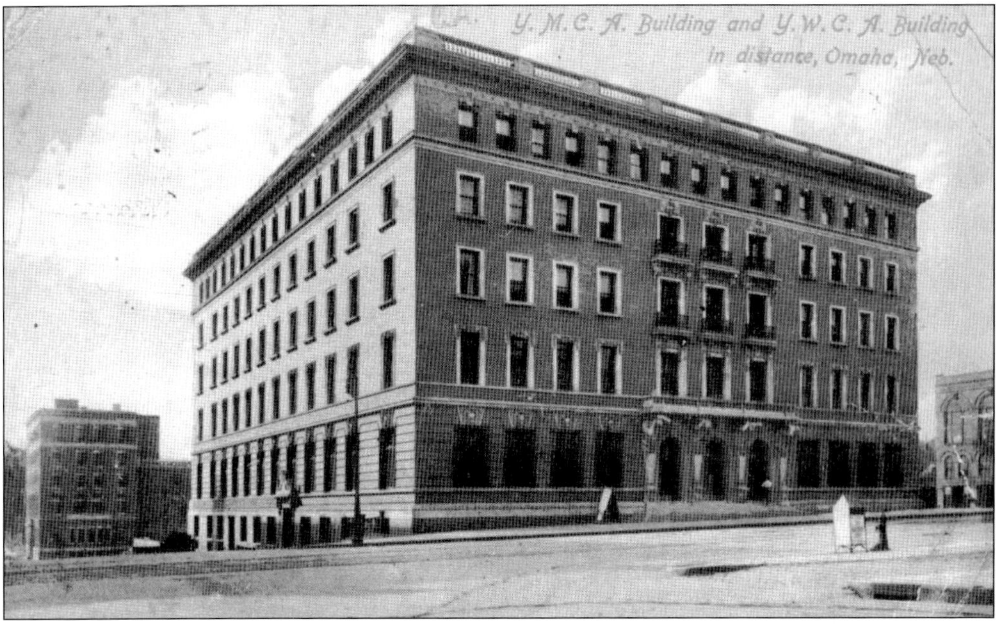

YMCA Building and YWCA Building (in Background). Founded in London in 1844, the YMCA came to Boston in 1852 and Omaha in 1865. This 1907 building at Seventeenth and Harney Streets was located near the main library at 1823 Harney Street (dating from 1891) and was the YMCA's third downtown location. The YMCA used this building until 1968. The YWCA is at left. This card is postmarked 1912.

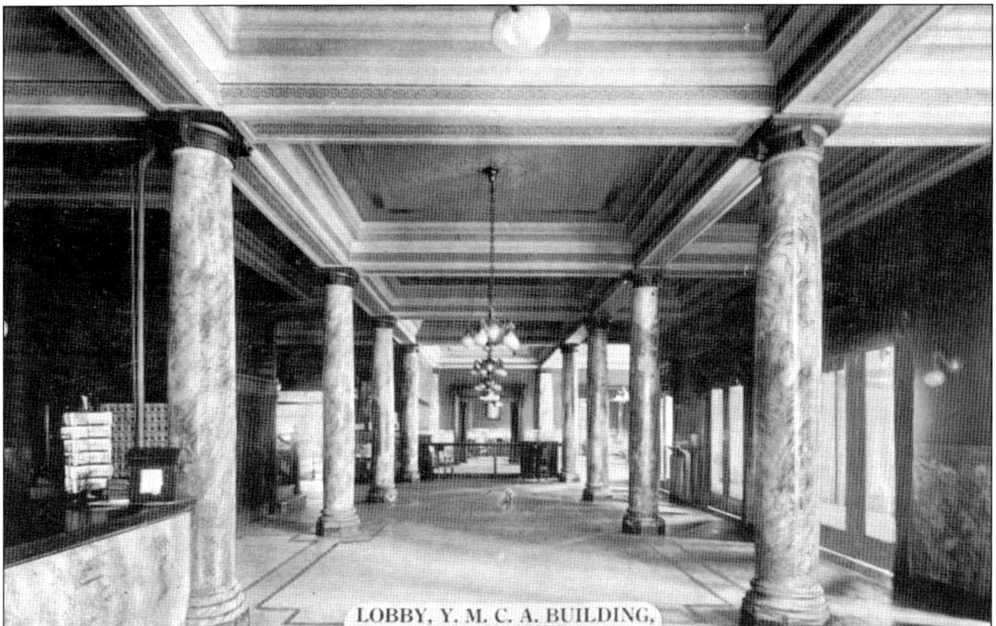

YMCA Lobby. Columns or pillars are structural and cultural artifices; they evoke Greece and Rome, grandeur, seriousness, and valor. Omaha Electric Light & Power Co. rented the ground floor of the YMCA building. The Grand Central Hotel, Paxton Hotel, YWCA, and Brandeis had columns. The Joslyn Art Museum has magnificent specimens. This card is postmarked February 24, 1915.

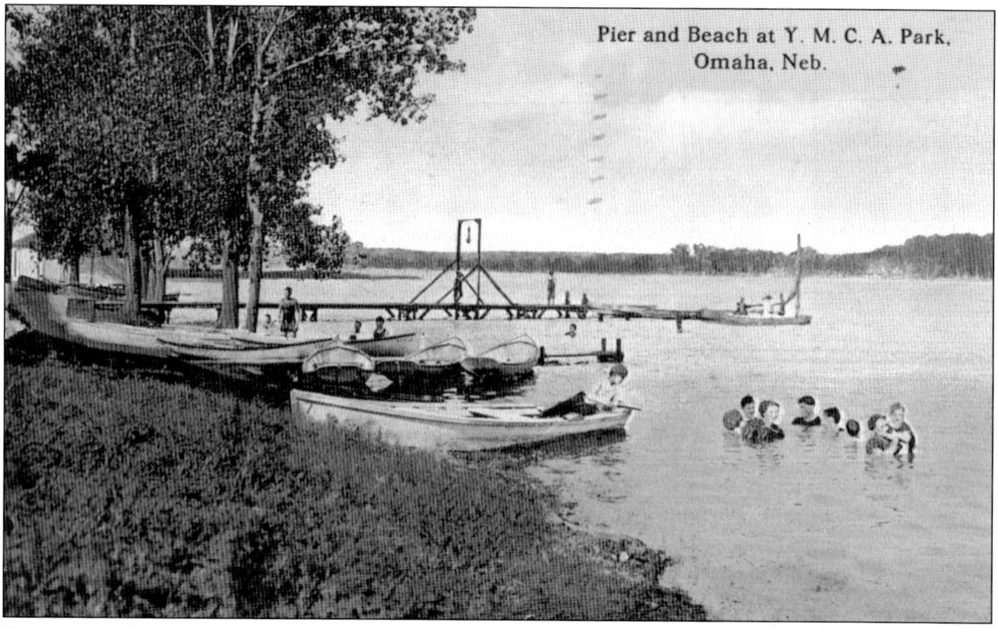

Pier and Beach at YMCA Park. YMCA Park opened in May 1894 with the sounds of a band and speeches. The facilities included fields for baseball, football, lacrosse, and quoits; a quarter-mile bicycle track; and a grandstand. It occupied the field of a former professional baseball team. Getting away from the city, stretching limbs, and promoting physical vitality animated the Boy Scouts and YMCA. Summer camps were private and exclusive reserves involving gender, class, race, ethnicity, and faith. This scene contains a sailboat, rowboats, fishing gear, and boys in the water.

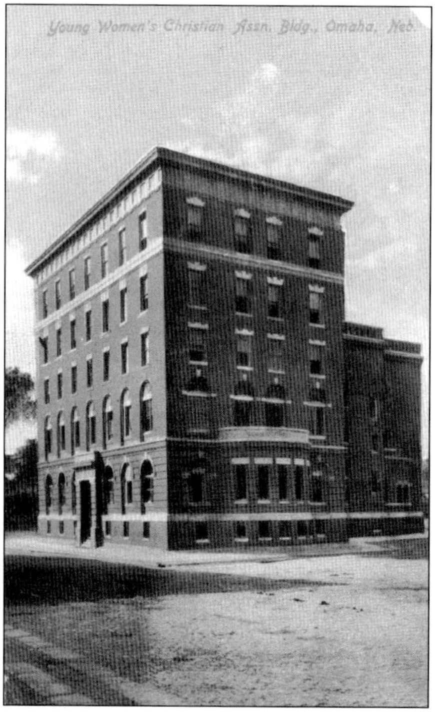

YWCA. Eleven years after the founding of the YMCA, a women's version emerged in England in 1855, the United States in 1858, and Omaha in 1893. George Prinz designed this building at Seventeenth and St. Mary's Streets. It opened in 1909 and had athletic facilities. Although it lacked sleeping quarters, locals would show it to visitors with pride. The sender of this card writes to Lena in Silver City, Iowa (30 miles away): "Am sending you a couple of pieces of [sheet] music which I hope you will like." This building was demolished in 1970.

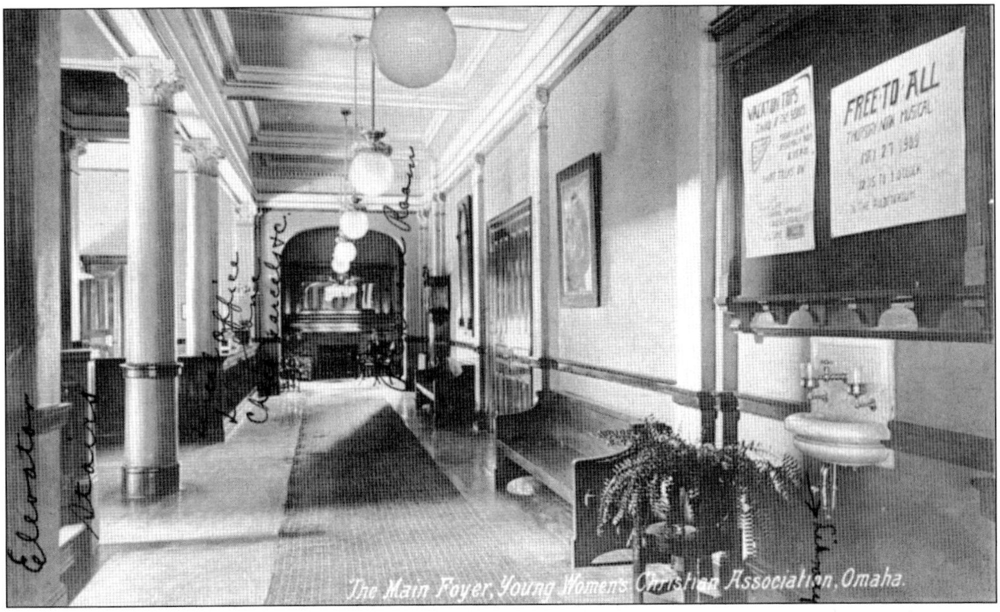

Main Foyer, YWCA. This well-lit foyer with columns, seating, greenery, water fountain, bulletin board, office, parcel room, elevator, and stairs welcomed many women, suffragettes, and feminists for committee meetings and educational and entertainment programs. The building contained a basketball court, gymnasium, auditorium, and swimming pool.

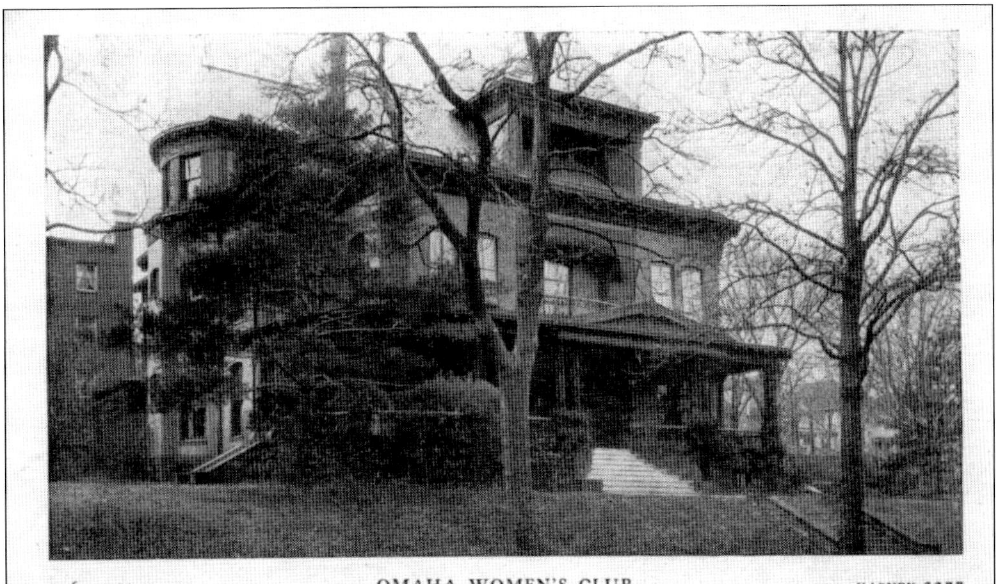

Omaha Women's Club. The American Association of University Women was founded in 1881. The Chicago World's Fair encouraged organizing. The Omaha Women's Club, formed in 1893, facilitated the establishment of the Nebraska Federation of Women's Clubs in 1894. It advocated for children, suffrage, and education and held book discussions, occasional teas, and ice cream socials. In 1896, they met at Unity Church, then spent 14 years at the First Congregational Church. They leased the Metropolitan Hall at Twenty-third and Harney Streets in 1911. The club acquired this building at 206 S. Thirty-second Avenue in 1926.

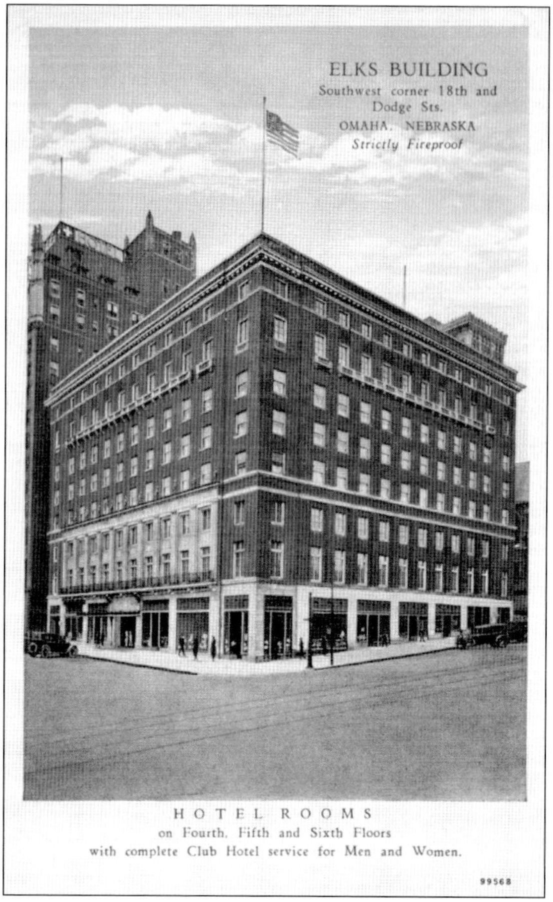

ELKS CLUB HOTEL. The Benevolent and Protective Fraternal Order of Elks, founded in 1868, used hotels as club headquarters and rented out rooms. In 1910, Gould Dietz dedicated the eight-story building at Eighteenth and Dodge Streets, two blocks west of the post office. Hotel rooms were on the fourth through sixth floors. The fireproof building had a cocktail salon and bowling alley. The Elks had hotels in several cities, including Springfield, Illinois; Brainerd, Minnesota; and Huron, South Dakota.

ELKS MULTIVIEW. To dispel the notion of male exclusivity, matchbooks noted that venues were "open to the public for men and women." If a member's wife stayed in Omaha, he might take comfort in the fact that she stayed at her husband's club, "the ideal place of refinement for ladies and gentlemen . . . where friends meet friends." The Pine Board Liquor Store, a package store, was a watering hole where melodies from a fine Hammond organ accompanied the libations.

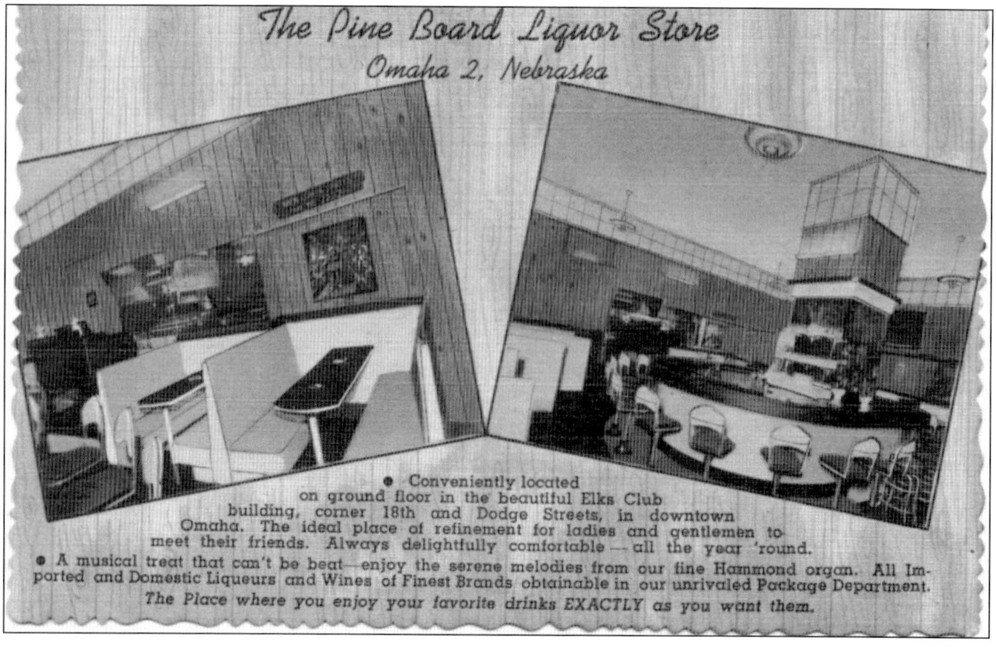

OMAHA ATHLETIC CLUB. John Latenser and Sons designed this $750,000 ten-story club, which opened in 1918 at 1714 Douglas Street. It had a dining room, grill, ballroom, bowling alley, billiard room, pool, nine-hole golf course (in the basement), and handball and squash courts (on the roof). The pool had separate hours for men, women, and children. Rooms were available for guests. It closed in 1970, sold in 1977 and again in 1983, and was demolished in 1992.

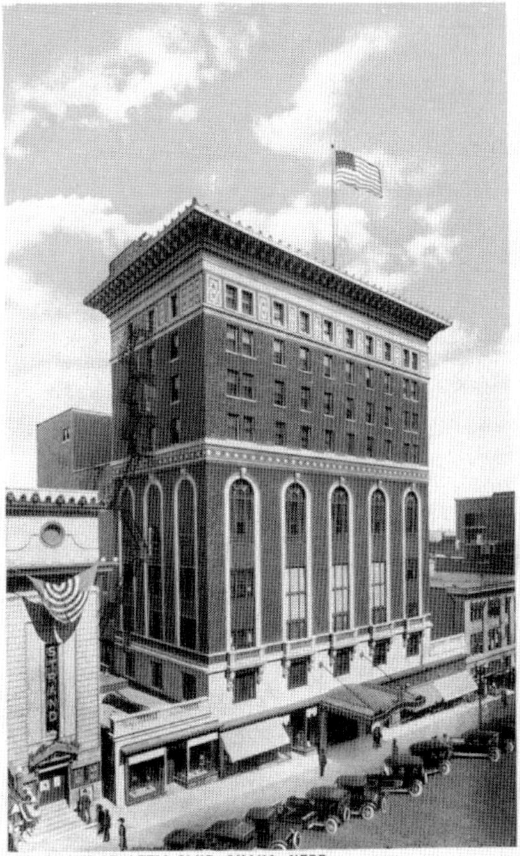

OMAHA ATHLETIC CLUB, OMAHA, NEBR.

OMAHA FIELD CLUB. The Omaha Field Club, founded in 1898 (as the Omaha Cricket Association) at 3615 Woolworth Avenue, claims to be the oldest country club west of the Mississippi River. Country clubs, by their nature, are elitist and exclusive. "EES" in Tamora in Seward County wrote to Hillsboro, Texas, in June 1907: "I know you had a fine trip. Gerald was so pleased to receive three cards. We were in Omaha last week. Ellen was married there Sat eve."

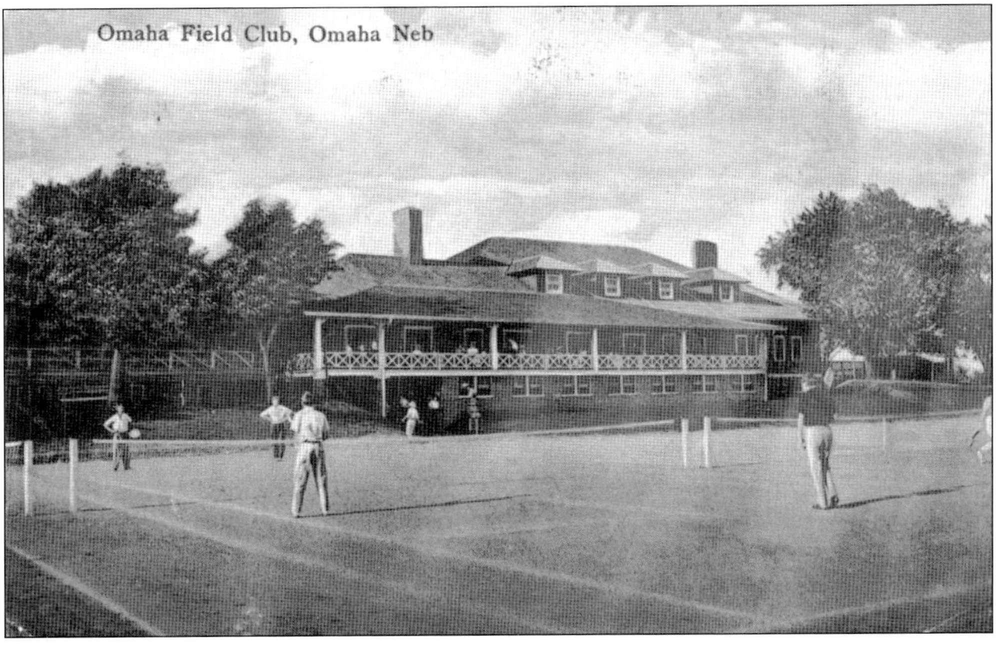

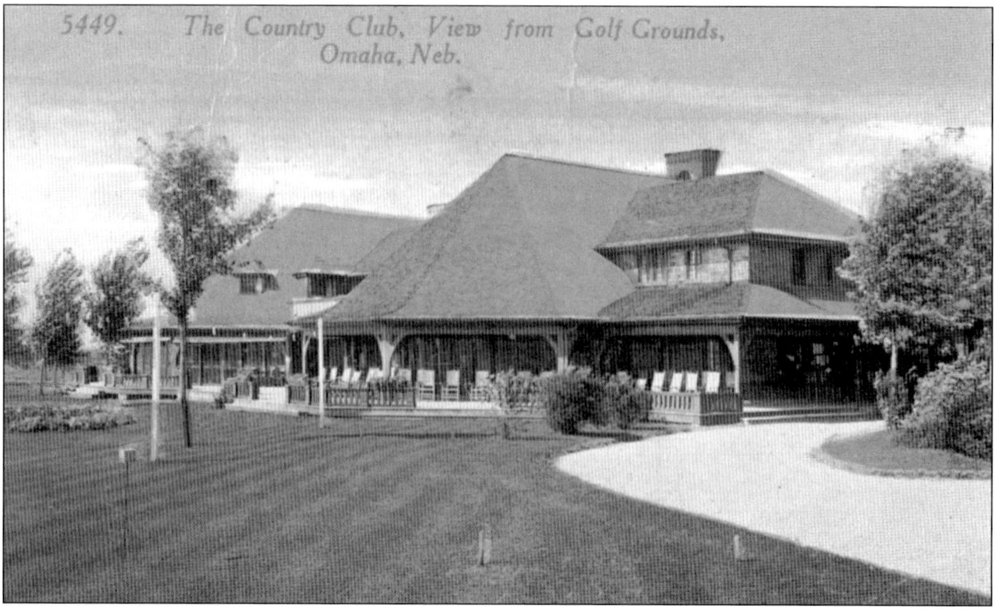

THE COUNTRY CLUB, VIEW FROM GOLF GROUNDS. The Omaha Country Club, founded in 1899, began as a golf and dining club. It moved to 300 acres at 6900 Country Club Road in 1925 and established the course in 1927. Country clubs offered tennis, swimming, and other outdoor recreation. Indoor socialization included card games, food, a bar, and other activities. M.R. wrote to Havelock, Nebraska, on September 28, 1908: "Dear Alice. I thought you would come in for the carnival. I suppose you are going to school every day. Alice we are all well. I remain M.R."

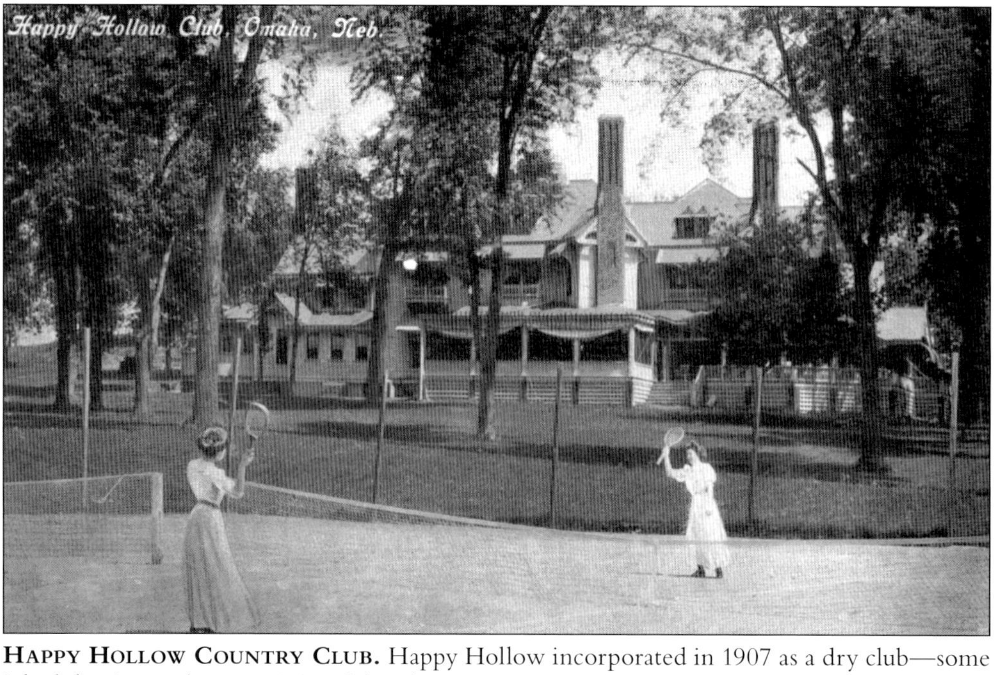

HAPPY HOLLOW COUNTRY CLUB. Happy Hollow incorporated in 1907 as a dry club—some joked that it was the grape juice club. These two women are playing tennis at the original club. Brownell-Talbot School now occupies this land. Although the club moved west in 1927 to 1701 S. 105th Street, it kept the name of its original neighborhood.

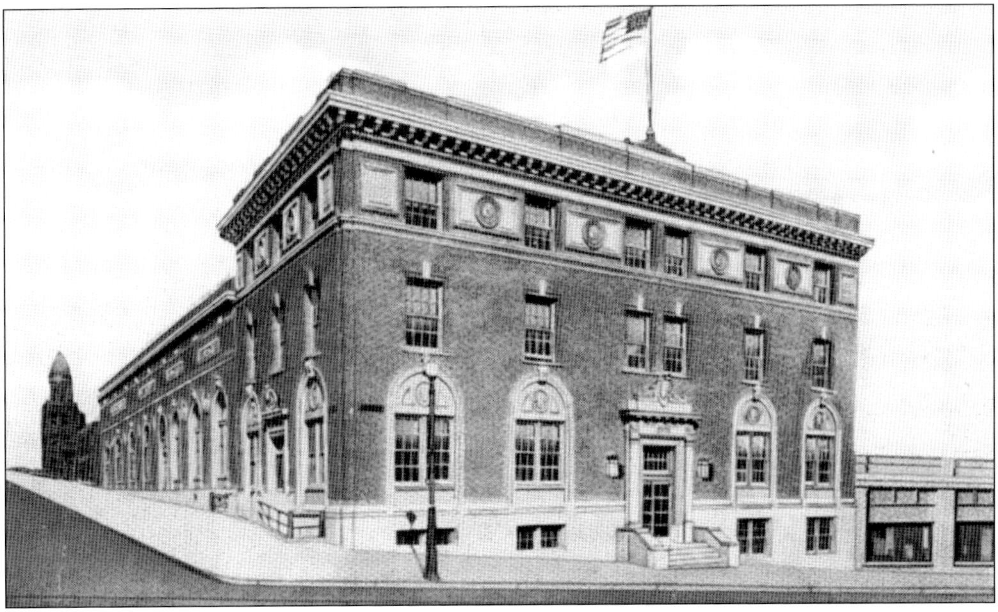

Jewish Community Center (JCC). The 1913 tornado and World War I interrupted fundraising for a Jewish community center. It opened in 1926 at Twentieth and Dodge Streets across from Central High School. The Jewish Highland Country Club, established at 132nd and Pacific Streets in 1922, became Ironwood in 1999 and closed in 2010. In 1973, westward suburban growth led to the abandonment of the downtown JCC and relocation to a 28-acre campus at 333 S. 132nd Street. (Nebraska Jewish Historical Society.)

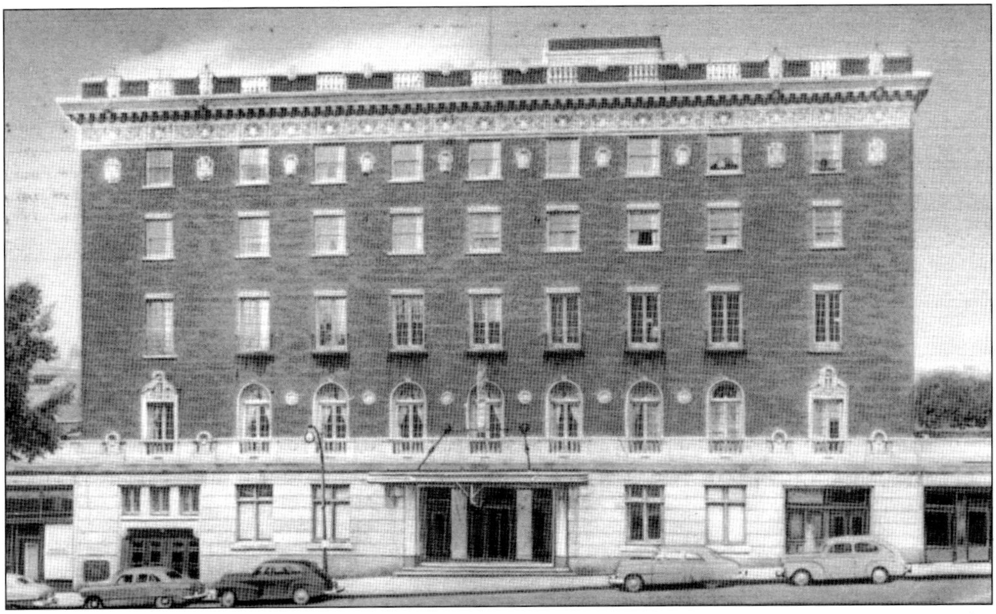

Knights of Columbus/American Legion Building. Over 1,100 members attended the opening of this Knights of Columbus clubhouse built in 1927 at 2027 Dodge Street. In 1928, they offered Thanksgiving turkey for $1.25 and chicken for $1. The efficient hotel service included baths and showers. The American Legion, chartered by Congress in 1919, leased space and later acquired the 75-room Knights building in 1945.

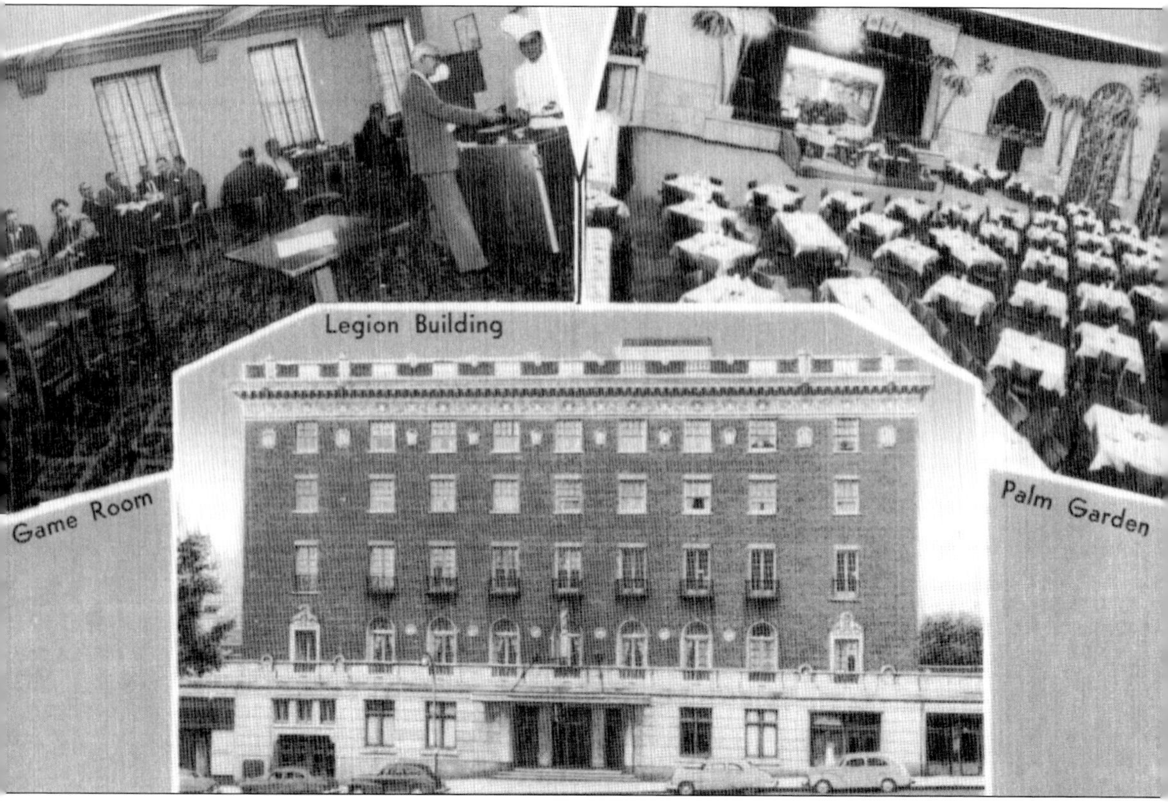

AMERICAN LEGION BUILDING. Post 1 claimed to be the "World's Largest Legion Post." It hosted the national conventions in 1925 and 1943. Members ran for political office, and politicians sought endorsement from the group. The Palm Room featured "dancing every night to the finest music in the Middle West." They had the "largest bar in Omaha" and maintained a "service office where any veteran may obtain counsel and assistance." George and Joe wrote to Richard in Hamilton, Ohio, in 1955: "Had a good trip out. Saw lots of interesting things." Northern Natural Gas purchased this building in 1956 for $475,000.

Five

Entertaining Excursionists and Tourists

The lure of the city, the model of civilization, stems from fine arts, architecture, music, and parks and zoos (nature in the city). "Excursionist" was a popular term in the late 18th and early 19th centuries. The European grand tour visited ancient sites and moribund civilizations. Improved free and toll roads and bridges, canals, railways, and steamships facilitated oceanic and continental human migration and settlement. Commerce is the lifeblood of the city, and the culture of consumerism includes theater, restaurants, museums, and shops. Although there are a finite number of lodgings, Omaha tourist experience possibilities approach the infinite.

Events such as the Presbyterian Ministers Assembly in 1887, the 1898 Trans-Mississippi Exposition, the Black Ministers Conference in 1954, the Ak-Sar-Ben horse racing season, the Berkshire Hathaway Annual Meetings, the College World Series, the NCAA basketball semifinals, and the Olympic swim trials, among others, have attracted and continue to attract tens of thousands of visitors and millions of tourist dollars to Omaha.

Attractions need venues and hotel accommodations. Union Station was repurposed into the Durham Museum. TD Ameritrade Park was built in 2011 to keep the College World Series in Omaha. Rosenblatt Stadium was demolished. The Holland Performing Arts Center opened in 2005 at 1200 Douglas Street, gloriously supplementing The Orpheum and the Joslyn's Witherspoon Recital Hall. Horse racing has gone, but other sports have moved into new venues. Baseball, hockey, basketball, soccer, and football are played in state-of-the-art facilities. New construction includes Quest Center (2003), Werner Park (2011), Ralston Arena (2012), and Baxter Stadium (2015).

Conveying Omaha's allure, the big city's bright lights keep it attractive for inhabitants and visitors. The rich had country clubs, while the public had parks and municipal golf courses. Major public events serve as attractions for both residents and tourists. The Visitors' Bureau, Greater Omaha Chamber of Commerce, Nebraska Film Office, and similar agencies work arduously to popularize Omaha's attractions to lure visitors and investors.

Council Bluffs, Iowa, located across the Missouri River, had the traditional conglomeration of downtown hotels and highway motels. The development of Iowa's gaming industry in the 1980s with casinos and hotels on the river changed the cityscape. Hotel Chieftain, Grand, Grove, and Kiel Hotel are gone; Ameristar Hotel, Harrah's, and Harvey's Casino thrive. Legalized gambling in Nebraska is very limited. They say you can hear the whoosh of dollars going across the bridge to the casinos.

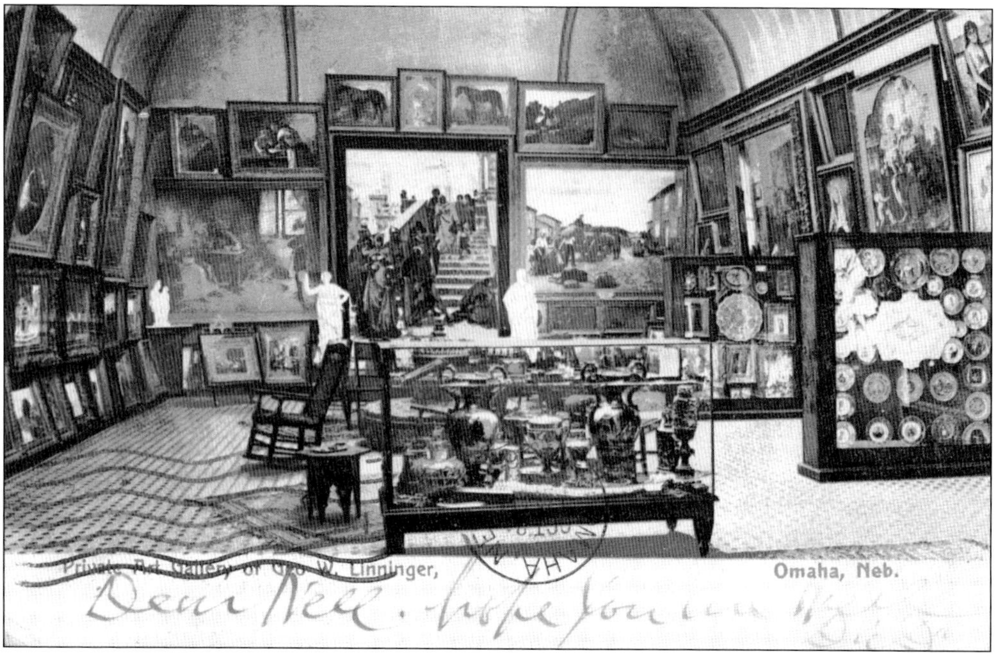

Private Art Gallery of Geo W. Lininger. Lininger, a farm implement dealer, opened his "Palace of Art" to the public in 1879. An 1893 Baedeker guide praised the Lininger Art Gallery located at 221 N. Eighteenth Street. It was open to "strangers [the public]" on Thursday and Sunday and by appointment. Visitors could view works by Fra Angelico, Guido Reni, Guercino, Del Sarto, Solimena, Giordano, Rembrandt, Zurbaran, Bouguereau, Detaille, Meissonier, Schreyer, Lefebvre, "and several modern masters."

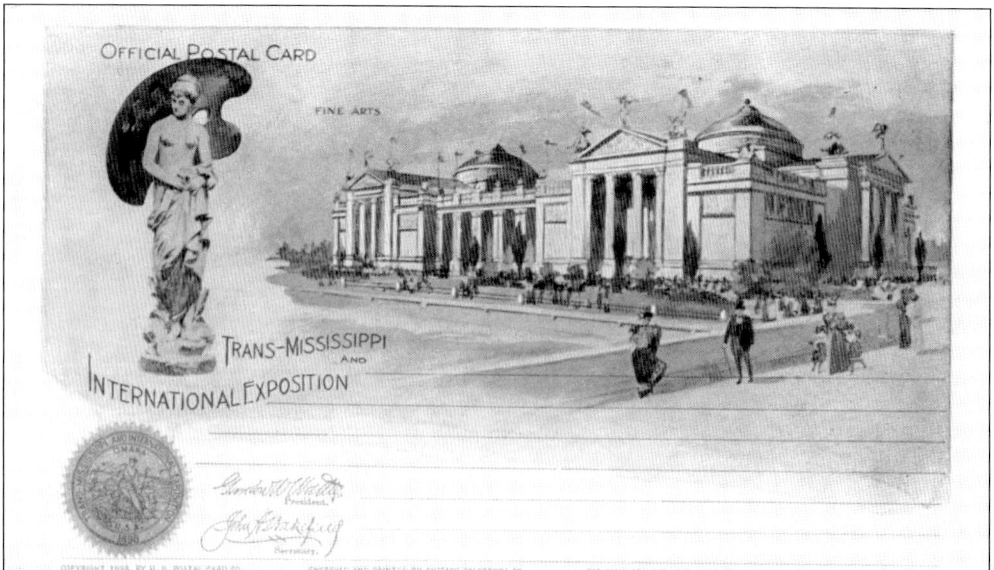

Official Postal Card, Trans-Mississippi International Exposition. The 1898 Trans-Mississippi and International Exposition has been called "Omaha's Greatest Event." Exposition buildings were dedicated to human endeavor. A 25¢, 134-page catalog guided visitors through the Fine Arts exhibition hall.

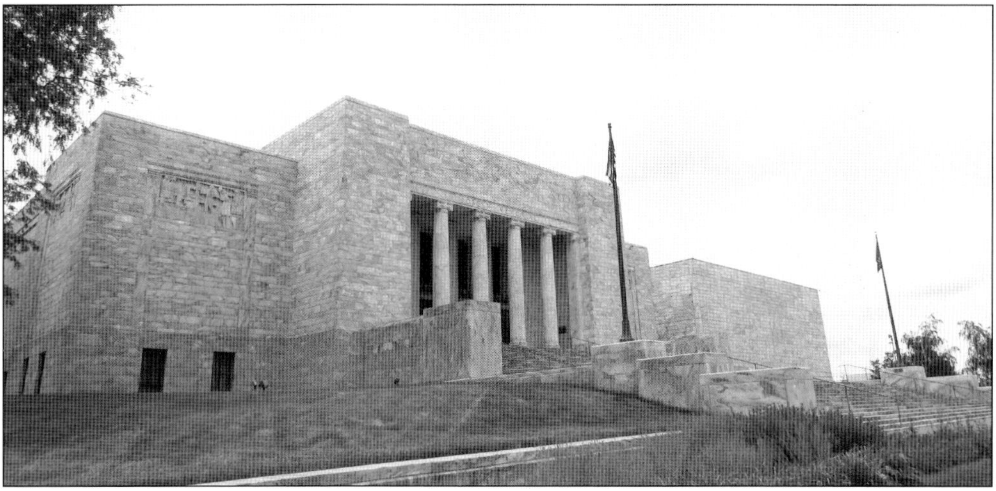

Joslyn Memorial Art Museum. Alan McDonald designed this $3.5-million marble and brick museum. After opening in 1931, it enhanced access to art and became an icon of Omaha's cultural life. Upon the death of George Joslyn, owner of Western Newspapers, his wife, Sarah, donated funds for his memorial. Architect Norman Foster designed the 1994 addition. Widows played a significant role in Omaha philanthropy. Edward Creighton's widow, Mary Lucretia, established Creighton University. Henry Doorly's widow, Margaret Hitchcock, improved the zoo.

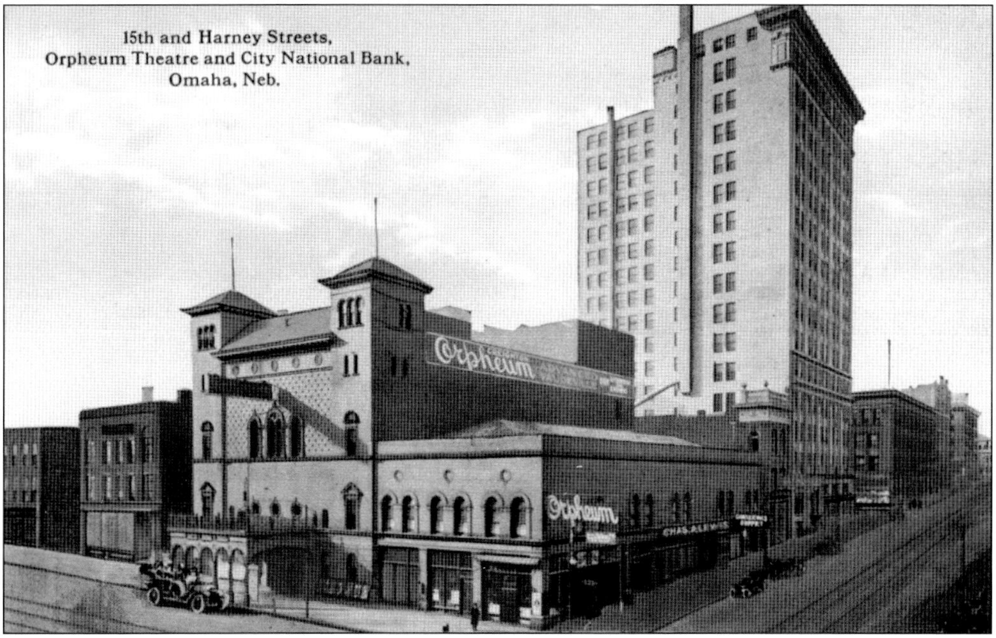

Orpheum Theatre. The Orpheum Theatre at 409 S. Fifteenth Street, built in 1895, was rebuilt in 1927. In the early years of the 20th century, theaters featured vaudeville, burlesque, recitals, traveling companies, films (silent, then with sound and color), political rallies, debates, and other events. Local venues included Grand, Redick, and Boyd's Opera Houses; Brandeis, Burwood, and Gayety Theatres; Douglas, Empress, Lyric, American Music Hall, Music Box, Omaha, Roseland, Dundee, Paramount, Rialto, Ritz, Astro-Riviera, State, World, Muse, Ambassador, Indian Hills, Dundee, and Film Streams, among others. Multiplex theater owners, like hoteliers, must respond to consumers to remain relevant. (Omaha Public Library.)

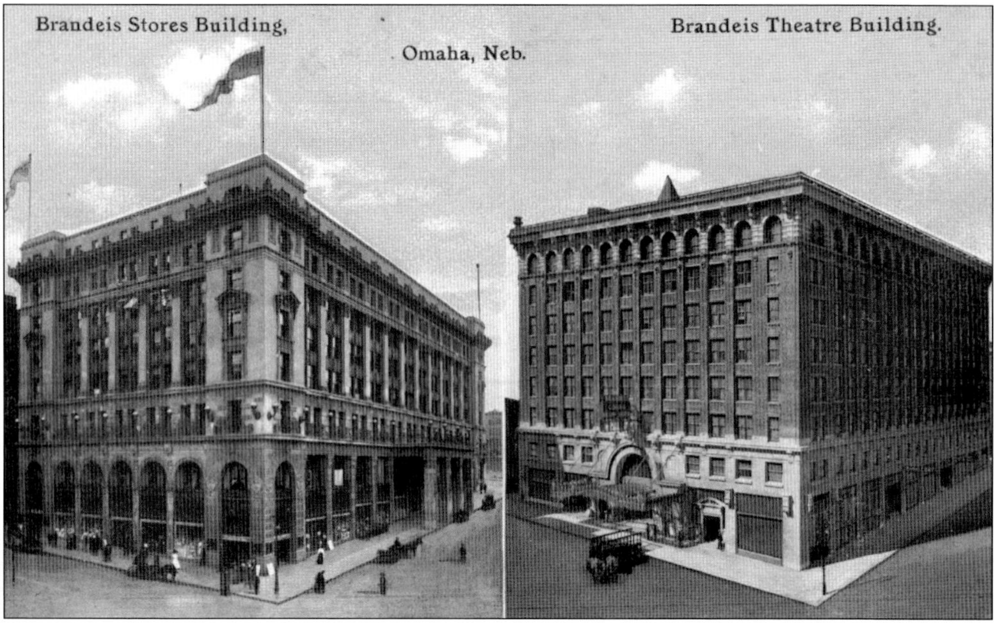

BRANDEIS STORE BUILDING AND THEATRE BUILDING. A concierge guided guests to restaurants, entertainment, and shopping—Brandeis offered all three. The Fair and Boston Stores were Brandeis predecessors. The eight-story Brandeis Store building opened in 1906 as "the largest store in the west." It expanded to 10 stories in 1921 and now houses condominiums. The eight-story theater opened in 1910. In 1959, a parking garage replaced it. The department store had several restaurants.

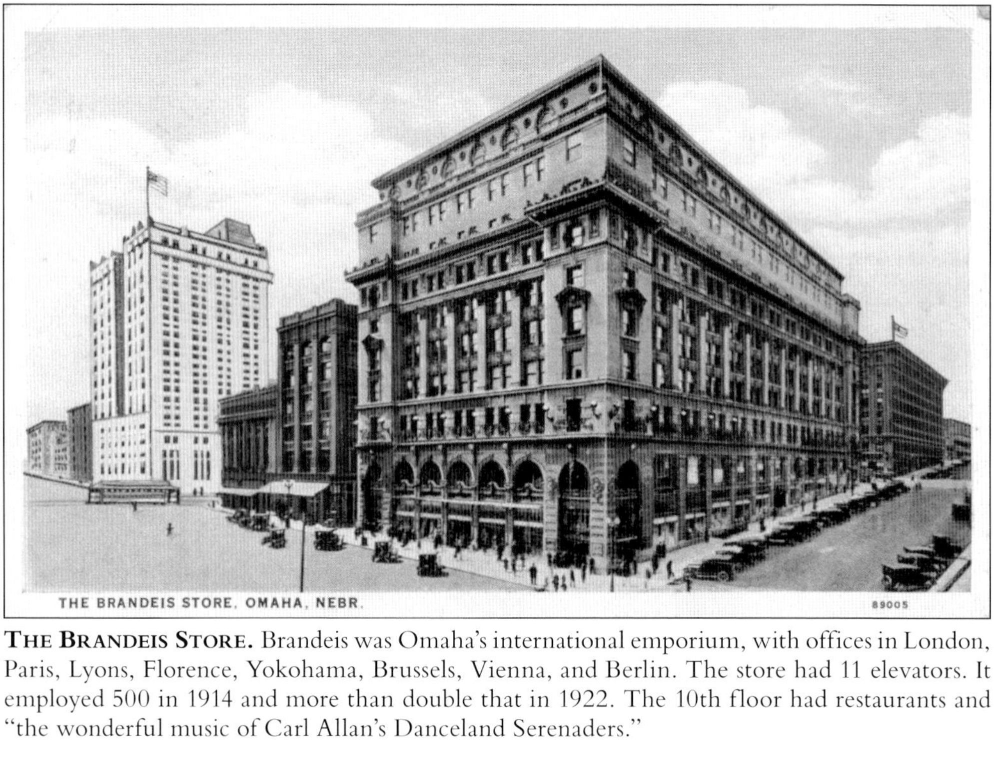

THE BRANDEIS STORE. Brandeis was Omaha's international emporium, with offices in London, Paris, Lyons, Florence, Yokohama, Brussels, Vienna, and Berlin. The store had 11 elevators. It employed 500 in 1914 and more than double that in 1922. The 10th floor had restaurants and "the wonderful music of Carl Allan's Danceland Serenaders."

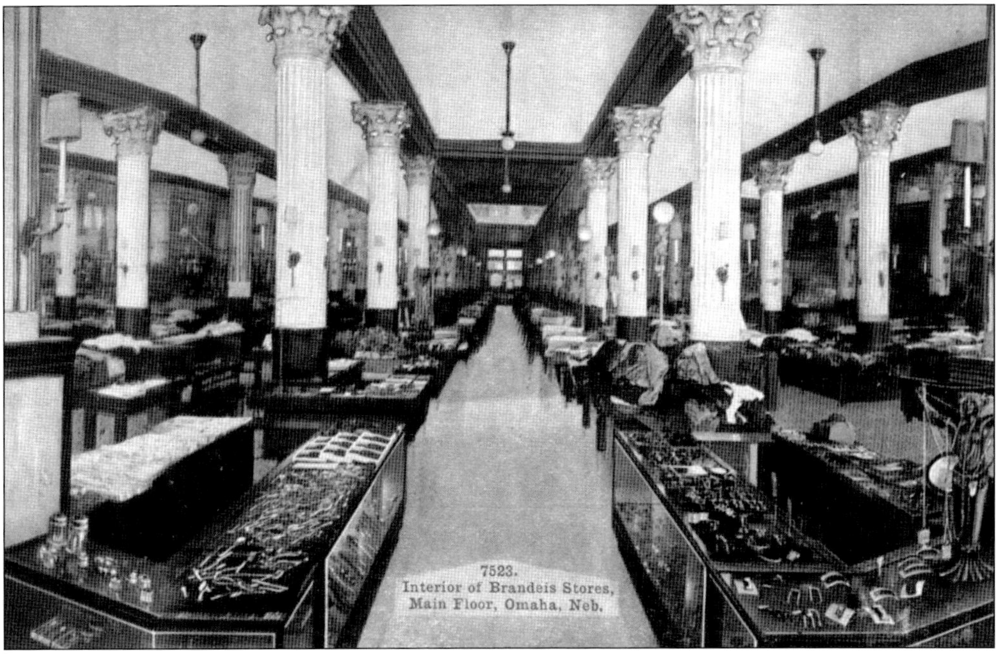

INTERIOR OF BRANDEIS STORE, MAIN FLOOR. The displays and counters reeked of accessible opulence. People adored the dressed store windows. Grandmothers, mothers, daughters, and girlfriends rendezvoused at the Tea Room. Younkers purchased Brandeis in 1987 and closed it. Gertrude wrote in March 1915 to an Omaha friend at St. Joseph Hospital: "I am glad to hear you are improving and hope you will continue. We are having a little nice weather again."

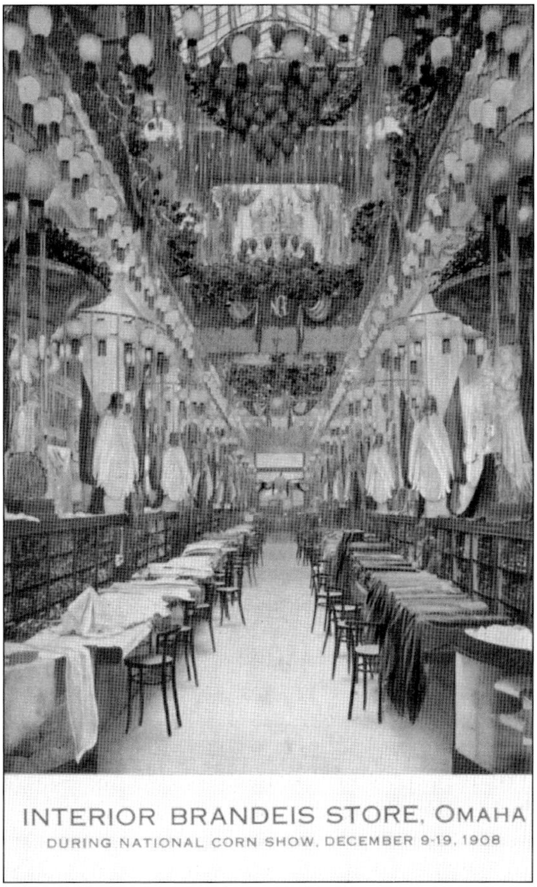

BRANDEIS STORE DURING NATIONAL CORN SHOW, DECEMBER 9–19, 1908. Chicago hosted the first National Corn Exposition in 1907; Omaha hosted the second. Organized by Gurdon W. Wattles, who had inspired the 1898 Trans-Mississippi Exposition, the 10-day show attracted more than 100,000 people. Omaha hosted again in 1909, and after that, it went to other cities. The slogan for this agricultural booster was "Prosperity Moves on Crutches When Crops Go Wrong." Eugene D. Funk headed the National Corn Association. (Omaha Public Library.)

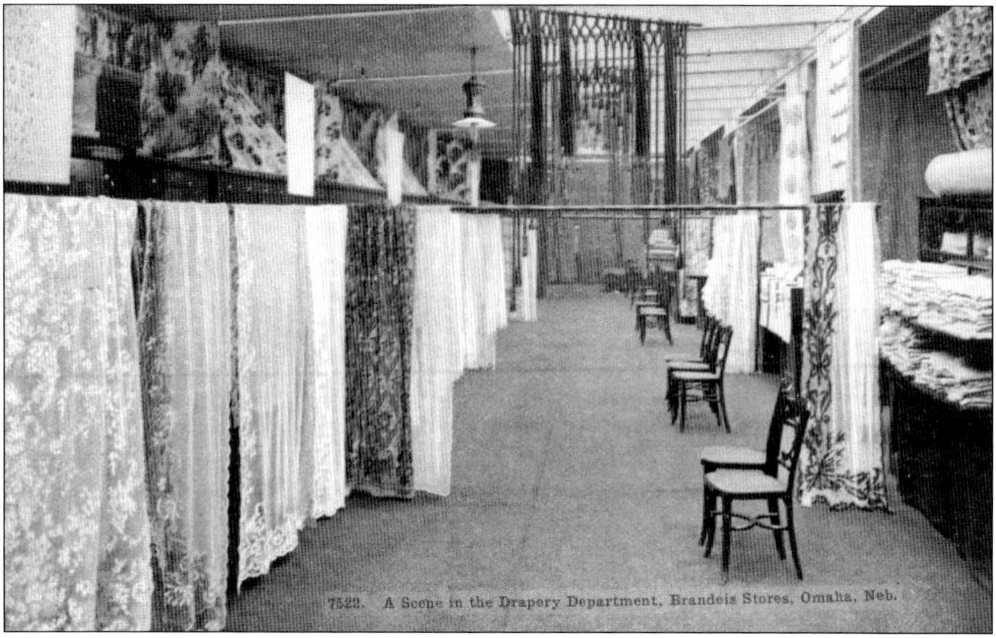

A Scene in the Drapery Department. This large room is filled with a profusion of broad swaths of colorful fabrics that salespeople displayed to a buying public at the Brandeis Store. Cotton, silk, linen, and wool—all natural fibers—fueled interior designers, drapers, window dressers, milliners, haberdashers, and the home seamstress. These fabrics could brighten the house and the person. Drapes enhanced privacy and cut down on drafts.

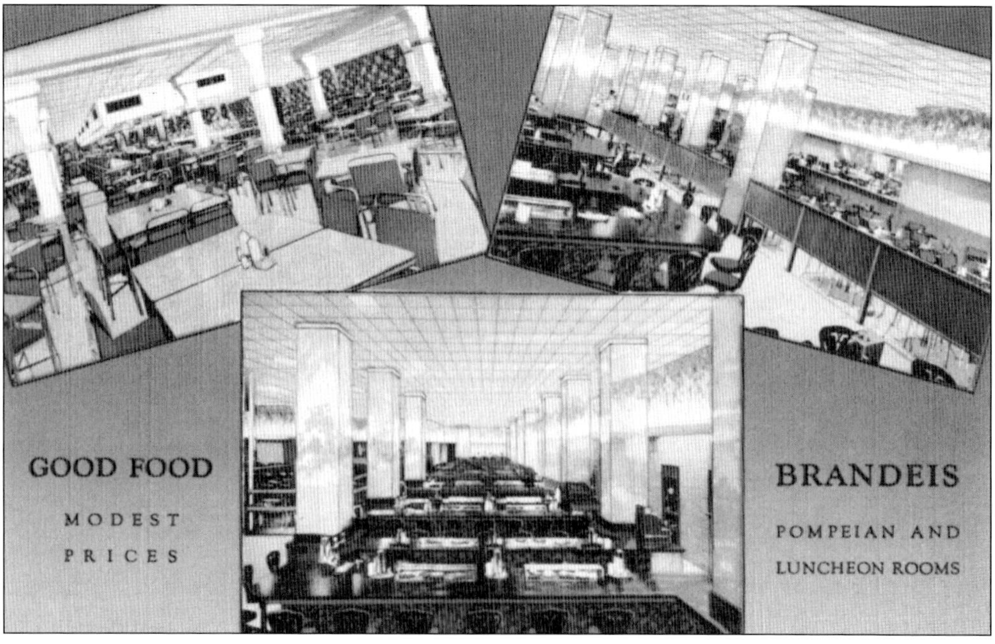

Brandeis, Pompeian, and Luncheon Rooms. The Pompeian Room entrance included a fountain, ornamental greenery, four columns, and an arch, simulating a Roman bath. Brandeis maintained a cafeteria, a much-remembered Tea Room, the Green Room Cafe, an Edwardian Buffet, the Men's Grill, Hamburger Haven, and J.L.'s Attic.

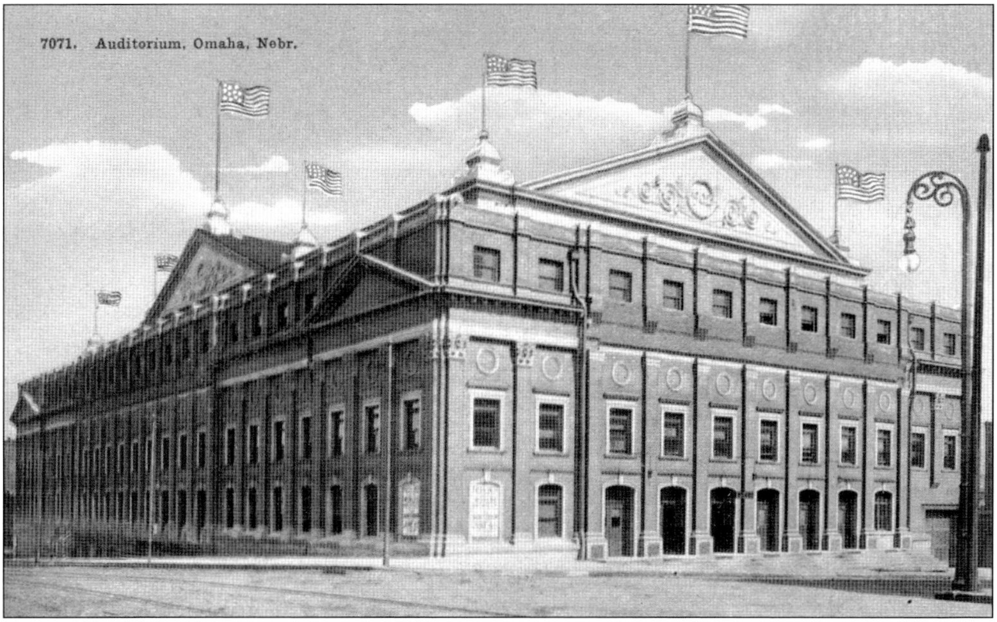

OMAHA AUDITORIUM. John Latenser Sr. designed the Omaha Auditorium, which opened in 1904 at Fifteenth and Howard Streets. It hosted the National Corn Exposition, First National Electric Show (1908), International Lions (1924), and the National Flower and Garden Show (1936). Presidents Theodore Roosevelt, Taft, and Wilson addressed thousands here. The Civic Auditorium superseded it in 1954, and the Omaha Auditorium was demolished in 1963.

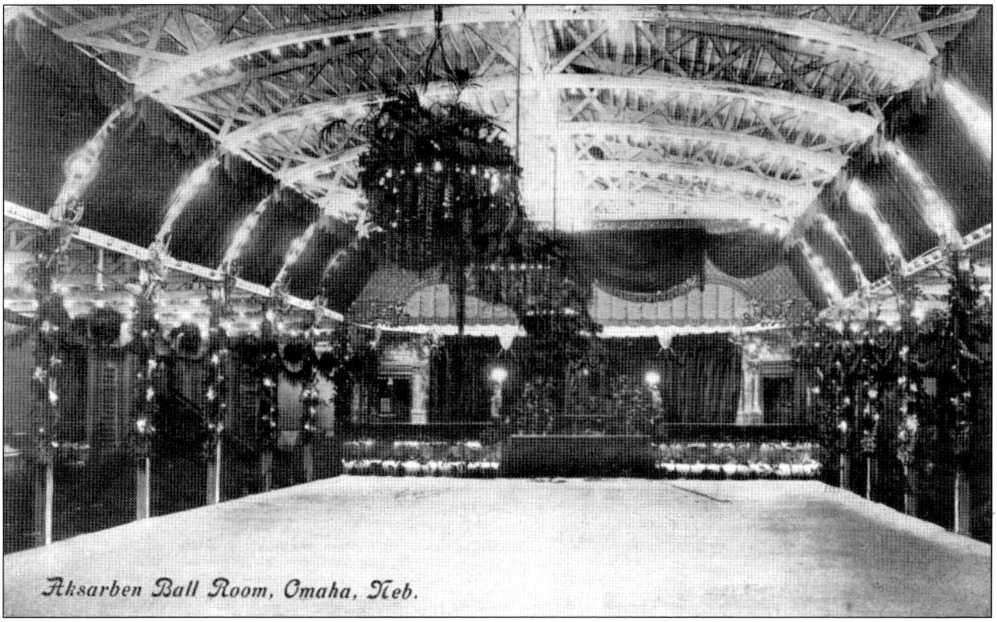

AK-SAR-BEN BALLROOM. The Knights of Ak-Sar-Ben, a philanthropic organization founded in 1895, held an annual ball here. The ballroom hosted circuses, rodeos, and the opera *Aida* complete with live elephants. A racetrack operated from 1919 to 1996, when legal gambling nearby undercut profits. The buildings were demolished in 2005. Ak-Sar-Ben Village and the University of Nebraska at Omaha now occupy the site.

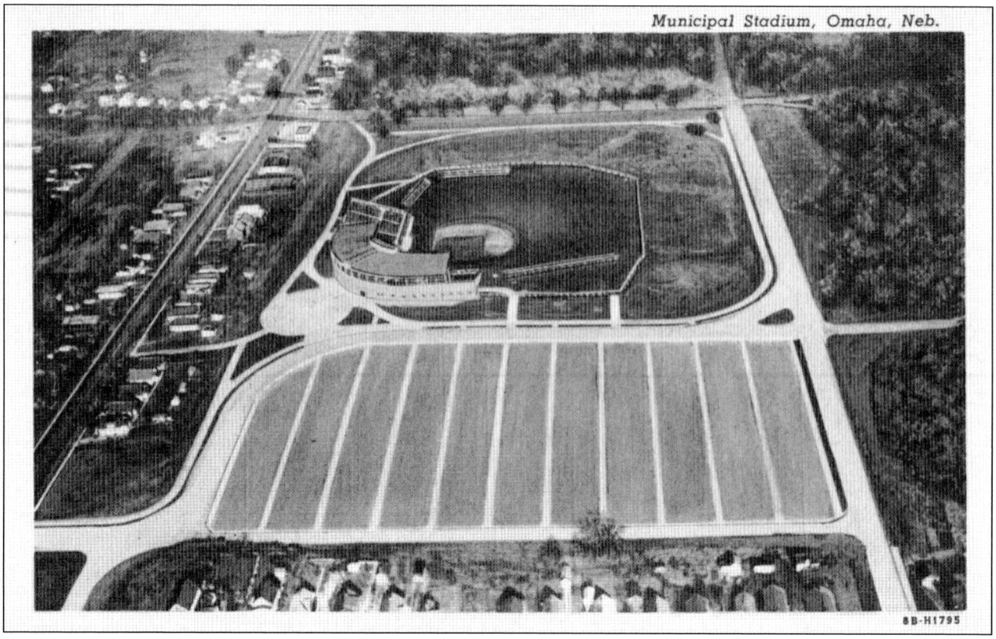

MUNICIPAL STADIUM, ROSENBLATT STADIUM. This stadium was built in 1947. Omaha had Triple A clubs and became the home of the NCAA College World Series in 1950. The stadium was renamed in 1964 to honor John "Johnny" Rosenblatt, Omaha's mayor from 1954 to 1961 and an avid sportsman. The College World Series moved downtown to TD Ameritrade Park in 2011. Rosenblatt was demolished in 2012, and Henry Doorly Zoo received the land.

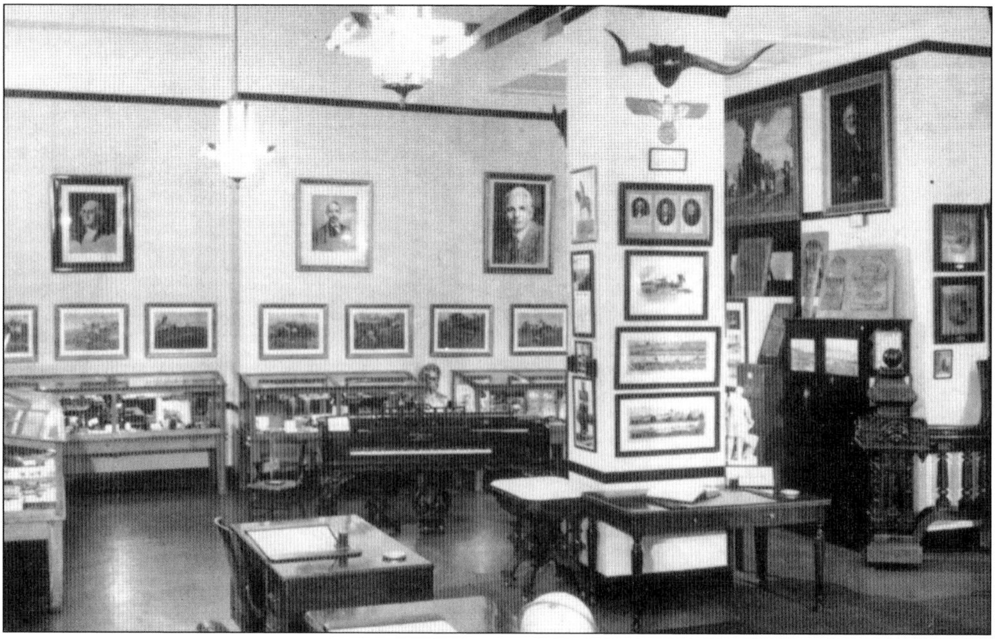

UNION PACIFIC MUSEUM IN OMAHA. According to the museum's brochure, visitors could "inspect the collection which portrays the history of the colorful pioneer west and the building and progress of the Union Pacific Railroad." The museum "contains a wealth of valuable pieces recording the struggles and triumphs of the old west." The museum moved to Council Bluffs.

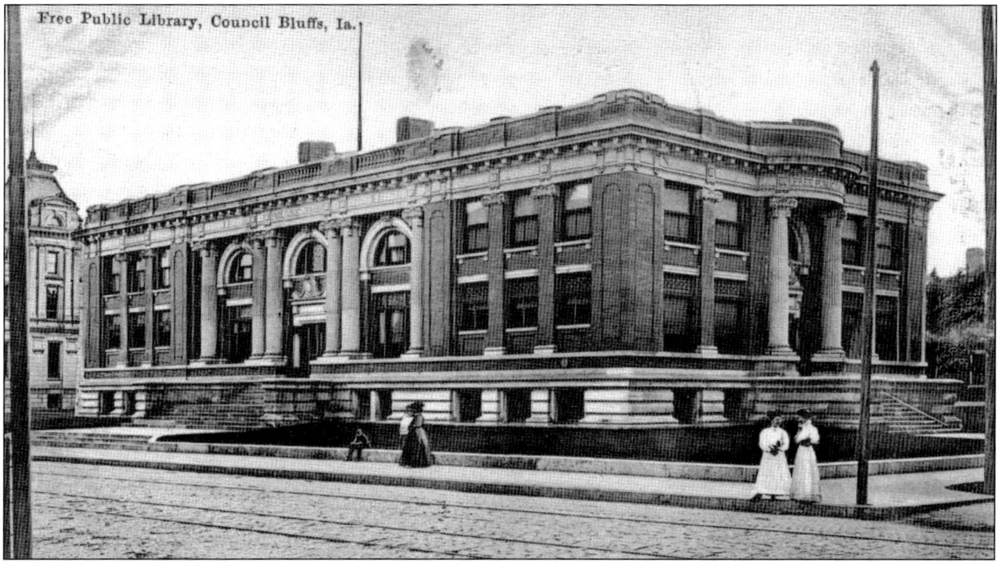

UNION PACIFIC RAILROAD MUSEUM IN COUNCIL BLUFFS, IOWA. In 2003, the Union Pacific Museum moved from Omaha to the former 1905 Carnegie Library in Council Bluffs. Andrew Carnegie built 2,509 libraries worldwide between 1883 and 1929, including 101 in Iowa and 69 in Nebraska. Most are still standing, although some have been repurposed. The Council Bluffs location recognizes the intertwining of two cities divided by a river. Streetcar tracks connected Council Bluffs and Omaha. (Union Pacific Museum.)

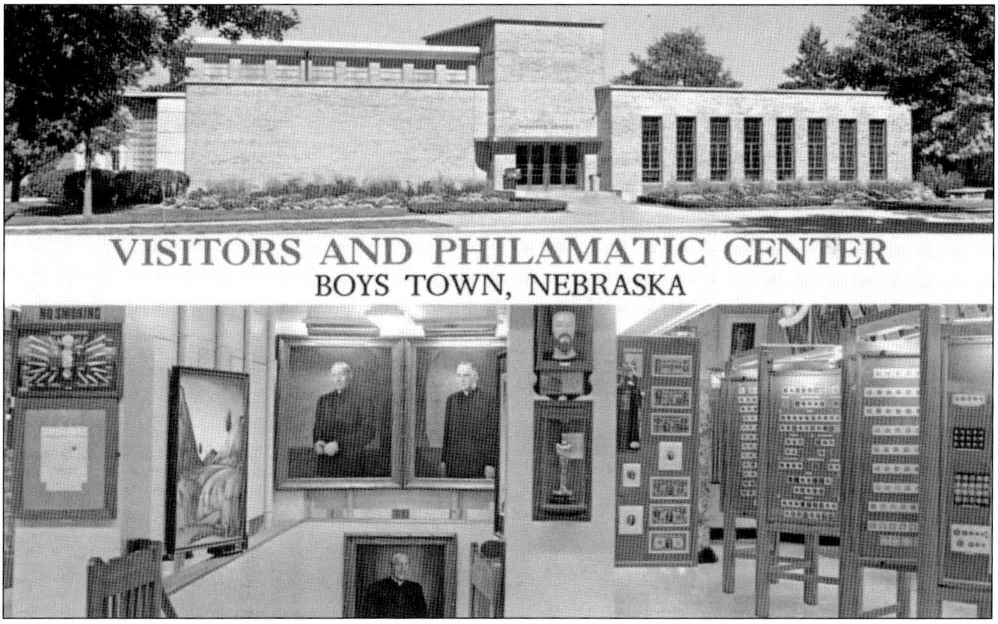

BOYS TOWN PHILAMATIC MUSEUM. Fr. Edward J. Flanagan, a stamp collector, shared his passion with the boys. The center opened on Memorial Day in 1951 and was renamed the Leon Myers Stamp Center in 1989. In the early 1950s, the Stamp Club constructed the world's largest ball of stamps, which weighed 600 pounds, contained four million stamps, and was 32 inches in diameter. The US Postal Service issued a 4¢ stamp commemorating Father Flanagan in 1988. The Boys Town Hall of History opened in 1986. Boys Town celebrated its centennial in 2017.

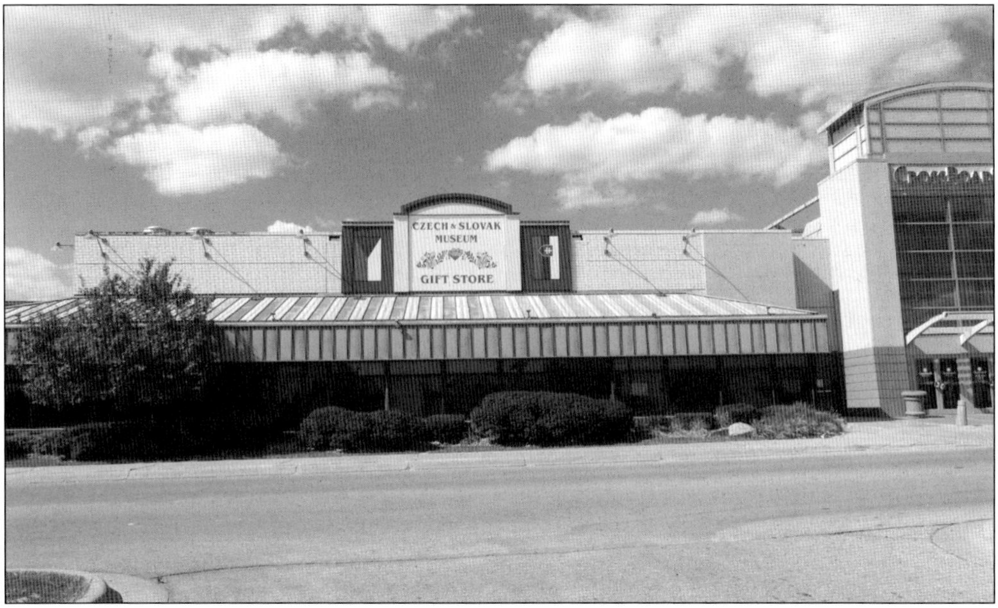

CZECH AND SLOVAK EDUCATIONAL CENTER AND CULTURAL MUSEUM. Museums flourish in a diverse cultural atmosphere. This museum in Crossroads Mall, located at Seventy-second and Dodge Streets, opened in 2014 several miles from the Czech community's South Omaha roots. This storefront location is in a former Chili's restaurant. Among Omaha's nearly two dozen museums are the Great Plains Black History Museum, El Museo Latino, and Nebraska Jewish Historical Society Riekes Museum. Museums record the vital roots of diverse communities.

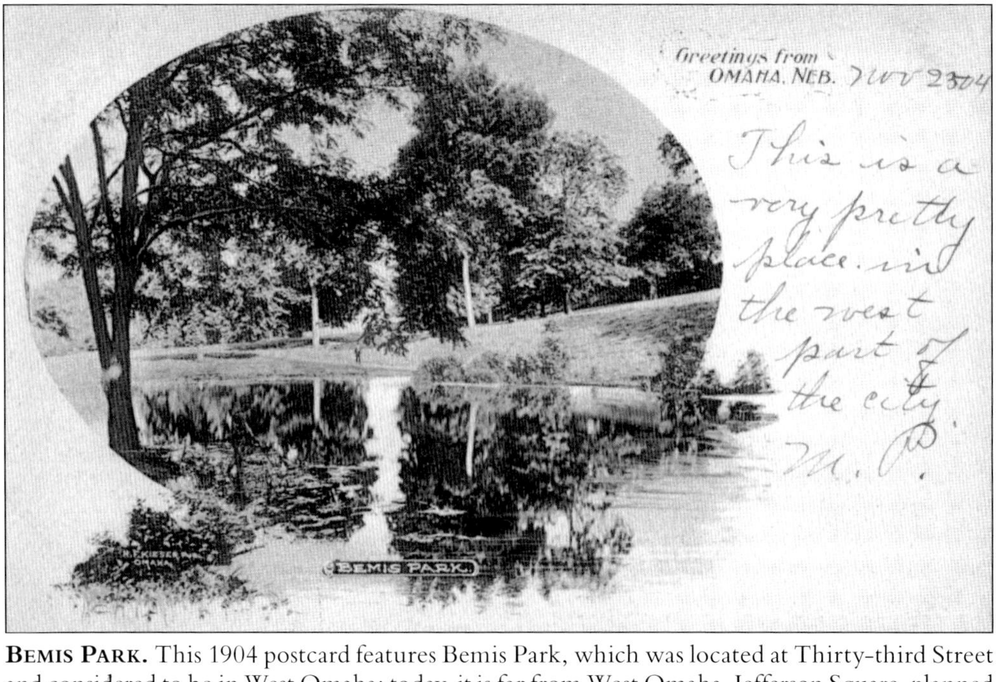

BEMIS PARK. This 1904 postcard features Bemis Park, which was located at Thirty-third Street and considered to be in West Omaha; today, it is far from West Omaha. Jefferson Square, planned in 1854 and opened in 1856, was paved over in 1969 for Interstate 480. Heartland of America Park opened in 1990, adjoining ConAgra, on the land that once housed Jobbers Canyon.

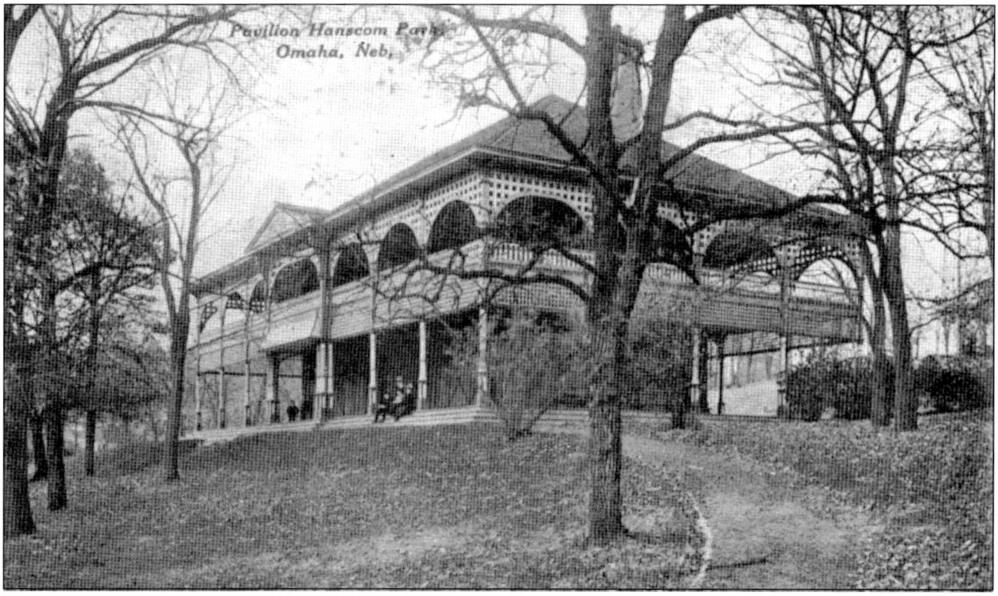

PAVILION, HANSCOM PARK. Opened in 1889, this park wins the prize for the greatest variety of postcards—about 50. Anna wrote Lula, her sister in Hagerstown, Maryland on September 10, 1908: "We are still in Omaha. Expect to go to Chicago Sat. Having a very nice time yet. Still plenty to see." A July 21, 1927, letter to the *Omaha World-Herald* included a poem: "Omaha fair Omaha / I love your verdant hills: / I love your parks and flowery dells / The bird with music fills."

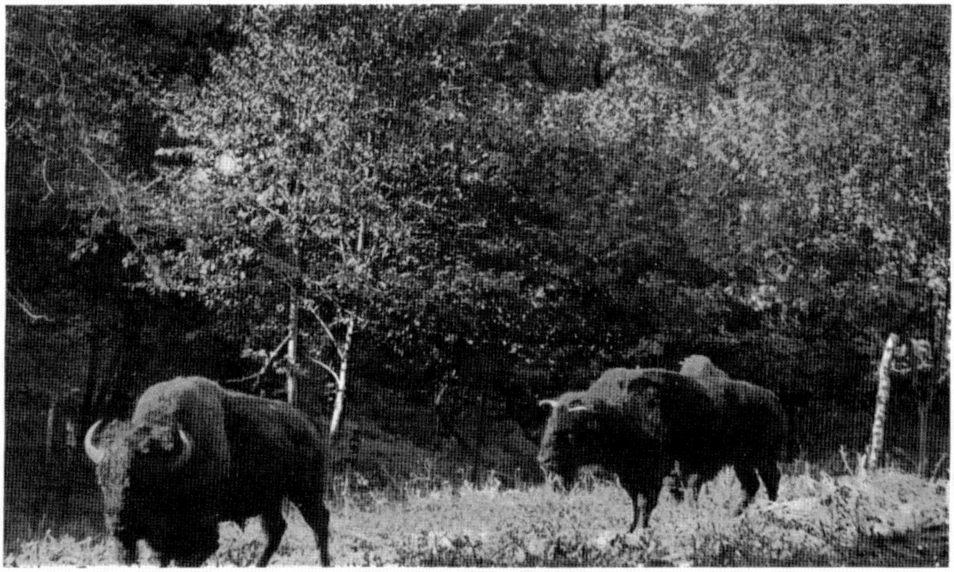

BUFFALOES, RIVERVIEW PARK.

BUFFALOES, RIVERVIEW PARK AT HENRY DOORLY ZOO. Pioneers called them buffalo, but they are bison. Riverview Park, created in 1894, housed Omaha's first zoo, which had about 120 animals, including bison, deer, and a grizzly bear. Another card displays deer—not quite as exotic. In 1962, Margaret Hitchcock, wife of *Omaha World-Herald* editor Henry Doorly, donated $750,000, and it became the Henry Doorly Zoo. It acquired additional land from the demolished Rosenblatt Stadium in 2012.

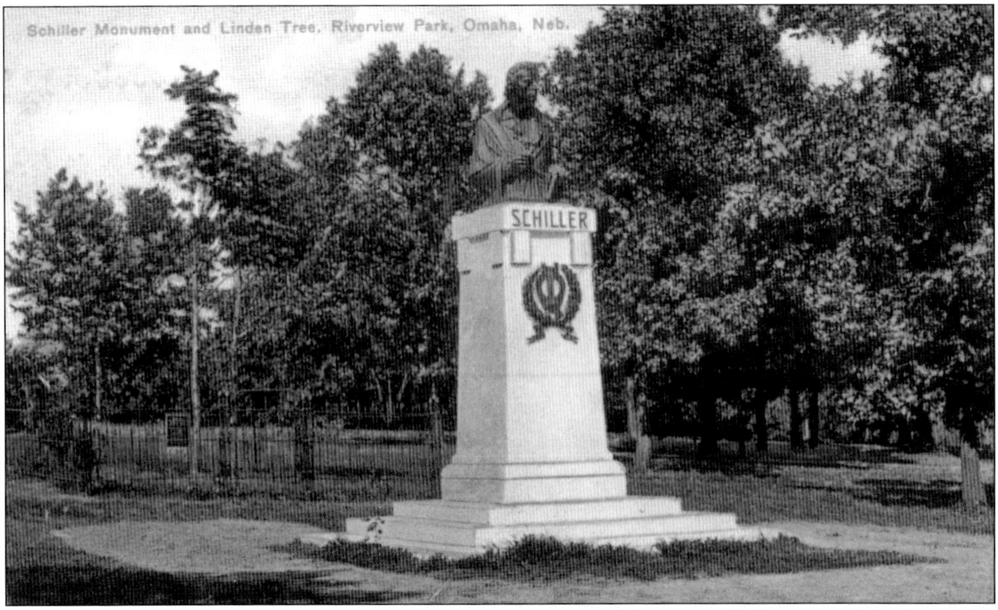

RIVERVIEW PARK. SCHILLER MONUMENT AND LINDEN TREE. Friedrich Schiller (1759–1805) was a German cultural icon. Nebraska had a substantial German population. Schiller's statue was dedicated with pomp and circumstance in May 1907. It was packed away in July 1918 because of the war and returned to the park in July 1922. In October 1942, an *Omaha World-Herald* letter to the editor suggested Schiller be melted down for the scrap drive. The German-American Society now has the statue.

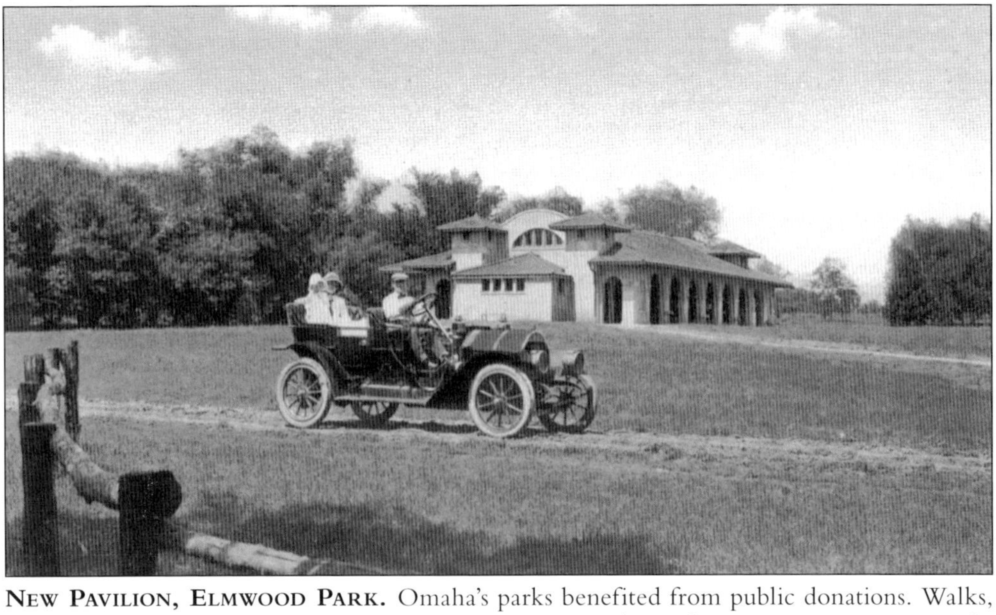

NEW PAVILION, ELMWOOD PARK. Omaha's parks benefited from public donations. Walks, hikes, golf, baseball, softball, volley ball, badminton, tennis, horse shoe, soccer, swimming pools, reunions, picnic tables, barbecues, parties, benches, playgrounds, swings, slides, merry go rounds, sandboxes, bridle paths, bandstands, gazebos, lagoons, ponds, creeks, lakes, flowerbeds, bicycle trails, and dog parks fill the green spaces. The Union Pacific menu on page 27 used an image of the Elmwood Park pavilion. Riverview, Hanscom, Kountze, and Miller Parks also had pavilions.

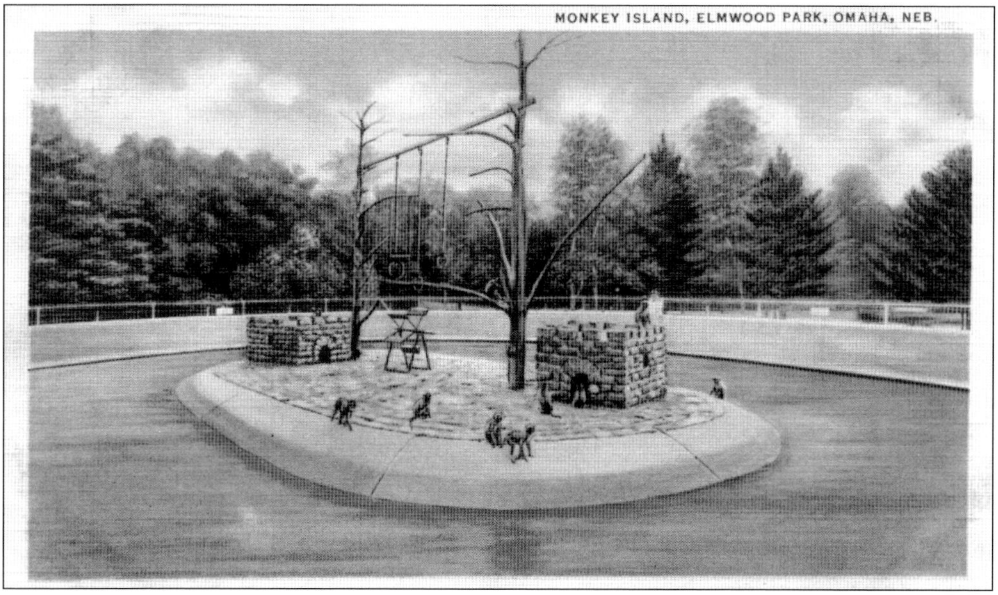

MONKEY ISLAND, ELMWOOD PARK. At least 19 Tarzan movies appeared between 1918 and 1932. In June 1933, the parks commission converted some golf-course parking into Monkey Island, a 60-foot strip with a bungalow to house monkeys. The fence kept spectators out but did not keep the monkeys in. In August, a concrete wall was built, and Commissioner Frost was assured that the animals wouldn't get away again. Monkey Island closed in 1936, and about 20 monkeys were returned to Riverview Park cages.

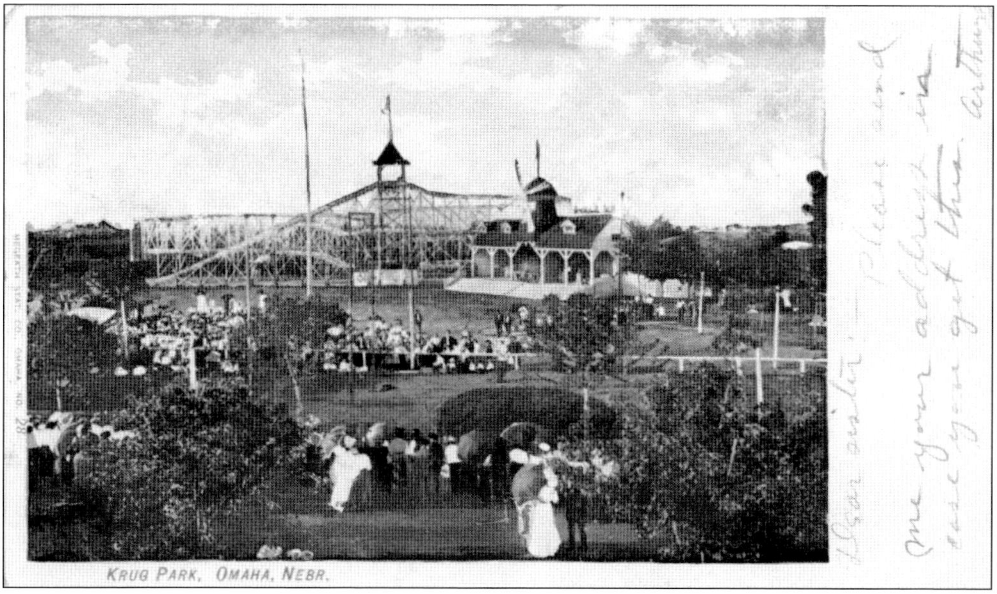

KRUG PARK. Tietz Park in Benson, located at 2936 N. Fifty-second Street, dates from as early as 1891. In 1896, brewer Frederick Krug wanted to turn it into a "first class summer garden" with a museum, menagerie, and concert hall. The Sensation Supreme roller coaster was running by 1904. Krug was advertised as "Omaha's Polite Resort." Four roller coasters ran off the rail in 1930, killing four and injuring 17—the deadliest roller coaster mishap in US history at the time. Krug Park closed in 1940. It was renamed Gallagher Park.

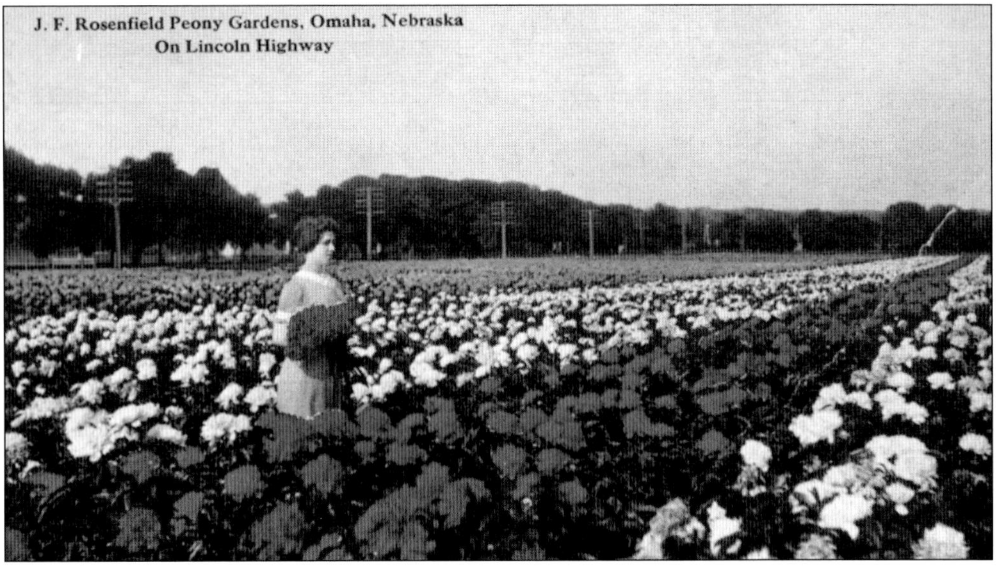

PEONY PARK. J.F. Rosenfield grew peonies in West Point. He purchased 25 acres in Omaha and grew peonies adjacent to the Lincoln Highway, one block north of Seventy-eighth and Dodge Streets. He sold the property to Detroit developers in 1917. Peony Park opened in 1921 as a 35-acre amusement park. In 1955, the Omaha Urban League complained about racial discrimination at the swimming pool. Peony closed in 1994. The park was redeveloped and now houses apartments, a supermarket, a bank, restaurants, and parking lots.

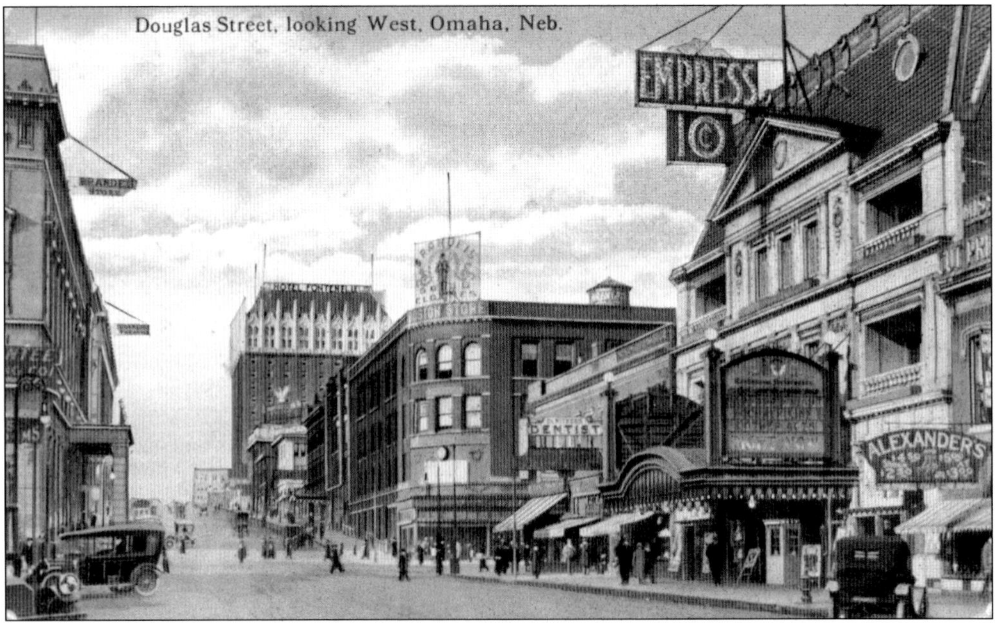

DOUGLAS STREET, LOOKING WEST. Postcards are echoes from the past. This card captures Alexander's clothing, Empress Theatre, the Brandeis sign, Boston Store, and the Fontenelle looming in the background. The overwhelming majority of postcards, letters, and parcels sent through the postal system arrive safely and on time. Exceptions result in consternation and frustration. In 1916, the sender of this card wrote, "What's the matter with the Postmaster there? The letter was probably there when we inquired for mail."

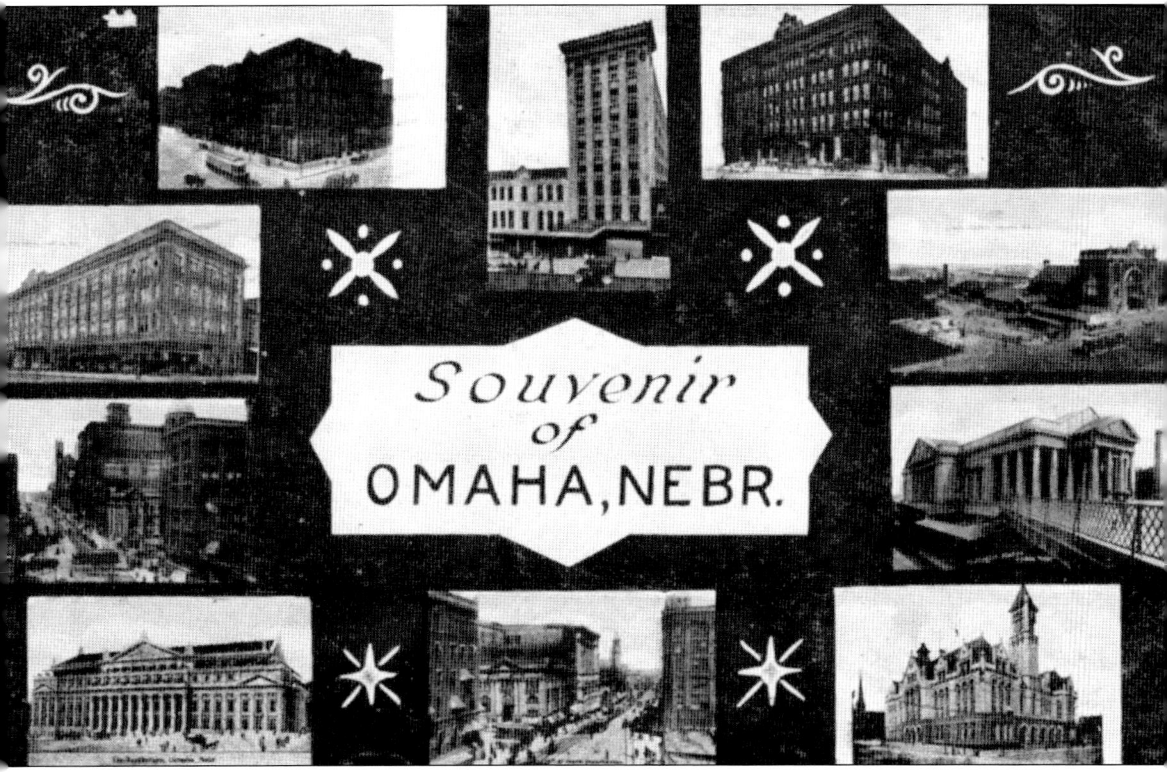

"SOUVENIR OF OMAHA" MULTIVIEW. These 10 thumbnail images feature the Burlington and Union Stations; post office; auditorium; and the Paxton, four-column Henshaw, Rome, and Loyal Hotels, representing transportation, government, and hospitality. The Burlington and Henshaw still survive today. On September 2, 1909, the sender wrote to West Virginia: "Hello Lena. How are you all. I am all OK at present and I am in Omaha N.B. It is pretty cold here but It is so awfully cold up north." Compare the images on this early 20th century souvenir card to the mid-century greetings card on the back cover. Today, 21st-century greetings postcards reveal fresh attractions. (Douglas County Historical Society.)

Bibliography

Belasco, Warren James. *Americans on the Road: From Autocamp to Motel, 1910–1945.* Cambridge, MA: The MIT Press, 1979.

Bristow, David L. *A Dirty Wicked Town: Tales of 19th Century Omaha.* Caldwell, ID: Caxton Press, 2000.

Groth, Paul. *Living Downtown: The History of Residential Hotels in the United States.* Berkeley, CA: University of California Press, 1986.

Jakle, John A. and Keith A. Sculle. *America's Main Street Hotels: Transiency and Community in the Early Auto Age.* Knoxville, TN: University of Tennessee Press, 2009.

Jakle, John A., Keith A. Sculle, and Jefferson S. Rogers. *The Motel in America.* Baltimore, MD: The Johns Hopkins University Press, 1996.

Larsen, Lawrence H., Barbara J. Cottrell, Harl A. Dalstrom, and Kay Calamé Dalstrom. *Upstream Metropolis: Urban Biography of Omaha & Council Bluffs.* Lincoln, NE: University of Nebraska Press, 2007.

Luebke, Frederick C. *Nebraska: An Illustrated History.* Lincoln, NE: University of Nebraska Press, 1995.

Omaha City Architecture. Omaha, NE: Landmarks and the Junior League, 1977.

Otis, Harry B. and Donald H. Erikson. *E Pluribus Omaha: Immigrants All.* Omaha, NE: Lamplighter Press, Douglas County Historical Society, 2000.

Peters, Robert C., ed. *A Comprehensive Program for Historic Preservation in Omaha.* Omaha, NE: Landmarks Heritage Preservation Commission, 1980.

Pollak, Oliver B. "Dining at the $1,000,000 to $1,500,000 Fontenelle Hotel, February 25, 1915." *The Connection.* Douglas County Historical Society, 1(2018): 4-6.

————. "Omaha Hotels in the Matchbook Era." *The Connection.* Douglas County Historical Society 2 (2017): 4-5.

Sandoval-Strausz, A.K. *Hotel: An American History.* New Haven, CT: Yale University Press, 2007.

Van Orman, Richard A. *A Room for the Night: Hotels of the Old West.* New York, NY: Bonanza Books, 1966.

The *Omaha World-Herald* has published several volumes on Omaha history, including *Omaha Times Remembered* (1999, 2002) and *Greetings from Omaha, Nebraska* (2001), as has Jeffrey Spencer, including *Building for the Ages* (2001), *Historic Photos of Omaha* (2007), and *Remembering Omaha* (2010).

Newspaper sources include Chronicling America (*Omaha Daily Bee*) and Genealogybank.com (*Omaha World-Herald*). Useful blogs include "My Omaha Obsession" by Miss Cassette; Northomahahistory.com, Adam Fletcher Sasse; "Adventures in Omaha History," Micah Evans; Omahahistory.blogspot; and Omababe.blogspot.

Index

Discover Thousands of Local History Books Featuring Millions of Vintage Images

Arcadia Publishing, the leading local history publisher in the United States, is committed to making history accessible and meaningful through publishing books that celebrate and preserve the heritage of America's people and places.

Find more books like this at
www.arcadiapublishing.com

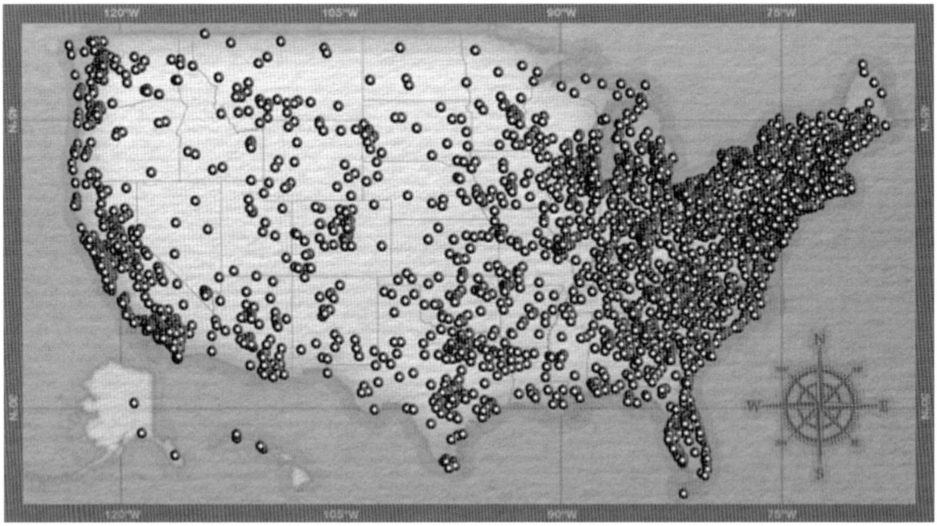

Search for your hometown history, your old stomping grounds, and even your favorite sports team.

Consistent with our mission to preserve history on a local level, this book was printed in South Carolina on American-made paper and manufactured entirely in the United States. Products carrying the accredited Forest Stewardship Council (FSC) label are printed on 100 percent FSC-certified paper.